PRINCE
OF THE TIMES

PRINCE OF THE TIMES

Ado Bayero and the Transformation
of Emiral Authority in Kano

Omar Farouk Ibrahim

Africa World Press, Inc.

P.O. Box 1892

Trenton, NJ 08607

P.O. Box 48

Asmara, ERITREA

Africa World Press, Inc.

P.O. Box 1892
Trenton, NJ 08607

P.O. Box 48
Asmara, ERITREA

Book design: Krystal Jackson

Library of Congress Cataloging-in-Publication Data

Ibrahim, Omar Farouk.
    Prince of times : Ado Bayero and the transformation of emiral authority in Kano / [Omar Farouk Ibrahim].
        p. cm.
Includes bibliographical references and index.
    ISBN 0-86543-951-6 (hardcover) -- ISBN 0-86543-952-4 (pbk.)
    1. Ado Bayero, Emir of Kano, 1930- 2. Kano State (Nigeria)--Kings and rulers--Biography. 3. Kano State (Nigeria)--Politics and government.
I. Title.
    DT515.9.K32 .I37 2001
    966.9'7805--dc21
                                    2001002814

 PRINTED IN CANADA

Dedicated to

*Sarkin Kano Alhaji Abdullahi Bayero:
A Perceptive Emir*

CONTENTS

FR D

Prince of the Times is a befitting chronicle of the glorious reign of one of Nigeria's most revered traditional rulers. Alhaji Ado Bayero, the Emir of Kano, is royalty personified, an exemplary symbol of monarchical excellence, and a man of the people — adored and loved almost to a point of deification.

The Emir's activities since he ascended the throne of his fore-fathers, which I had the opportunity to attend over thirty-five years ago, have proved the best commentary on the background of a great royal offspring. It is a vivid manifestation of the dictum that says that "it is the attitude as well as the aptitude that determine the altitude."

The plentiful showers from the bounty of the Almighty have seen the Emir preside over unprecedented development in the city of Kano. Alhaji Ado Bayero has always used his good offices to mediate in conflicts amongst traditional rulers all over the country. As a matter of fact, in consent, consort and concert like a good number of traditional rulers in the country, for instance the Obi of Onitsha, and the Ooni of Ife, the Emir has for long believed, that the people of the North, East and West of our dear country would not only see themselves as brothers and sisters but would always love to live together as one family. Towards this, he has put unceasing efforts and drive. This is also a belief that I hold.

Alhaji Ado Bayero has warmed himself permanently into the hearts of more than ninety-nine percent of the entire Nigerian citizenry. His sense of humility is inimitable. He has proved that the virtues of humility coupled with firm and resolute disposition are major indices of assessment of a ruler's leadership qualities. It may interest all Nigerians to know that but for this God-fearing paramount ruler, along with a very few others, Nigeria as a country would have gone into pieces between 1966 and 1970 and also between 1993 and 1998. He is God-fearing, forgiving, patient, benevolent, contented and peace loving.

It is gratifying to note that the book *Prince of the Times* has vividly captured those characteristics of the Emir that have made him unique among Nigerian traditional rulers.

The author and publishers deserve commendation for this publication. And for me, a long-standing friend of more than forty years, it is my honor and privilege to provide this foreword.

Alaiyeluwa Oba Okunade Sijuwade
Olubuse II
The Oluaiye and Ooni of Ife
The Royal Court of Ife
May 1999

Preface and Acknowledgments

He symbolizes different things to different people. To some he is the pillar of that "anachronistic" institution that has for decades made the nation's quest for modernity a mirage. To some others he personifies an institution that is increasingly becoming irrelevant in a world where democracy is the fad. To yet others, he represents that single institution unto which the nation has always fallen back in its moments of crisis; moments when the voices of modern leadership are drowned by the loud protests of the people. And to yet others, he is simply the dAmirthe leader, both social and religious, who therefore deserves unquestioned loyalty.

Emir Ado Bayero is an enigma. Most people who have formed opinions about him have never met him. They have mostly formed their opinions from what they have seen from a-far or what they have been told; usually by people who have not, themselves met him. And this observation applies as much to the common folk as the elite.

The various and sometimes contradictory perceptions of Emir Ado Bayero notwithstanding, one basic fact acknowledged by all, even if grudgingly, is that although constitutionally the Emir's powers have over the years since independence been completely whittled away, he still commands the kind of respect that few leaders, whether at the state or national level can lay claim to. Virtually every Nigerian leader has sought his advice from Alhaji Abubakar Tafawa Balewa to Chief Olusegun Obasanjo on key national issues. Even where his advice is not sought explicitly, the government has often intimated him of the reasons why certain policies or decisions are taken. And on all matters, his support has been sought. Depending on the issue at hand, Emir Ado Bayero has been very supportive, barely supportive or absolutely opposed to the policies or decisions.[1]

Emir Ado Bayero has seen many changes of regime in his thirty-seven years reign so far. From the conservative and professedly pro-traditional institution, Northern Regional Government of the Northern People's Congress (NPC) in the First Republic, 1960-1966, to the radical and professedly anti-traditionalist Kano State Government of the People's Redemption Party (PRP) in the Second Republic, 1979-1983. Also from civilian democracies to military dictatorships, the pendulum has swung back and forth, throwing off eleven[2] Heads of State and sixteen Regional and State Governors[3]. All the while Emir Ado Bayero sits comfortably on his throne protected from the vagaries of political instability by his charisma, his calculated response to issues, the sheer resilience of the institution he has come to personify and, as the Emir himself and the people of Kano would say, the will of Allah.

Very few traditional rulers have lived through the fundamental, though gradual, process of abridgement of the powers they exercised at the time of their appointment. Emir Ado Bayero is one of the few. At the time he ascended the throne of Kano in 1963, Emir Ado Bayero presided over the most powerful Native Authority (NA), in Nigeria. With a population of 4,949,868 in a territory covering 33,496 square kilometers, a staff strength of 5,083 persons, a fiscal budget of £2,149,128, 99% of which was internally generated, the Kano Native Authority was the most populous, and economically most buoyant. It was also the largest employer of labor among the sixty-six NAs in the then Northern Region[4]. As head of the Kano NA Emir Ado Bayero controlled the police, the courts and prisons in addition to land matters. But now, thirty-six years later, the Kano NA has been fragmented into fifty-three independent administrative units called local governments[5]. The NA Police Force has been dismantled and in its stead is the Nigeria Police Force. Also the courts have been taken over by the federal and state governments, while the prisons now belong to the federal government.

In spite of the diminishing of the constitutional powers of the Emir, Alhaji Ado Bayero has continued to loom even larger in the eyes of his subjects and indeed Nigerians. It is a paradox that the seeming impotence of the institution that the series of reforms have brought about, also contain the very strength that has helped the Emir to survive all the vicissitudes especially under the People's Redemption Party-controlled government of Kano State during the Second Republic. The Emir's handling of volatile situations affecting him or his subjects has continued to endear him to many people.

What have been the Emir's most difficult periods on the throne? What have been his most memorable periods? How did he react to the various situations he found himself in? Did regime type, military or democracy, radical or conservative make different impacts on the institution of emirship? What formal or informal structures exist within the modern system to protect traditional institutions from unmitigated assault? Are the days of the institution numbered or are better days yet to come? What is it about Emir Ado Bayero that has endeared him so much to his subjects, and made him admired and respected even by people who have never lived in his domain? How do his subjects see him, and how do other Nigerians perceive him? These are some of the questions addressed in this study.

When I first discussed undertaking this study with Emir Ado Bayero as long ago as February 1987, I had in mind writing an essentially academic work. I was then teaching at Bayero University, Kano. But since then, I have gone into journalism. Naturally, ten years of writing in the newspapers has made an impact on my writing style. I have thus tried to blend some serious academic writing with the popular style of the journalist.

I have written a rather lengthy introduction, and it takes up about a quarter of the entire book. It sets the background to the study, particularly about the institution of kingship in Kano. It is against that background that readers will better appreciate the fundamental changes that the institution has gone through. Those who are academically inclined may find that chapter useful. Other readers may wish to skip it and go straight to Chapter Two, without losing much.

I have in a number of places avoided identifying my source of information. I have done that in deference to some of my informants who requested anonymity for now. As I came to appreciate in the course of this study, it is not easy getting people who know about royalty to speak frankly to you about it. Those who speak normally do not know. And those who know hardly speak. When they agree to speak therefore, their wishes become our commands.

I wish to acknowledge my sincere appreciation to His Highness, the Emir of Kano, Alhaji Ado Bayero, for his support in the course of this study. From the day he consented to my request to undertake it, His Highness has been most generous with his time for me. Quite a lot of the materials for this study were collected from personal observations of the Emir and the court over a period of more than ten years, but especially during the large part of 1996 when the Emir graciously offered me a "seat" in the Kano Emirate Council. I was also admitted as a "member" of the Emir's court. With these two privileges, I was in a vantage position to observe how the Emir conducted affairs of the Emirate Council as well as in his various courts. As an observer at those meetings, I took copious notes from which I compiled questions for the Emir and some of his councilors. I also had many interview sessions with the Emir, spanning a period of over ten years. On several occasions, I was in the Emir's entourage on official tours outside Kano City.

Next to the primary data collected from interviews and observations, I made extensive use of archival material from the Kano State History and Culture Bureau, the National

Archives, Kaduna, the Arewa House, Kaduna, and the Africana Section of the Ahmadu Bello University Library, Zaria.

Among individuals whose assistance made this project a reality I must mention His Majesty Alaiyeluwa Oba Okunade Sijuwade Olubuse II, The Oluaiye and Ooni of Ife, Mai Martaba Sarkin Daura, Alhaji Muhammadu Bashar, and Mai Martaba Sarkin Gumel Alhaji Ahmad Muhammed Sani. I must mention His Highness, the Shehu of Borno, Alhaji Mustapha Umar El-Kanemi, His Eminence Alhaji Ibrahim Dasuki, the 18th Sultan of Sokoto, and Mai Girma Sarkin Karshi, Alhaji Ismaila Danladi Muhammed. I must also mention the following hakimai of Kano emirate: Masu Girma Magajin Gari, Alhaji Inuwa Wada; Galadima Alhaji Tijjani Hashim, late Ciroma, Alhaji Muhammadu Aminu Sanusi; Sarkin Bai, Alhaji Muhtari Adnan; Wali, Alhaji Mahe Bashir; Wambai, Alhaji Abbas Sanusi; Matawalle, Alhaji Aliyu Ibrahim; Mai Unguwar Mundubawa, Alhaji Aminu Yusuf; Sarkin Dawaki Mai Tuta Alhaji Aminu Babba Dan Agundi; Sarkin Dawakin Tsakar Gida, Alhaji Sanusi Ado Bayero; Tafida, Alhaji Nasiru Ado Bayero; Ma'ajin Watari, Alhaji Abba Ahmed and the late Magajin Garin Sokoto, Alhaji Aliyu (who died in a motor accident barely forty eight hours before I was scheduled to interview him). Finally, I must mention Yeriman Zazzau, Alhaji Mannir Ja'afaru, the Sarkin Hatsi, Sallama Alhaji Aminu Kwaru, and the Secretary and deputy secretary of the Kano State Council of Chiefs, Alhaji Mahmud and Alhaji Sarki Waziri respectively.

Equally, the contributions of the following persons is graciously acknowledged: Generals Yakubu Gowon, Olusegun Obasanjo, Muhammadu Buhari, and Ibrahim Babangida. Each of these former heads of state graciously granted me interviews on the subject. More than that, all four, despite their very tight schedules found time to read either all or parts of the manuscript and made useful suggestions. In this regard, I am particularly grateful to General Obasanjo who still found time, barely three weeks to his inauguration as the democratically elected President of Nigeria's Fourth Republic, and with all the pressure on his time, to read sections of the manuscript and made useful comments.

Air Vice-Marshal Hamza Abdullahi a former military Governor of Kano State deserves special mention for the many interviews he granted me, for reading and making incisive comments on the manuscript and for facilitating my meeting with General Babangida. The following former Governors of Kano State also spoke to me at length on the project: Colonel Sani Bello, Muhammadu Abubakar Rimi, and Kabiru Gaya. Similarly Audi Howeidy, Sule Yahaya Hamma and Guda Abdullahi, who were all secretaries to the Kano State Government at various times were helpful with interviews and materials. I benefited immensely from the insights of Dan Masanin Kano, Yusuf Maitama Sule, Talban Bauchi Ibrahim Tahir, Salihu Abubakar Tanko Yakasai, and Shehu Mohammed Shanono. Dr. Attahiru Mohammed Jega and Mallam Ibrahim Muazzam were generous to me with their personal libraries. Alhaji Uba Lida, Dr. Muhammadu Uba Adamu, Colonel AbdulRazzaq A. Muhammad-Oumar Ph.D., Professor Abdullah Uba Adamu, Dr. Dahiru Yahya, and Dr. Ibrahim Datti Ahmed also deserve my gratitude just as Chief Emeka Odumegwu Ojukwu who granted me many interviews and commented on sections of the manuscript he had read. The undotted i's and uncrossed t's of the manuscript could not escape the eagle eye of A'isha U. Yusuf.

There is a second group of people who also deserve my appreciation for constantly prodding me into working on this project. They built such great expectations on me that I felt I could not afford to disappoint them. In this category are: Abubakar Abdul-Rasheed, Abdullahi C. Ibrahim, Haruna Mohammed, Tijjani Borodo, Bashir M. Wali, Mansur and Hadiza Muhtar, Onyema Ugochukwu, Chidi Amuta, Malama A'ishatu, Ngozi Anyaegbunam, Ahmad Rufa'i Ibrahim, Suleiman Ibrahim, Salisu Iliyasu, Farouk U. Mohammed, Muhammad L. Yusuf, Biodun Aladekomo, Ad'Obe Obe, Bisi Akindiji, and members of my family, Safiya, Ummul-Khairi,

Safina, Sagira, Ahmad Rufai, Amina and Ansar. A special gratitude goes to Alhaji Iliyasu Suleiman Mazawaje, Group Captain Aliyu Mohammed and Ali Mohammed. General Aliyu Mohammed Gusau was helpful in many ways.

Mr. Tunji Okegbola, the Chief Librarian of The Daily Times of Nigeria, Turaki Nasir Ado Bayero, Mallam Muhammad Danyaro of the Kano State Ministry of Information, Chris Mammah, and Alhaji Uba Lida dug into their archives to make available the photographs.

To Barbara C. Pollack, C.S. Whitaker, Jr., Sam Oyovbaire, and Larry Diamond, I owe a debt of gratitude for intellectual development. Rose Obi Mbatha and Sidi Hamidu Ali deserve my commendation for pioneering the studies on Emir Ado Bayero. Emeka Akaezuwa was most helpful in many ways—from getting a publisher to arranging all the meetings and shipping the books. Kassahun Checole of The Africa World Press, my publisher, deserves special commendation for pioneering the reawakening of interest in African Studies in the new millenium. There is yet another set of people whose love and reverence for Emir Ado Bayero know no bounds. These people—Turaki Nasir Ado Bayero, V. Golpi and J. Dueni and Matawalle Aliyu Ibrahim—offered financial assistance for the completion of this project.

Omar Farouk Ibrahim

NOTES

1. See Chapter Ten for instances of each of the three positions taken by the Emir.
2. The heads of state were: Nnamdi Azikiwe (with Abubakar Tafawa Balewa as Prime Minister and Head of Government), 1963 - January 1966; General J.T. Aguiyi Ironsi, Jan 1966 - July 1966; Lt. Colonel, Later General Yakubu Gowon, July 1966 - July 1975; Brigadier, later General Murtala Muhammed, July 1975

- February 1976; Brigadier, later General Olusegun Obasanjo, February 1976 - October 1979; Alhaji Shehu Usman Aliyu Shagari, October 1979 - December 1983; General Muhammadu Buhari, January 1984 August 1985; General Ibrahim Badamasi Babangida, August 1985 - August 1993; Chief Ernest Shonekan, August 1993 - November 1993; General Sani Abacha, November 1993 to June 1988; General Abdulsalami Abubakar, June 1998, to May 1999. Olusegun Obasanjo, who returned as a democratically elected President on May 29, 1999 is the 12th.

3. These were: Premier Ahmadu Bello, 1963 - January 1966; Major Hassan Usman Katsina, 1966-1968; Alhaji Audu Bako, 1968-1975; Colonel Sani Bello, 1975-1978; Group Captain Ishaya Aboi Shekari, 1978-1979; Muhammadu Abubakar Rimi, October 1979 - May 1983; Abdu Dawakin Tofa, May 1983- September 1983; Aliyu Sabo Bakin Zuwo, October 1983 - December 1983; Air Commodore Hamza Abdullahi, 1984-1985; Colonel Ahmad Muhammad Daku, 1985-1986; Group Captain Muhammed Ndatsu Umaru, 1986-1988; Colonel Idris Garba, 1988-1991; Kabiru Ibrahim Gaya, 1992-1993; Colonel Muhammadu Abdullahi Wase, 1993-1996; and Colonel Dominic Oneya 1996 to 1998; Col. Aminu Isa Kontagora, 1998 to May 1999. Alhaji Rabiu Kwankwaso, the 17th Governor has been in office since May 29, 1999.

4. Figures from Northern Nigeria Local Government Yearbook 1966, (Zaria, Gaskiya Corporation, 1966).

5. These comprise all the 44 LGs in present Kano State and the following nine in present Jigawa State: Ringim, Babura, Garki, Birnin Kudu, Jahun, Dutse, Kiyawa, Gwaram, and Taura.

INTRODUCTION

HISTORICAL BACKGROUND

The history of Kano Emirate as a state system dates back to 999 AD when Bagauda, a son of Bawo, a Daura prince and son of Bayajida, brought together the various clans living around the hills of Dala, Gwauron-Dutse, Panisau, and Magwan under one political authority.[1]

Although begun as a small city-state, many factors contributed to making Kano expand into a great city, and later one of the greatest kingdoms of Africa. First among the factors was the location of Kano. The land was blessed with fertility, having abundant rainfall, and as a result, food was plentiful all year round. This attracted many people to the area. Secondly, the land was blessed with iron ore. This contributed to the rise of craftsmen who produced various commodities ranging from farming implements to war armaments. The mass production of farming implements (hoes, axes, cutlasses, etc.) and the development of the technology of food preservation (construction of barns, drying of some perishable food items) boosted food production thus making for increase in the population of the kingdom. At the same time, the production of war armaments (spears, arrows, shields, armors and later guns) ensured the safety and security of the kingdom and its inhabitants from external aggression. The Kano Chronicle records that by the reign of Sarki Kanajeji (1390-1410) Kano warriors were using *lifidi* or quilted armor, *kwalkwali* or iron helmets, and *sulke* or coats of mail. The net result of these advancements in the military sphere was that people felt generally secure and embarked on various activities of wealth creation. In fact, as early as 1098 when Gajemasu became king, Kano had become the envy of other kingdoms. That prompted Gajemasu to begin the process of fortifying Kano city by initiating the building of the famous Kano city walls.[2]

As its power increased, Kano began to expand its territories through conquest, sometimes through negotiation, but sometimes at the request of smaller settlements. Hadejia and Gaya, for example, voluntarily put themselves under Kano's rule in the 15th century.[3] With population and territorial expansion came more elaborate forms of government. The territories were divided into districts, each of which comprised a number of villages. The districts and villages were each assigned a head. Kano city, the capital of the kingdom was also divided into administrative wards, each with a ward head. The main responsibility of the district, village and ward heads was ensuring the safety and security of the lives and property of the residents of their areas. The king, or *sarki* as he was called, was at the apex of the pyramid of authority.[4] Next to him were the district heads, then came the village heads and then the ward heads in that order.

Next to establishing territorial administration, the government also instituted tax administration in order to raise the revenue needed for governance. The Kano Chronicle identifies such taxes as *kudin kasa*, sometimes-called *kharaj* or poll tax, *kudin aure* or marriage levy, and *kudin kasuwa* or market tax. There was also *kudin karofi*, literally pond tax, which Fika likens to industrial or excise tax.[5] King Kutumbi is reported to have introduced *jangali* or tax on animals in the early 17th century.[6] To ensure the proper administration of taxes he also appointed an official, the Sarkin Shanu, and entrusted him with the responsibility of assessment and collection of that tax throughout the kingdom[7]. From all indications, Sarki Bagauda and his successors established a solid foundation for the growth of Kano as a prosperous agricultural, commercial and industrial kingdom.[8]

Whereas Bagauda and his immediate successors, especially Guguwa, set out to destroy Tsumburbura, the idol that the various clans living around Kano were worshipping, there is no evidence that they did so because they wanted to establish Islam. Dokaji suggests that the first Hausa King to accept Islam was Yaji (1359-1396), when he received forty Wangara missionaries from Mali. Among them were Abdurrahman Zaite who was made *alkali* or judge, and Mandawari who was made chief imam.[9] From that time until Muhammadu Rumfa became King in 1463[10] Islam's fortunes in Kano rose and fell with changes in the occupants of the throne.

THE LEGACY OF MUHAMMADU RUMFA

Muhammadu Rumfa's accession to the throne of Kano marked a radical departure in the philosophy of governance of the kingdom. Celebrated as an innovator, Rumfa "created a totally new kind of state in Kano."[11] Beginning with Islam, Rumfa declared it the state religion. Next, he decided to relocate the seat of power from near Dala, where there were still some influences of traditional religion, to a virgin area in the southeastern corner of the city. There he built Gidan Rumfa, the present palace. He then put up a juma'at mosque north of the palace. Further north still, he established the now famous Kurmi market. He encouraged Islamic learning, and opened the doors of his capital to scholars, merchants and artisans. Rumfa also began the practice of celebrating the bi-annual Muslim Eid festivals with pomp and pageantry. Those days of festivities were declared public holidays throughout the Kano kingdom. For the first time in Kano moreover, Rumfa introduced *kulle,* or purdah.

During the reign of Muhammadu Rumfa a very famous Muslim scholar from Morocco called Sheikh Muhammad bin Abd al-Karim al-Maghili al-Tilmisani, arrived in Kano. He was very well received by Rumfa, who requested his guest to help him establish a very sound foundation for Islamic government. In response to Rumfa's request, al-Maghili wrote *The Obligations of Princes: An Essay on Muslim Kingship*.[12] Al-Maghili's treatise became the first written constitution of Kano. It dealt with virtually every topic normally contained in the constitutions of modern states, from the conduct of the ruler to the rights of citizens, but from an Islamic perspective. In view of the indelible impression that al-Maghili's treatise has made on the institution of emiral authority in Kano, it will be useful to highlight some of its salient propositions.

Al-Maghili begins with a discussion on the essence of power and admonishes the prince thus: "God has not invested you with power that you may lord it over your subjects and dominate them; He has put you in authority only to foster their spiritual and material well-being." He then discusses the proper appearance and behavior of the prince. According to Al-Maghili, "Every prince should put on the mantle of dignity... manifest your love for what is excellent and worthy of people, show your hatred for corruption and corrupt people. Sit cross-legged when you seat yourself; be still as far as you are able, and do not fidget even with your hand... be covetous of silence always, for seldom is the talker safe. If you must speak, be brief and clear.... Two most shameful things are arrogance in a learned man and falsehood in a prince.... If the king is slack in enforcing his orders weakness appears in all his affairs, the whole of his authority among men is enfeebled, and he casts off his garments of majesty and excellence. Do not approach your council chamber and your work meanly attended in the eyes of the people, for a man's retinue is his garment."

Al-Maghili further discusses the duty of the prince in the organization of his realm, stating that, "authority rests on wise management in government. The prince should have wise men as counsels, trusted men to collect and spend public wealth, scribes and accountants to keep records, viziers who fear none but God, governors who love to pay God's

4

due..." Al-Maghili admonishes the prince that kingly power is seductive and caution is its shield. Al-Maghili also emphasizes the need for probity stating that, "the prince must watch his governors vigilantly in all their works, weigh carefully their statements and examine their conditions. He will estimate their wealth before appointing them and will watch their conduct on all occasions. If any of them is the object of repeated complaints, albeit the evidence is not clear, he will change him if he can find a substitute... the prince should investigate the case of anyone who is strongly suspected of corrupt practices, should these be duly attested.... look into every matter and be cautious of your allies in all things." The treatise also lays down rules about righteous judgement, where it states that, "royal authority has two pillars of support, justice and charity. Justice means that the prince shall pay every claimant his full due, both from himself and others; charity means that he is bounteous with his own substance, not with the property of others." The treatise advises rulers about lawful and unlawful collection of revenue. Al-Maghili warns that "the essence of bounty is for the prince to keep his hands from the people's goods. Restraint therein causes the realm to endure in beauty; covetousness makes it quake and fall in ruins... Gifts may not be accepted from subjects for they open the door to all corruption. When a prince permits a present from a man of doubtful character he has chosen fire for his portion and the burden is his.... It is oppressive to punish by taking fines as from a thief or adulterer. Neither oppressors nor extortioners will enter paradise."

As can be seen from this brief summary, most of what are today described as unique conventions in the Kano palace have their roots in Al-Maghili's treatise. The custom of the emir sitting in court cross-legged, without moving and seldom or only briefly speaking, for example, is traceable to Al-Maghili's advice[13] and is unique to Kano emirs. So are the paraphernalia of office, which are exclusive to the emirs of Kano like ostrich feather sandals, trumpet, the twin spear and the practice where spare horses accompany the emir on every outing.

Muhammad Rumfa's reign witnessed great strides in commerce, industry and learning in Kano. Because he ruled according to Islamic precepts, he was able to establish peace and security throughout his kingdom. The common people felt contented and the rich felt secure. Many people from far and near, especially Arabs from North Africa, came and settled in Kano. They contributed significantly to the development of international trade, industry and education in the kingdom. The development of education was further helped by the location of Kano, sandwiched between Borno and Gao, two centers of Islamic learning and both major actors in the trans-Saharan trade. So great did Kano become that it was described as "one of the three main towns in Africa at par with Fez and Cairo.[14]

But that era was not to last forever. Sarki Kutumbi (1623-1648), the tenth king after Rumfa, introduced *jangali*, a tax on cattle. Some fifty years later, 1703, Sarki Sharefa imposed even more onerous taxes on the people. He introduced a marriage tax, which was paid to the state by every man taking a wife, and a market tax, paid by all who transacted any business in the market.[15]

The tyranny of the rulers set in train a decline in the power of the kingdom. Sarki Kumbari (1731-1743) is reported to have so rigorously enforced the collection of the taxes introduced by his predecessors, that many Arab settlers decided to leave Kano for Katsina. Similarly many Kano people moved out to other kingdoms.[16] As a result of these developments Kano became so weak that when Borno invaded the kingdom in about 1740, the Kano forces could not repel them. The Borno army camped at Fagge, just outside the city walls, until a Mallam Dahiru Bindoma appealed to them to leave Kano alone.[17] Ringim also successfully revolted against Kano, conquering some towns of the kingdom. Ringim is reported to have set out to attack Kano city when Sarki Kumbari was saved by the arrival of Jarmai Tagwai, who led Kano to subdue Ringim.[18]

Things continued to get worse for the mass of the people. The rulers abandoned the *shari'ah*—the Islamic legal code—in their administration. They practiced an ostentatious lifestyle that could not be sustained with their legitimate income. They had to resort to extortion and that, in turn, increased the alienation of the rulers from their subjects. The situation continued until the jihad of Shehu Usman Dan Fodio swept away the ruling class and established a new system of government based on Islam.

BACKGROUND TO DAN FODIO'S JIHAD

While the masses of the people of Kano were groaning under the tyranny of their rulers, a revolution was brewing in Gobir—some seven hundred kilometers away to the north-west. There, a religious reformer by name Usman Dan Fodio, popularly called Shehu, which is the Hausa version of the Arabic word sheikh or great scholar, had emerged calling on the people to abandon their ungodly ways for the straight path. Shehu Usman Dan Fodio had begun his preaching career in the last quarter of the 18th century, a time when decay was becoming entrenched in most of Hausaland. Beginning in the Gobir and Zamfara areas of Hausaland, the Shehu gradually gathered around him a large following of students and admirers.

The fame of the Shehu spread so far and wide that the king of Gobir, Bawa Jan Gwarzo, recruited him to teach his sons. Although he accepted to teach at the court of Gobir, Shehu Usman Dan Fodio refused to compromise on religious matters. Before long, the increasing popularity of the Shehu began to be a cause for worry for the Gobir rulers. When Nafata became king, he resolved to curtail the influence of the Shehu. He issued a proclamation to the effect that:

a. No man should be a Muslim except those who had inher-ited the faith from their fathers, and that all others should return to that faith which they had inherited.

b.   No man should wear a turban.

c.   No woman should cover her head with a cloth (veil).

The persecution of Muslims continued throughout the reign of Nafata. But it took an even more frightening turn on the accession of Yunfa to the throne. Sarki Yunfa felt threatened by the growing influence of the Shehu. He also resented the Shehu's preaching in which the ills of the society, including those of its rulers, were openly criticized. Yunfa then planned to kill the Shehu. When he failed, the Shehu fled to Gudu, symbolizng the hijra, and the beginning of the preparation for a jihad, or Islamic holy war. Among the ills of Hausa society, which Shehu Usman Dan Fodio identified and sought to correct, were:

a.   Syncretism: The Shehu observed that Islam as practiced in Hausaland during his time was mixed with traditional religions, or acts of unbelief.

b.   Tyranny and extortion of the rulers: The Shehu noted that the mass of the people lived in perpetual fear of their rulers because of the absolute power they wielded over their subjects. He condemned the onerous taxes that the rulers imposed on the people. He identified recognized sources of state revenue according to the *shari'ah*, and condemned every other source not approved by Islam.

d.   The position of women: The Shehu also criticized the practice of denying education to women. He came down forcefully on this issue when he addressed Muslim women thus:

Muslim women, do not listen to the speech of those who are misguided and who sow the seed of error in the heart of others; they deceive you when they stress obedience to your husbands without telling you of obedience to God and to His Messenger (May God show him bounty and grant him salvation), and when they say the woman finds her happiness in the obedience to her husband.

8

They seek only their own satisfaction, and that is why they impose upon you tasks which the law of God and that of the Prophet have never specially assigned to you. Such are the preparation of meals, the washing of clothes and other duties which they like to impose upon you, while they neglect to teach you what God and the Prophet have prescribed for you....[19]

c. The practice whereby men stayed at home and their women went to trade or engage in other activities to earn income for the family.

d. The practice whereby ignorant men or women were allowed to engage in trade and business. According to the Shehu, trade and business had laws governing them. And it was gross negligence of the *shari'ah* to allow ignorant people to engage in them.

e. The appointment of unqualified and corrupt people to such important positions as the *qadi* or judge and other important state offices.

After the Shehu's hijra to Gudu, the battle line appeared to have been drawn. It was not whether, but when the fight would begin. Meanwhile, Yunfa's persecution of the Muslims was intensified. Many fled and joined the Shehu's jama'at. The news of the Shehu's hijra soon spread to the neighbouring Hausa states and many more people left their homes and joined the Shehu. Just before the Shehu formally declared the jihad, he issued a manifesto titled *Wathiqat Ahl al-Sudan*. This justified in twenty-seven points the jihad, which he was about to prosecute.[20] Copies of the manifesto were dispatched to all the Hausa kingdoms and beyond. Thus the jihad began in 1804. Many delegations came to the Shehu from various kingdoms for his blessing for them to go and wage the jihad in their respective states. To each delegation a flag, symbolizng Islamic theocracy, was given. The delegation from Kano was led by Mallam Danzabuwa.

THE JIHAD IN KANO

Unlike Gobir, where Shehu Usman Dan Fodio took some time to prepare for the jihad, calling people to his side and justifying what he was about to do, the jihad in Kano was neither planned, nor organized. All the ills that the Shehu was preaching against were also manifest in Kano. Settlers, and even citizens, as we noted during Kumbari's reign, were fleeing the kingdom because of the pervasive oppression and tyranny of the rulers. Many left because they found the taxes imposed by the rulers too onerous to bear. For various reasons different social groups easily identified with the jihad. The majority of the people, who were Hausa, saw the jihad as their saving grace from the despotism of their rulers. The Fulani, like their Hausa counterparts, also felt aggrieved over the onerous taxes imposed on them, especially the *jangali*. Islamic scholars, both Hausa and Fulani, also had their reason for supporting the jihad. They had been preaching against the same ills that the Shehu identified. When the news of the Shehu and his preaching spread to many Hausa states the emirs, fearing for their thrones, sought to silence the preachers in their midst. Many Muslim Hausa rulers also resorted to unIslamic practices in the hope of securing protection for their thrones.

In Kano the king, Alwali, was said to have consulted fortunetellers to tell him what the jihad portended for his kingdom. When told that trouble was imminent, he asked the fortunetellers to tell him who was going to succeed him. The fortunetellers returned with instructions to the king that early the following morning, he should go out to the entrance of the palace. Whoever he first saw there would be the one to succeed him. The following morning, king Alwali did as instructed by his soothsayers. He went out to the south entrance of the palace. There, he saw a student carrying a mat and some books on his way to where he took lessons. He looked around but did not see anyone else. He reported to the soothsayers and they advised him to repeat the exercise the following morning. He did so and saw the same person. He reported to them again, and they suggested he repeated the exercise for the third time. Again he saw the same person. Alwali then decided that for the next outing he was going to use another entrance, the north entrance. Meanwhile, the student that Alwali had been seeing in the past three days had also become frightened of his successive encounters with the king, and had decided to change his route from the south to the north entrance. By coincidence, the king saw the same person that morning too. An indignant Alwali called the student and warned him never to come near his house again. But it never for a moment crossed king Alwali's mind that that "poor and wretched student" was going to succeed him.

Mallam Danzabuwa, who collected the flag from Shehu Usman Dan Fodio, went as a representative of all the major Fulani clans in Kano. These were the Sullubawa under the leadership of Mallam Jamo, the Danejawa under Mallam Danzabuwa, the Jobawa under Mallam Bakatsine, and the Danbazawa under Mallam Dabo. These clan leaders led the jihad in Kano. After terminating the Hausa dynasty and killing Alwali at Burum-Burum in 1807, the four leaders sent to Shehu Usman Danfodio to appoint a leader for Kano. The Shehu enquired who was the most learned man around. None of the four clan leaders agreed he was the most learned. So Sulaiman, who was their student, was recommended. Sulaiman, incidentally, was not from any of the four major clans who sent Mallam Danzabuwa to the Shehu for the flag, but from the Mundubawa clan. Shehu Usman Dan Fodio then appointed Sulaiman the first amir of Kano.[21] The four clan leaders then came to constitute the electoral college of Kano Emirate. They sat to deliberate and nominate a successor from among the eligible candidates, in the event of death or abdication of an amir. Their nomination is sent to the Caliph for approval. When more than one name was submitted, the Caliph's control over the selection was, according to Adeleye, "real and final."[22]

According to Muhammad Bello, Shehu Usman Dan Fodio's son and successor, Sulaiman was appointed the first Amir of Kano because he was pious and just—qualities that would help him establish a good foundation for justice, equity and fairness in the administration of the new Kano emirate.[23]

Amir Sulaiman's reign, which lasted from 1807 to 1819, brought about a very fundamental change in the perception of Kano people about *sarauta* or the institution of kingship. He demystified the institution by doing away with all that protocol that surrounded the ruler. He made himself easily available to all who wanted to see him. He did not sit on the throne unless he was at court, and his advisors all sat on sheepskins on the floor around him. Immediately after the court session, they all returned to their occupations, as farmers, weavers, or teachers.

Amir Sulaiman lived a very simple life. He continued to impart knowledge to his students as well as leading the juma'at prayers. In addition, he earned his living from his orchard and from writing.[24] He ensured that only religiously sanctioned taxes were collected in his emirate and they were expended as specified in the Shari'ah. He is reputed to have kept his distance from the public treasury. It is reported that there was a year when Amir Sulaiman fell ill and therefore could not work on his orchard to save enough money to buy a ram for the sacrifice of *Eid al-Adha*. But he did not tell anyone nor ask anyone for assistance. Everybody went to the Eid praying ground where the prayers were offered. Traditionally, the amir would slaughter his ram at the Eid Prayer Ground, and the rest of the faithful would then go home and slaughter theirs. But on that particular occasion, when the prayer had been concluded, and everybody was expecting the amir to slaughter his ram Sulaiman announced to the congregation that anyone who had a ram should go home and slaughter it. As for him, Allah had not given him the means of buying one.

Initially, the jihad leaders advised Amir Sulaiman against moving into Gidan Rumfa, arguing that such a move would corrupt their government. But a Hausa elder who understood the psychology of Kano people advised the Amir that unless he moved into the palace, he would not succeed in controlling Kano people. Kano people, he argued, believed in grandeur and they always wanted to be different. They wanted to be pacesetters especially in clothing and housing. Amir Sulaiman therefore sought permission from Shehu Usman Danfodio to move into Gidan Rumfa. In granting the permission the Shehu also sent to Amir Sulaiman a knife and a sword with a mandate that whoever rebelled against him should be put to death. Amir Sulaiman died in 1819.

Once again the leaders of the four clans met to choose a new amir. Each of them, as before, declined the position. Mallam Ibrahim Dabo, twenty-eight years old and a younger brother of Mallam Jamo of the Sullubawa clan, was saddled with that responsibility. His name was sent to Caliph Muhammad Bello who approved the appointment.[25]

THE RETURN OF MONARCHY

Upon assuming office Amir Dabo was confronted with many problems, which he sought to overcome. In the first place the office of the Sarki [26] had, as a result of late Amir Sulaiman's policies and style of leadership, lost its mystique and become bare. The sarki had become just like any ordinary citizen or *talaka*. As a result of the demystification of the office of the sarki, it lost its reverence among the people. That loss of reverence translated into general loss of respect for authority, law and order. In Amir Dabo's analysis of the situation, a vast majority of the common people respected authority and abided by law and order either because of the reverence they had for the sarki, or because of the fear of him that they felt. Amir Dabo was therefore confronted with the problem of getting his subjects to respect him or to fear him so that law and order could be established.

At another level, Amir Sulaiman's policies had neglected state building. In trying to avoid concentration of powers in his own hands, Amir Sulaiman had given the rulers of Kano's outlying districts and towns a great measure of autonomy. He had also ignored the military threats posed by neighbouring states. The result was that Dan Tunku seized Danbatta while Borno under Sheikh Al-Amin El-Kanemi nearly ransacked Kano.

Amir Dabo, like Sulaiman before him, was reputed to be very learned in Islam. He was also learned in psychology and sociology. Early in his administration Amir Dabo identified the demystification of the office of *sarki* as a major source of weakness of his government. He reasoned that if he was to succeed in strengthening Islam in Kano, as he was required to by his position, he needed first to establish an effective authority. Amir Dabo therefore sought permission from Caliph Bello to re-introduce some of the pre-jihad customs and traditions of the Hausa rulers, which although not un-Islamic had been discontinued by Sulaiman. Amir Dabo thus reintroduced most of what Al-Maghili had recommended as exclusive symbols of the king such as the use of ostrich feather sandals, the holding of the twin spears, maintaining some physical distance from the ruled, exhibiting dignity in apparel and mannerisms, and sitting cross-legged in court. Amir Dabo also introduced a new style of wearing the turban, with two ears protruding from the back, a style, which was exclusively reserved, to the Amir and princes. It was one of Amir Dabo's ways of distancing the royalty not only from the *talakawa* but even the aristocrats.

The actions of Amir Dabo began to give concern to some of the original surviving Fulani clan leaders. They thought that Amir Dabo was deviating from their original goals, and that he was paying more attention to worldly, than to spiritual affairs. To check the situation Mallam Dabo Danbazau, who, like the others, had earlier declined the office, sent word to the Caliph, Muhammad Bello, informing him that he had changed his mind and that he was interested in the office. But the Caliph sent back a message to Mallam Dabo Danbazau saying that it was too late at that time as he had already approved the appointment of Mallam Ibrahim Dabo. The Caliph however assured Mallam Dabo Danbazau that should he survive Amir Dabo, the office would be given to him. As it turned out, Amir Dabo outlived Mallam Dabo Danbazau.[27]

Meanwhile, Amir Dabo consolidated his rule by waging wars and appointing to strategic offices of state, his children, kinsmen and other trusted friends. Amir Dabo spent twenty-seven years on the throne and was succeeded by his son Usman. That was the beginning of the Dabo dynasty, which has survived to-date.[28] Usman was succeeded by his younger brother Abdullahi who ruled from 1855 to 1883. After Abdullahi's death, his brother Bello was appointed Amir. He too ruled from 1883 to 1892. Thus, three sons of Amir Dabo, became Amirs. On the death of Bello the Caliph, against the advice of the Kano kingmakers, popular opinion in Kano and his own vizier, directed the latter to turban Tukur, the son of Bello as the Amir of Kano. The vizier complied with the Caliph's instructions and Tukur was turbanned. But he never had a stable reign. His cousins, who felt that Tukur was an imposition, rebelled against him and by implication the Caliph. They were led by Yusuf; the son of Abdullahi and for eleven months Kano was involved in a civil war. Just on the eve of the victory of the rebels, Yusuf, their leader, died. He was succeeded by his younger brother Aliyu who regained Gidan Rumfa as the 7th post-Jihad Amir of Kano in 1894. Amir Aliyu reigned until the British conquered Kano on February 3, 1903. The British appointed Abbas, the son of Abdullahi and a brother of Aliyu as the first colonial Emir of Kano in April 1903. When he died in 1919, he was succeeded by his brother Usman, whose reign lasted until 1926. Abdullahi Bayero, the son of Abbas became Emir in 1926, and was succeeded by Muhammadu Sanusi, his eldest living son in 1953. Emir Sanusi was forced to abdicate in 1963. He was replaced by Muhammadu Inuwa, the son of Abbas. Emir Inuwa's reign lasted only seven months and he was succeeded by Ado Bayero. Thus, since 1819 Ibrahim Dabo, his sons and direct descendants have ruled Kano.

Although during the caliphate years many amirs became very powerful, various mechanisms existed to check their possible excesses. For example, the amirs were constantly reminded that the *raison d'être* of their office was Islam. They were there to strengthen the religion and the only justification for having overthrown the Hausa rulers was the Hausa rulers' straying from Islam. If the Fulani rulers were to follow the same path, then they would equally lose their legitimacy to rule. Another check on the amirs was caliphal authority. The Caliph, through his vizier, supervised the various amirs ensuring that they did not tyrannize their subjects. The vizier sat in the courts of the amirs whenever he was on tour, which he did often, and people brought petitions and appeals before him. He could, and did sometimes, overrule the verdict of the amirs' courts. There were also instances when the Caliph deposed amirs for misgovernment and insubordination as happened with Amir Abdullahi and Amir Abdul-Qadir, both of Zaria.[29] A third mechanism for checking the possible excesses of the rulers was emigration from the territory of the despotic ruler to another. This mechanism, as we noted, had existed long before the jihad. But the Jihad gave it a religious sanction with the Qur'anic injunction "Was, then, Allah's earth not wide enough for you to flee from the domain of oppression" (Holy Qur'an 4:97).

The final mechanism by which the rulers were restrained from arbitrary use of power against their subjects was the fear of revolt by the people. This mechanism was considered a last resort, and was rarely used, perhaps because before the legitimacy of an amir had eroded to the extent that his subjects would openly defy him, the Caliph would either have warned him to behave or removed him from office. But where none of the three mechanisms succeeded, revolt could occur.[30]

EMIRATE ADMINISTRATION IN KANO

The post-jihad leaders of Kano retained the political structures and institutions that they had inherited from the Kano kingdom. Although at the initial stages during the reign of Amir Sulaiman he did not effectively control all the territory of the kingdom, the reign of Amir Dabo witnessed the consolidation of the power of the state in the whole territory. Thus in territorial extent the Kano Emirate was not different from the Kano kingdom.

Administratively, the political institutions and structures developed by the Hausa kings, which were essentially abandoned at the time of Amir Sulaiman, were revived by Amir Dabo. District, village and ward heads were recognized in the administrative set up. But in contrast to the situation prevailing before the jihad or during the reign of Sulaiman, the autonomy of the major towns and their district heads was effectively curtailed. At the head of the political system was the Amir. Directly under him were his councilors or *hakimai*, the important ones being the Makama, Sarkin Bai, Madaki, Galadima, Sarkin Dawakin Tsakar Gida, Sarkin Dawaki mai Tuta, Wambai, Dan Iya and Ciroma. These officials constituted the Tara ta Kano or Council of Nine, who were the chief advisors to the Amir. Although the Amir could appoint persons of his choice to any of these offices when it became vacant, he could not depose such an official without reference to the Caliph. This requirement helped to ensure that the Amir did not surround himself with mere sycophants as advisors.

The amir's councilors were assigned portfolios with the Waziri as chief advisor on all matters. He was therefore expected to be very learned in the Qur'an, hadith (or the traditions of the Holy Prophet) and fiqh (or Islamic jurisprudence), and at the same time be a skilled administrator. The Ma'aji was the emirate treasurer and he kept the accounts of all the proceeds from taxation, royal farms, court fines etc. The Madaki was the commander of the emirate cavalry. Since wars were fought mainly on horseback, the madaki was for all practical purposes the Chief of Defence of the emirate.

Many of the councilors were assigned territories called *gunduma* or districts to administer, even though they continued to live in the emirate capital. The *hakimai* were assisted in the administration of the territories by village heads or *dagatai* and ward heads or *masu unguwa*. The authority structure was pyramidal with the amir on top followed by the *hakimai, dagatai* and *masu unguwa* in that order.

Amir Dabo's many wars of consolidation, increased the demand for revenue. So also his decision to dignify the office of amir, and by extension the court and other important offices of state, through keeping a very high profile in dressing, feeding, and in the affairs of state. This was continued by his successors. In the absence of *ghanima* or religiously sanctioned war booty, due to the fact that Kano was virtually surrounded by Muslim states, resort to the old taxes of the *ancien regime* was made. The most common of these taxes was *kharaj* or poll tax. Some detailed examination of the *kharaj*, particularly the method of its assessment and collection during that period, might help to shed some light on the changes that it later underwent as a result of colonial rule.

ASSESSMENT AND COLLECTION OF *KHARAJ* IN THE KANO EMIRATE UNDER THE CALIPHATE

With the approach of the rainy season each year, the Amir of Kano and his senior advisors would sit to discuss how much would be needed for the administration of the emirate. In arriving at that decision, they were guided by the experience of the previous year and prospects of harvests in the coming year. If the prospects for the current year looked promising, the *kharaj* was made to reflect the economic boom. On the other hand, if the prospects were poor the *kharaj* was accordingly reduced. After the total amount for the emirate had been decided on, it was broken down amongst the various districts of the emirate—population being at this stage the most important determinant of how much a district was required to raise. Thereafter, each district head was informed of how much was expected from his district. After that, dates were fixed for the Amir to go round the districts to announce the taxes or *fasa haraji* (literally "breaking the tax"). It is interesting to note that the district heads were not allowed to simply go and raise the taxes due from their territories after the meeting with the Amir. The Amir himself went out to each district and announced how much was due from the people. He also informed the people what the average rate, or *kudin goro*, was. The Amir would implore the people to endeavour to pay their taxes as soon as they had disposed of their harvested crops—usually two to four months ahead. And finally, the Amir would pray to Allah to give them a bumper harvest, to let peace reign, and to protect the emirate from all evils.

The next stage in the assessment and collection of the *kharaj* lay with the district heads, who assembled their village heads and formally informed them about the total amount due from their district as a whole and the *kudin goro*.[31] This meeting was held in the presence of the Amir's *jakada* or agent.[32] Based on the number of households in the villages, the *kudin goro* was shared out among the village heads. These village heads then went back to their villages and with the help of their ward heads (in the case of big villages) an updated list of taxable persons was prepared.[33] The amir and district head were represented at this stage of the exercise by their own agents, who were expected to ensure compliance with the directives issued by their respective masters. A day was then fixed and the people of a village were all invited to an open place—usually the village head's residence or the market place. The village head then formally informed his subjects that the amir had "broken the tax." He also informed them what the average rate was.

In theory the tax burden was shared equally among the taxable adults. But in reality, the rich paid more than the poor did. The practice was that the village head, in the presence of the agents and all the people, brought some nuts or pebbles. The total number of the units was equal to the amount of tax expected from the village. The people were then called upon to go and share out the nuts among themselves. The poorer people took fewer of the nuts or pebbles, while the richer

ones took more. Neither the village nor the ward head inter-
fered in that distribution of tax burden. It was left to the people who knew the economic status of each other. If some nuts
remained after everybody had taken what he thought was his
fair share of the tax burden, the community members usually
approached the wealthy people among them and implored
them to take more—usually praying that Allah might make
them richer and their wealth beneficial to their families and
community. After all the nuts had been taken, each ward or
village head proceeded to record against his name what each
member had taken. This, then, is the process by which taxes
were assessed. After the harvest, everybody was expected to
pay to his ward or village head what was recorded against his
name. That practice continued until the British conquered
Kano and introduced policies that compelled the traditional
rulers to change the methods of assessment and collection of
the tax, as we shall see shortly.

BACKGROUND TO THE BRITISH CONQUEST OF KANO

On January 1, 1900, in the confluence city of Lokoja, in what
is now Kogi State, Captain Frederick Dealtry Lugard, who
later became Lord Lugard, took the first practical step
towards bringing the Kano Emirate under British colonial
rule. On that fateful day Captain Lugard lowered, for the last
time, the flag of the Royal Niger Company, and in its stead
hoisted the British Union Jack. With that symbolic act accomplished, Lugard declared a protectorate over the whole of
what later came to be called Northern Nigeria. Next, Lugard
set out to accomplish his mission. This was to take effective
control of the rest of the lands and peoples in the region to
which Britain had claimed sole right according to the terms
agreed by the various European powers at the Berlin
Conference on the partition of Africa in 1884-85.

Within three years of Lugard's declaration of a protectorate over Northern Nigeria, he had largely accomplished
his task of subjugating that territory. Sokoto, the seat of the

Usmaniyya Caliphate was brought under effective British rule. So were Kano, Zaria, Ilorin, Yola, and other major emirates that made up the caliphate. How was this vast area of 281,273 square miles (three times the size of Britain) brought under British rule with such speed considering especially that colonial occupation took over fifty years to be effected in the Southern protectorates and colonies, whose combined territory is only a third of the North's? What accounts for the difference in the pace of occupation?

Was it, as Margery Perham argued, because the Fulani rulers were so tyrannical and despotic in their rule that made the Hausa subject class to see the British as their possible redeemers, and therefore assisted rather than opposed the British troops against their rulers?[34] Or was it, as Lady Lugard argued, that "they [the Hausa] were easily defeated because they had none of that permanent resisting power which is drawn from the love of a people for its liberty, its territory, its institutions."[35] We will not attempt any detailed critique of these explanations here. It suffices to note that these explanations failed to see any relationship between, on the one hand, the amount of time spent preparing for that event, the amount of money expended, the number of soldiers involved in actual combat, and on the other hand, the speed with which the occupation was effected. It is interesting to note that virtually all the major studies on the subject mention that Lugard was chosen for the job of subjugating Northern Nigeria in 1897. He was then instructed to raise an initial army of 2000 strong; and that the British government voted £200,000 (a sum unprecedented in British imperialist history in West Africa) for a military expedition to bring Northern Nigeria under British rule.[36] Why the sudden interest by imperial Britain in subjugating Northern Nigeria at the end of the 19th century? Before answering that question we shall briefly examine the imposition of colonial rule in Southern Nigeria. This is to provide a background to our discussion of the imposition of colonial rule in the North.

THE ESTABLISHMENT OF COLONIAL
RULE IN SOUTHERN NIGERIA

The European presence along the coast of Nigeria dates back to the 15th century, when the Portuguese first began to trade with the coastal peoples. At first, from the late 15th to the early 16th centuries, trade was conducted in commodities, the Europeans exchanging rum, cloth, gunpowder, etc. for African gold and pepper. Then from the mid-16th century, the trade in human traffic came to replace commodities, and for the next 300 years and more, until the 19th century, slaves were the dominant commodities Europeans bought from Africa.

In 1807 the British government abolished the slave trade, forbidding British subjects to engage in it. Thirty years later, in 1837, it abolished slavery too. In formulating a law abolishing the slave trade two problems were created for the British government. The first was how to enforce the law to ensure that slaves were not brought into Britain or British territories and sold. The second was how to develop "legitimate" trade for the benefit of the new industries of Britain. The solution to either of these problems appeared to require a British presence in the area, which served as the source of the slaves, and in the area where "legitimate" trade was to be developed. Britain therefore sent gunboats to the West African coast to patrol the area, seize any slave ship, and free the slaves. At the same time, British merchants were encouraged to go and start legitimate trade, with the Africans in such commodities as palm oil. The British merchants were assured of government protection against the natives. With that assurance the British traders began to penetrate the interior of the coasts to transact business directly with the producers of the commodities they needed, thereby cutting off the coastal peoples and their chiefs from the trade. The coastal peoples resented being eliminated from the business and therefore began to disrupt the flow of trade. Consequently, the British government made good its promise to its nationals when in 1849, it declared the area today known as the Eastern Coast of Nigeria as a British Protectorate with the name of the

Oil Rivers Protectorate, and Calabar as its administrative head-quarters. A British Consul was appointed for the Protectorate. That was the first step in the colonisation of Nigeria. Thirteen years later, in 1862, the British took the opportunity of a succession dispute concerning the occupant of the throne in Lagos to declare Lagos a British colony. Thereafter, calculated efforts were made to bring as much of the surrounding land and peoples as possible under the British Raj. Benin was taken in 1897. By the turn of the 20th century, most of Yorubaland was under effective British occupation. The Egbas were the last of the Yoruba states to come under British rule with the signing away of their nominal independence in 1914.[37]

Those areas that Britain occupied in the hinterland of Lagos were not made part of Lagos colony. Rather, they remained as separate administrations called protectorates.[38]

At the same time that inroads were being made into the hinterland from Lagos, similar developments were taking place in the East with the Oil Rivers Protectorate. In 1893, the Oil Rivers Protectorate was extended into the hinterland on both banks of the Niger River and renamed the Niger Coast Protectorate. With the formal naming of the territory "Nigeria" on January 1, 1900, by Britain, the Niger Coast Protectorate was renamed the Protectorate of Southern Nigeria. Despite the declaration of a protectorate over the whole of the area called Nigeria by Britain, the three different administrations continued as autonomous political entities until 1906. It was then that the colony and protectorate of Lagos were amalgamated with the protectorate of Southern Nigeria, and designated the colony and protectorate of Southern Nigeria. Eight years later, in 1914, Lugard amalgamated the Northern and Southern Protectorates to form the Colony and Protectorate of Nigeria.

ESTABLISHMENT OF COLONIAL RULE IN NORTHERN NIGERIA

In contrast to the gradual process of occupation in the South, the occupation of the North was effected with lightening speed. Within three years an area three times the size of the South had been largely brought under British colonial rule. What accounts for this change of policy from gradualism to immediate action? The following, is what I believe best explains the immediacy with which the North was conquered, as opposed to what Orr, Geary, Perham, Lugard and others would want us to believe.[39]

There seem to be at least three factors, which, together, may offer a more fruitful explanation to this question. The first was a change in the climate of public opinion in Britain with regard to the acquisition of colonies. The second was the British perception of the Sokoto caliphate. Finally there were certain developments within the caliphate at about the turn of the century including the caliphate leaders' perceptions of the British and their war machine. I will examine each of these factors to see how it contributed to the swiftness in the conquest of Northern Nigeria.

BRITISH PUBLIC OPINION AND COLONIALISM

Colonialism was not a new phenomenon in British history by the 19th Century. Many centuries earlier, parts of North America had been colonised. So also were New Zealand, Australia, and Canada. However, by the end of the 18th century, after America had fought for and won its independence, British public opinion did not favour acquiring any more colonies.[40] This climate of opinion prevailed until sometime after 1870[41] when, due to a series of developments both domestic and external to Britain, a new wave of support for imperialism sprang up. This second surge of imperialism came to be called "the new imperialism," and a vast body of literature was produced to explain the new phenomenon. This body of literature can be classified under three broad schools or paradigms. The first is the economic-deterministic school. This body of theories attempts to explain the new imperialism in an economically deterministic way. The crux of its argument is that the new imperialism was embarked upon by the nations of Europe at the time they did from economic necessity, namely the need for raw materials as well as markets for their manufactured goods. It was argued that by the late 19th century, when the new imperialism was at its peak, most of the European powers and America had industrialised. Capitalism, being a progressive economic system, needed new outlets for expansion.[42] Hence, the competition among the industrialised nations of Europe for control of the lands and peoples of Africa—the new imperialism.

The second body of theories comes under what Schumpeter called social atavism.[43] This group of theories attempts to explain the rise of the new imperialism by reference not to the immediate and prevailing political, social, economic and industrial conditions in Europe in the last quarter of the 19th century, but to unchanging human nature. The new imperialism, according to this school, was not caused by developments in Europe in the 19th century, as throughout history powerful nations had sought to conquer and dominate less powerful ones. The new imperialism was therefore explained as just a continuation of what had always been the stuff of history.[44]

The final group of theories, which have been variously, called the "theory of moral responsibility" or the *"mission civilizatrice"* or the "white man's burden" attempted to explain the new imperialism in ideological terms. The expansion of Europe into Africa and Asia, and the forcible colonisation of these continents was, according to this school, a moral duty Europe owed to the Africans and Asians, i.e. the moral obligation to raise them "up" to the European level. Because all the colonial powers emphasized this variant of the causes of the new imperialism at the expense of the other two, we shall look at this theory in some greater detail.

THE IMPERIAL THEORY OF MORAL RESPONSIBILITY

Three developments, spanning some four centuries, shaped the European theory of moral responsibility. The first was

Christianity and its proselytizing mission. The second was the industrial revolution. And the last was intellectualism. We will briefly examine each of these developments and how it contributed to imperialism and the imperial theory of moral responsibility.

CHRISTIANITY, PROSELYTISM AND IMPERIALISM

Some critics of imperialism have argued that Christian missionaries did the groundwork for the later colonisation of Africa. Christian missionaries were alleged to have encouraged their home governments to establish, initially, some form of presence so as to protect them against the natives should the need arise, and later to occupy the lands of the natives.[45] It has also been argued that at the Berlin Conference on the partition of Africa, one of the criteria used for determining which European nation got which piece of African territory, was the extent to which missionaries from a particular European nation were already effectively established in the territory. This was usually signified by the granting of permission by the local rulers to the missionaries to settle in their lands.[46]

These two historical facts have made European missionaries less able to extricate themselves from charges of conspiracy with their national governments to subjugate Africans. While these charges are undeniable, I think that the role Christian missionaries played in the colonisation of Africa and Asia was far greater than these two incidents, and in fact, long predated the era of the new imperialism itself. The greatest impact of the Christian missionaries on the new imperialism did not come from what they said or failed to say, or what they did or failed to do. Neither did it come from what was done because of them. The greatest impact, I think, came essentially from an idea they created, but which was later popularized by others in pursuit of different goals. That idea was the belief in the correctness or moral rightness of converting others to Christianity. There is no doubt that the

Christian missionaries sincerely believed that Christianity was superior to all other religions. They believed that it was the one and only right way to heaven. For this reason those peoples or races who had not embraced it were either completely ignorant of it or did not know much about it. In either case, the Christian missionaries believed that it was their moral and religious responsibility to guide those "lost peoples or races" to the right faith.[47] This belief in the moral responsibility of those who had seen the "light" to lead others still in the dark to see the same light, all in the name of God, was later in the 19th century to be revived. But this time the light was not God's, but that of Western civilization. The analogy drawn was that if religious superiority carried an obligation to convert the heathen to Christianity, then cultural superiority equally carried an obligation to convert the barbarian to civilization. Hence, the French idea of *"mission civilizatrice"* or civilizing mission.

What then made the Europeans to see themselves as culturally superior to the Africans?

INDUSTRIALISM AND IMPERIALISM

The industrial revolution which started in England in the early 18th century and spread to other parts of Europe by the 19th century greatly transformed European society. No aspect of European life was left unaffected by this development. Tom Kemp describes it as a "fundamental revolution in the history of mankind which led to the development of the world as we know it today." He argues that the revolution or industrialization brought into existence "those forms of labor and styles of living distinguishing the modern world from the past, the advanced from the "backward" ones".[48] The way politics was conducted was changed. The economy underwent a radical transformation and so did the social structure.[49] Material progress in all respects—medicine, agriculture, weaponry, transportation, etc.- came not only to change the material life of European people, but also their ways of thought. Old beliefs, especially about some diseases, were discarded as medicine came to prove them wrong. The reality of "human progress" became evident. It was this reality, which gave rise to the third development connected with the new imperialism, namely, scholarship or developments in the "scientific" study of man (his physiology and psychology) and his societies (with their various cultures).

INTELLECTUALISM AND IMPERIALISM

The developments in the intellectual field in Europe from the late 18th century through the 19th, seemed to support the view that great philosophies or doctrines do not arise in a vacuum; they always arise as responses to specific crises of their times.[50] The missionaries' i dea of the superiority of the Christian faith over all other faiths (particularly African religions), coupled with the material progress that industrialization bestowed on Europe in the 19th century began to create a crisis in the thinking of Europeans with regard to other peoples and races. Why should Europeans be the only race to develop materially? Why have other races not been able to develop too?

These and other questions occupied the minds of many of Europe's intellectuals at that time. Before long, a series of studies purporting to answer these questions were being produced. Among the notable ones was H.T. Buckle's *A History of Civilization*[51]. This study attempted to handle human society by the methods of the physical sciences. It purported to trace a causal connection between climate and forms of social organization, size of population, and even the production and distribution of ideas. Next came Walter Bagehot's *Physics and Politics: Thoughts on the Application of the Principles of Natural Selection and Inheritance to Political Society*[52], to be quickly followed by Joseph Gobineau's *Essay on the Inequality of the Human Races*.[53] Finally, the most significant of all, in terms of its impact on European thought at that time, Charles Darwin's *The Origin of Species*.[54] Most of these "scientific" studies arrived at some common conclusions.[55] The first was that race was a fundamental determinant of all history and culture. Secondly, racial superiority led to cultural superiority. And, finally, the white race was superior to all other races. Hence, there was an explanation for the white race's cultural (ideational, material, and technological) advancement while other races were still backward. The general conclusions drawn from these positions were that a) inferior races will wither away in the struggle for survival (Darwin's survival of the fittest); or, in the alternative, b) inferior races should be provided with some chivalric protection accorded to women and other weaker forms of life. Morally, the second option was preferable to the extinction of a whole race. Imperialism, according to imperial theorists of the moral responsibility school, was a means of actualizing this preferred alternative.

THE WHITE MAN'S BURDEN

If the only alternative to the extinction of the inferior races was for some members of the white superior race to take the burden of civilizing them, European nations felt they should carry that burden. After all, their missionaries had for centuries been doing the same thing, but the missionaries had acted in the name of religion. Jules Harmand summarized the general belief of the period thus:

> It is necessary, then to accept as a principle and point of departure the fact that there is a hierarchy of races and civilizations, and that we belong to the superior races and civilizations, still recognizing that, while superiority confers rights, it imposes strict obligations in return. The basic legitimization of conquest over native peoples is the conviction of our superiority, not merely mechanical, economic, and military superiority, but our moral superiority. Our dignity rests on that quality, and it under lies our right to direct the rest of humanity. Material power is nothing but the means to that end.[56]

On the question of the moral responsibility for civilizing the backward races as an end in itself, all the European races seemed to have been in general agreement. Where they differed was on the means to achieving that end. The British chose indirect rule, the French assimilation and the Belgians and Portuguese association.[57] All of them argued that their respective policies were concerned with the benefit of others, or at least with mutual benefits for the colonized as well as the colonizers.[58]

This then was the prevailing climate of public opinion in Britain at about the turn of the century when Lugard was chosen to bring the caliphate under effective British rule.

BRITISH PERCEPTION OF THE SOKOTO CALIPHATE

From various European sources—missionaries, traders, explorers etc., the British had known since the 19th century about the Sokoto Caliphate which was reputed to be a very highly centralized state with an efficient and effective administrative system.[59] Though a loose federation of states—called the caliphate—the bond of unity among the component states was strong. Islam brought them together, and it also (through Sokoto) held them together. All the leaders of the emirates owed allegiance to the Caliph at Sokoto, who was their religious and political leader.[60] Once or twice a year, each of the emirs visited Sokoto to pay homage and renew his allegiance. The Caliph could assemble a substantial army at short notice to fight his wars, which were always proclaimed religious wars or jihad.[61]

From their experience with other Islamic states, the British knew that Muslims, both rulers and ruled, would not easily give in to Euro-Christian rule. In the case of the Sokoto Caliphate, the British fear of the non co-operation of the rulers at a British request for "protecting" them was heightened by one other factor. Apart from the natural rivalry between the Muslim and the Christian, the rulers of the Sokoto Caliphate could not, even if they wanted to, readily accept British protection, for the simple fact that their legitimacy as rulers was rooted in their being custodians of the Islamic faith. They had come to power through Islam, and they were, at least in theory, sustained on their thrones because they were defenders of Islam. To give in to European occupation would be like handing over the Islamic community to unbelievers, presumably to destroy it.

The British also believed that, quite apart from the rulers the subject population would also fight to the death for its religion. The British could not have been unaware of the fact that Islam taught its adherents that martyrdom, or *shahada,* was a sure way to heaven. Given these perceptions, the British became convinced that occupying Northern Nigeria was going to require a lot more force than they had previously employed anywhere else. They also believed that swiftness in the execution of the occupation process was the key to success.

CONTRIBUTORY FACTORS WITHIN THE CALIPHATE

By the end of the 19th century, the bond of unity that had characterized the relationship among member emirates of the Sokoto caliphate had weakened. Sokoto did not wield the kind of influence it had previously wielded on the emirates especially in the early years of the jihad. Indeed, there had been occasions when some emirates disregarded directives from Sokoto. In Kano, as we have seen, Sokoto's role in choosing a successor to the late Emir Bello had led to an open defiance of the authority of Sokoto by a section of the Kano royal family. This development weakened the military base of the caliphate. It could not muster from the militarily powerful emirates at a short notice, the number of soldiers and the amount of armaments it would need to repel European invasion.

The second development was internal to some of the emirates. In emirates like Kano, the civil war in the last decade of the 19th century as well as constant raids by Ningi and

Damagaram had taken a serious toll on the military institution. Not only was a large number of the fighting force killed, but also the armaments that had been saved over the years had been depleted in the course of the wars. That was the background to the British conquest of the North and it is against that background that we are going to discuss the reaction of the emirs to the imposition of colonial rule.

EMIRS' REACTIONS TO THE
IMPOSITION OF COLONIAL RULE

Among the criticisms levelled against contemporary African traditional rulers is the allegedly shaky foundation of their legitimacy. The critics argue that contemporary traditional rulers lost their legitimacy when their parents or grandparents collaborated with the colonialists, first to subjugate their own people, and later to exploit, denigrate and commit various atrocities against them. They further argue that most of those who have paraded themselves as traditional rulers since the inception of colonial rule, even though they came from royal families, would not have qualified for those offices if the traditional values of their people had been strictly adhered to. To such critics, those traditional rulers who faced the Europeans head-on and as a result died or were exiled are the heroes to remember. On the other hand, those who put up feeble resistance or none at all, and decided to negotiate or collaborate with the Europeans, are painted as the villains.[62] But how fair is this judgement? Does it take into consideration the historical circumstances under which each group of traditional rulers took its decision to either resist or acquiesce? What were the options available to them at that time? For those who acquiesced, were they any less nationalistic than those who resisted?

The reactions of the various emirs of the caliphate to the British invasion of their lands were, to a large extent, influenced by four factors. These were the timing of the invasion, the treatment of previously conquered emirs, the presence or absence of a threat to the emirate, and the individual emirs' perception of the power equation between the emirate and the foreign invaders.

Generally, all attempts to subjugate the emirates before 1900 met with stiff resistance. The British were beaten back or met with very stiff resistance in their attempts to overrun the emirates of Bida, Muri, and Ilorin in 1897, and also Yola, Kontagora, Agaie and Lapai in 1900. They met with little resistance in Ilorin in 1900, Gombe, Zaria, Bauchi and Gwandu in 1902; and Katsina, Katagum and Hadejia in 1903. They also met with some resistance in Kano in February 1903 and in Sokoto the following month.

From the foregoing a pattern could be discerned. Attempts at subjugating the emirates before the actual declaration of a protectorate over the area, on January 1, 1900, were resisted. This could be attributed to the emirs' belief that they could successfully fight the forces of the Royal Niger Company. And in that they were right, for they did succeed in repelling the invaders. Equally, the rulers, being the first in the whole caliphate to be confronted with a situation where they were going to lose their independence to a non-Muslim power, felt that they had a duty to resist that development. After all, the *raison d'être* of their thrones was Islam—to protect it from infidels and strengthen it among the believers. But after the Union Jack had been hoisted, and the southern emirates of Ilorin, Yola, Kontagora, and Bauchi had been resoundingly defeated in battles with Lugard's forces, the message went out loud and clear. There was no stopping the British. It has been persuasively argued that the last quarter of 1902 was the turning point in the attitude of the emirates towards British conquest: that is, from an attitude of determination to resist to one of marked fatalism.[63]

Apart from the timing of the invasion, the way the British treated the vanquished people especially their emirs also influenced how other emirs responded to the "invitation" to be part of the British protectorate. The fact that in a number of emirates the British allowed the erstwhile emirs to continue to rule if only they were willing to accept a subordinate role was encouraging to the other emirs. At least, they stood a chance of retaining their office if they co-operated. Another encouraging fact was the assurance given by the British that they would not interfere with the Islamic religion. That assurance relieved the emirs of the religious obligation to fight a losing battle.

The third factor was the internal social and political situation in individual emirates. Where emirs felt threatened from either within or without, the tendency was for them to invite or accept the offer of assistance from the British. In most cases, the emirs ended up losing their power to the British. It happened to the emir of Zaria in 1902, when he gladly welcomed the British in the face of a threat from the fugitive emir of Kontagora.

Finally, the perception of the individual emirs, of the power relations between them and the British also affected their response. When the powerful states of Kano and Sokoto were conquered, smaller emirates such as Katagum, Hadejia, Daura, Gumel and Kazaure submitted more or less peacefully when the British arrived to occupy each of them between 1903 and 1904.[64] It can be safely argued that the relatively weaker emirates of the south put up stiff resistance because they did not know the extent of the might of the British. The more powerful emirates did not put up stiff resistance because they had seen from the others what the colonial war machine could do to uncooperative rulers. How did Kano respond to the British invasion?

THE CASE OF KANO EMIRATE

By 1902, the imminence of the British invasion of Kano was certain. What was uncertain, however, was how to respond to the situation. There is evidence that the Amir of Kano, Aliyu bin Abdullahi, popularly called Alu, had agonized over this issue for some time. For example, in 1902, the Sarkin Garko, seeing the fate that had befallen the emirates of Bida,

Kontagora, and Yola, was reported to have warned Amir Aliyu of the impending danger, and advised that the Kano walls should be fortified and strengthened. But the Wazirin Kano, Ahmadu, brother of the Amir, advised the Amir against entertaining any idea of resisting the Europeans, in view of the fact that powerful states like Damagaram and Bida had failed to resist them successfully.[65]

The Waziri's advice notwithstanding, when the Amir learnt of the arrival of the British at Zaria in 1902, he took immediate steps to fortify Kano by rebuilding the walls of the emirate capital. He also directed the authorities of subordinate towns between Kano and Zaria to repair their own town walls too. Furthermore, he intensified efforts at securing arms from Tripolitanian merchants as well as run-away mercenaries of Lugard's West African Frontier Force, WAFF. It has been suggested that by October 1902, Amir Alu was ready to attack the British at Zaria, but for the death of the Sarkin Musulmi Abdurrahman.[66] Three months after the death of Sarkin Musulmi Abdurrahman, Amir Alu set off for Sokoto ostensibly on a condolence visit and also to pay homage to the new Sarkin Musulmi, Attahiru bin Ahmad. Abubakar Dokaji has argued that the reason for Amir Alu's departure to Sokoto at the time he set off, apart from paying homage and visiting his grand-parents and the tomb of his mother, was to consult with the Sarkin Musulmi, Attahiru, on how best to tackle the imminent danger which the British posed, not just to his emirate but the whole caliphate and the Muslim Ummah. According to this source, Alu went to discuss with the head of the caliphate how to work out a strategy for the collective security of the caliphate.[67]

Some critics have suggested that Amir Alu's departure from Kano at that particular time was an indirect way of sur-rendering to the British. They argue that having seen how the British easily defeated the powerful state of Kontagora, and what had befallen the Etsu Nupe after his emirate had been captured, Alu must have thought it wise to avoid any direct confrontation with the British. He knew very well that Kano could not withstand their might.[68]

Mahmud Tukur cites the action of the Amir while on his way back to Kano, on learning for certain that his capital had been occupied, to support this position. Amir Alu first learnt of the occupation of Kano city by the British while on his way back to Kano from Sokoto, about February 5, 1903, at Faru. He proceeded to Birnin Goga where he had further confirmation of the occupation. Confronted with a fait *accompli*, Amir Alu was reported to have decided to spend the night with his *hakimai* and forces at Birnin Goga. While everybody was asleep, the Amir, with one of his wives and five trusted servants, slipped away from the camp. The following morning everybody gathered waiting for the Amir to come out for a decision to be taken on what to do in view of the latest developments in Kano. When it was discovered that the Amir had fled, a debate ensued among his *hakimai* on the best course of action. But a consensus could not be reached. Three distinctive positions crystalized. The first, advocated by Waziri Ahmadu, was direct confrontation with the British forces, even if it led to *shahada* or martyrdom. The second, advocated by Galadima Mahmud, a younger brother of Alu, was to return to Sokoto and presumably to join forces with those of the Sarkin Musulmi to fight the British. The third, advocated by Wambai Abbas, also a brother to Amir Alu, was to surrender to the British.

A rational justification has been advanced for each of the positions taken by the Amir and his chiefs in dealing with the occupation of Kano. According to Tukur, Amir Alu had decided on the futility of resistance long before Kano was captured.[69] He buttresses this view with the fact that "the emir did not even risk being held back from his flight by his chiefs...by simply leaving in secret...."[70] The evidence of the correspondence that took place between Kano and Sokoto in 1902 supports Tukur's argument. In one letter from Sarkin Kano Alu to Wazirin Sokoto, Muhammadu Buhari, the Amir suggested that they should leave the territories, as the infidels were poised to take it. "To assist our religion, earth and heaven, let us leave as these dogs have surrounded us and threaten to overcome us."[71] Tukur further argues that in taking that course of action, "Aliyu at once followed the dictates of his conscience, unilaterally absolved himself from responsibility for any course of action that his chiefs might later take. By the same token he has absolved those chiefs, collectively and severally, to follow the dictates of their own consciences."[72]

Arguing in the same vein, but giving it a religious tone, Dahiru Yahya posits that Amir Alu's flight could be analogous to a hijra or religiously sanctioned flight from oppression, as Prophet Muhammad (SAW), was directed by Allah (SWT) to do in the face of persecution from the people of Makka. Amir Alu's flight should, therefore, not be equated with cowardice or the abandonment of Islam to the infidels, argues Yahya. Citing the Holy Qur'an's admonition to Muslims who, because they were weak, allowed themselves to be compromised "Was, then, Allah's earth not wide enough for you to flee from the domain of oppression?"(Qur'an 4:97) Yahya absolves Alu from charges of cowardice or betrayal of the faith on account of his abandoning his emirate and people.[73]

The path of *shahada* or martyrdom chosen by Waziri Ahmadu cannot in retrospect be rationally justified especially when it is remembered that about a year earlier, he had advised against direct confrontation with the British forces. It is arguable that the flight of Amir Alu, which could indirectly be linked to his advice, left Waziri Ahmadu, as the most senior *Hakimi* available with the duty to surrender, as he had earlier advised, to the British. Waziri Ahmadu would rather have preferred to be behind Alu if the Amir had surrendered. Waziri Ahmadu was not ready to do the surrendering himself. That could explain his decision to fight to the finish.

Another impetus for the Waziri's act is the religious support for *shahada*. The Qur'an (2:154) says, "And say not of those who are slain in the way of Allah: 'they are dead.' Nay, they are living, though ye perceive (it) not." The significance of the religious motive can be seen from the description of the behavior of the Waziri's troops before the actual fight. Various accounts say that just before the battle at Kotorkoshi, the troops dismounted from their horses, performed ablutions, remounted their horses and then charged at the British troops. As for the Waziri, in addition to performing the ablution he also wore white clothes and rode a white horse.[74] So widely was the belief in their martyrdom in Kano that Waziri Ahmadu is popularly referred to as *Mai Shahada* or the martyr.[75] As expected, the Waziri's troops were resoundingly defeated.

The argument of Galadima Mahmud falls in between hijra and *shahada*, as they were retreating, but with the hope of joining a larger force to come and do battle.

The final option—surrender—was that taken by Wambai Abbas. This decision is rationalized on the grounds of the futility of resistance, since after all the emirate capital had been captured. Whatever arms they might have had in their armory were not in their control. If they were to fight, they were only going to fight with the weapons they had on them, and these were no match for the fire power of the British troops.

The surrender to a non-Muslim power actually did have an Islamic sanction. Dahiru Yahya notes that the Qur'anic provision on *taqiyyah,* or what he calls prudent consciousness is given by the Qur'anic verse, "Let not the believers take those who deny the truth for their allies in preference to the believers, and he who does this cuts himself off from Allah in everything unless it is to protect yourselves against them in this way. (3:28):" By this Qur'anic provision, surrender, or allying with the British was sanctioned.

Wambai Abbas therefore proceeded straight to Kano and submitted to the British. Two months after the fall of Kano, Wambai Abbas was installed the first Emir of Kano under colonial rule.

But how did Emir Abbas and subsequent emirs appointed by the British relate to their colonial overlords? Were they just "yes-men" or had they minds of their own? In what ways did colonialism change the position of the emir in the new political system of the Kano emirate?

CHANGING POSITION OF THE EMIR UNDER COLONIAL RULE, 1903-1960

By April 3, 1903, when the British formally installed Muhammadu Abbas ibn Abdullahi (Maje Karofi) ibn Ibrahim Dabo as the first colonial Emir of Kano, the position of the new emir in the new political system of Kano emirate had been outlined. Even if Captain Lugard had not made his famous policy statement on indirect rule at the installation of Attahiru II as the first Sultan of Sokoto,[76] a month earlier, it is safe to assume that Muhammadu Abbas had no illusions that whoever was eventually appointed the Emir of Kano by the British would have his powers greatly circumscribed. In that policy statement, Captain Lugard left no one in doubt about the new power relationship—the position of the Sultan vis-à-vis the emirs and that of both vis-à-vis the colonial government. Lugard had said:

> The old treaties are dead—you have killed them. Now these are the words that I, the High Commissioner, have to say for the future. The Fulani in old times, under Danfodio, conquered this country. They took the right to rule over it, to levy taxes, to depose kings and to create kings. They in turn have by defeat lost their rule, which has come into the hands of the British. All these things, which I have said, the Fulani by conquest took the right to do now pass to the British. Every sultan and every emir, and the principal officers of state will be appointed by the High Commissioner throughout this country. The High Commissioner will be guided by the usual laws of succession, and the wishes of the people and chiefs; but will set them aside, if he desires, for good cause to do so. The emirs and chiefs who are appointed

will rule over the people as of old time, and take such taxes as are approved by the High Commissioner; but they will obey the laws of the Governor, and will act in accordance with the advice of the Resident. It is forbidden to import firearms (except flint-locks), and there are other minor matters, which the Resident will explain. The alkalis and the emirs will hold the law courts as of old; but bribes are forbidden and mutilation and confine-ment of men in inhuman prisons are not lawful. The powers of each court will be contained in a warrant appointing it. Sentences of death will not be carried out without the consent of the Resident.

The Governor will, in future, hold the rights in land, which the Fulani took by conquest from the people, and if government requires land, it will take it for any purpose. The government holds the right of taxation, and will tell the emirs and chiefs what taxes they may levy and what part of them must be paid to government. The government will have the right to all minerals, but the people may dig for iron and work in it subject to the approval of the High Commissioner, and may take salt and other minerals subject to any excise imposed by law. Traders will not be taxed by chiefs, but only by government. The coinage of the British will be accepted as legal tender, and a rate of exchange for cowries fixed in consultation with chiefs and they will enforce it.

When an emirate or an office of state becomes vacant it will only be filled with the consent of the High Commissioner; and the person chosen by the council of chiefs, and approved by the High Commissioner, will hold his place only on condition that he obeys the laws of the protectorate and the conditions of his appointment...[77]

Lugard's speech has been quoted at length to show how it contained all the seeds of the destruction of the fabric of the emirate system—from the relationship between the emirates and Sokoto to the emirs and their *Hakimai*. Any intelligent observer would have known from that speech that the position of the emirs in the new political system was not going to remain the same as prior to Lugard's speech. For the speech, while clearly subordinating the emirs to the representatives of the colonial government, also, by a fiat, removed all the four mechanisms identified earlier as restraints on the arbitrary use of state power by the emirs. In the first place, Sokoto was no more the suzerain of the emirates. The Waziri of Sokoto could not therefore go round to ensure adherence to Islamic principles of governance in the emirates. Secondly, the emirs appointed by the colonial regime did not owe their position to the jihad. As such, their legitimacy was not rooted in Islam. Hence, they were not obliged to rule according to Islamic precepts.[78] The acquiescence of the new emirs in the colonial government's abolition of mutilation and death sentences was the first indication, at least publicly, of a departure from the *shari'ah* or Islamic law, whose emphasis on justice served as restraints on the possible excesses of the rulers.[79] And the final mechanism—revolt against or emigration from the territories of tyrannical rulers—was completely ruled out as long as the rulers were in the good books of the colonial overlords.[80] With these observations and background, we shall now examine the policy and practice of indirect rule, and how they affected the position of the emir.

INDIRECT RULE: THE THEORY

With the pacification of the major emirates of the caliphate and Borno in the opening years of the 20th century, Lugard's mission was largely accomplished. His next major problem was how to establish effective and permanent control over the conquered peoples and territories. This problem was real, especially if it is remembered that after the initial shock of conquest, a number of towns rose against the British.[81] One way to establish effective control was to take direct charge of the administration of the territories. But Lugard had little knowledge of the peoples to whom he had just become a master. Neither did he know the terrain of the vast territory— three times the size of his metropolitan state—he had conquered. Moreover, his problem was compounded by the lack of sufficient qualified Britons to engage in the direct admin-istration of the territories. A fourth major hurdle for Lugard was how to raise the money needed to administer such a vast territory, in view of the unwillingness of the British govern-ment to make any grants to foreign dependencies. It was with these teething problems that indirect rule as a system of administration was conceived and applied.

C.S. Temple, one of the main architects of indirect rule and a successor to Lugard, defined indirect rule as:

> A system of administration which leaves in existence the machinery which had been created by the natives themselves, which recognizes the existence of the Emirs, Chiefs and Native Councils, Native Courts of justice, Mohammedan courts, pagan courts, native police controlled by native exec-utives as real living forces and not as curious and interesting pageantry by which European influence is brought to bear on the native indirectly through his chiefs and not directly through European officers -political, police, etc.,and by which the European keeps himself a good deal in the background and leaves the mass of the native individual to understand that the orders which come to them emanate from their own chief rather than from the all-pervading whiteman.[82]

To administer Northern Nigeria according to the indirect rule policy as defined above, the British designated the whole ter-ritory as a single political entity called the Protectorate of Northern Nigeria. It was headed by the High Commissioner. For administrative purposes, the protectorate was divided into provinces—varying between eleven and seventeen at different times from 1900 to 1937. These provinces were fur-ther sub-divided into divisions. The divisions were in turn carved into smaller administrative units called districts. A number of these districts corresponded with the pre-colonial districts in the emirates, while the divisions usually corre-sponded with the emirates. But this was not always so. Kano Division, for example, was comprised of Kano Emirate only, whereas Katsina Division comprised Katsina, Daura and Kazaure emirates. To each of these levels of administration, European heads were appointed. At the District level the *hakimi*'s immediate superior, or shadow *hakimi,* was the European District Officer (generally called D.O.) to whom the *hakimi* became accountable and from whom he took his orders. Similarly, at the divisional level the Divisional Officer was the emir's immediate superior or shadow emir, to whom the emir became accountable. The only exceptions to this rule were the Sultan of Sokoto, the Shehu of Borno and the emirs of Kano and Zaria, who were permitted direct access to the residents of their respective provinces. In the structure of colonial administration, the last two units of administration, namely, village level (*dagaci*) and ward or hamlet level (*mai unguwa*) did not have complementary European heads. But they were recognized by the colonial regime.

In theory, the colonial officers were required to operate in the background. They were not supposed to be seen or heard by the subject population. Whatever instructions they had to give were supposed to be given to the traditional rulers who were required to present them to the people as if they (the instructions) actually emanated from them. And the traditional rulers were also required to see to the execution of the instructions.

INDIRECT RULE IN PRACTICE

British over-rule in the 20th century, like that of the Fulani in the previous century left intact most of the existing structures of political organization of the people it had conquered. Thus, just as the Hausa institutions and structures of government, including symbols of royal authority, survived the Fulani jihadists after their conquest, the British also retained the political organization of the Fulani whom they had conquered in 1903. Of equal significance in the continuity from Habe Kano to colonial Kano was the administrative structure of Kasar Kano, the land of Kano, or Kano Emirate. When the Jihadists conquered Kano and Sulaiman was appointed the first Fulani Amir, his area of authority remained the same as that of Alwali, the last Habe King of Kano. The ward, village, district and emirate levels of administration were retained.[83] This structure of political authority was also left intact by colonial rule. The Emir continued to be the administrative head of the emirate and was now designated Sole Native Authority. The British Resident was the political head in the sense that all policy matters emanated from him or had to have his approval. The emir had his traditional council and it continued to sit and discuss political and administrative issues as before. He also continued to administer justice through his court as well as the alkali courts. The prisons remained under the Native Authorities. From all outward appearances, the traditional rulers—emirs, district heads, *alkalai*, village heads and ward heads—continued to perform the same functions as before. This was a deliberate policy of the British, as exemplified by Governor Temple's memorandum to his lieutenants in which he stressed that, "it is essential for the success of indirect rule that European control be kept in the background and the prestige of the Native Authorities (traditional rulers) be maintained."[84]

To give effect to Governor Temple's advice, a change in the pre-colonial system of administration of Kano emirate was made. Since the colonial officials were not expected to deal directly with any native below the rank of a *hakimi*, it became necessary to post the *hakimai*, who had previously lived in the emirate capital, to their respective districts. This was to enable the British District Officer to get the right native officials with whom to deal directly. Thus in 1908 the Resident for Kano, Dr. Cargill, directed Emir Muhammad Abbas to send the fief-holding *hakimai* to live in their respective districts.

The effects of this policy change on the emirate political and administrative structures were very far-reaching. It affected the power relationship within the *sarakuna* class itself and also between the *sarakuna* and the *talakawa*. Within the *sarakuna* class, it lessened the grip of the Emir on the *hakimai*. The *hakimai* became virtually autonomous. With a D.O. in the same town as himself, the *hakimi* did not need to refer to the Emir in Kano for any policy guidelines. Nor was he accountable to the Emir. In fact, a few *hakimai* interpreted their redeployment to their own districts to mean the granting of political as well as territorial autonomy from the Emir of Kano. It took some stern warnings from the colonial officers to impress it on the district heads that they were not autonomous of the Emir of Kano. Secondly, it strengthened the grip of the *hakimai* on the *dagatai* and of the *dagatai* on the *masu unguwa* and the *talakawa*. Quite naturally, the village and hamlet heads did not like the presence of their overlords right on their territories. It not only constituted a check on their activities, but it also appeared to overshadow their own prestige. A third consequence of this policy was the disbanding of the emir's traditional council as a result of the posting out of the *hakimai*. As a matter of fact, a structural-functional argument can be made for the posting.

None of the reasons that made for their retention in the emirate capital in the caliphate era was tenable in the colonial era. In the first place, the Resident and the Divisional Officers took over the roles of advisors or policy-makers to the emir. Secondly, the instruments of ultimate coercion in the hands of the colonial regime took care of any possible revolt by anyone against the emir.

The district heads continued to stay in their respective territories until 1925 when Resident Lindsell, on the advice of the visiting Edward, Prince of Wales, reconstituted the emir's council and institutionalized a weekly meeting.[85]

Over the years, a number of laws were enacted by the colonial regime, the net effect of which was to strengthen the emir's position vis-à-vis his officials and subjects. For example, in 1910 a Land and Native Rights Proclamation Law was enacted. That law, in effect, nationalized all the land in Northern Nigeria and gave power of control to the colonial regime, which in turn vested the traditional rulers with these powers. Then in 1916, a Native Authority Ordinance was passed which confirmed emirs in their position as presidents of their respective judicial councils, which were designated as the highest legal institutions in the emirate with full executive powers of law enforcement.[86]

One of the features of Kano emirate administration that most impressed Lugard at the time of his conquest was the existence of institutionalized taxation in the form of *jangali,* and *kharaj.* These taxes, among others, constituted sources of state revenue. The colonial government therefore recognized these taxes with appreciation and introduced policies aimed at improving their method of collection. The impact of these new policies on the traditional rulers was felt in three ways. Firstly, whereas all taxes were, as before, imposed and collected in the name of the emir, the new policy gave the final say on how much was to be collected to the British Resident or District Officer. Secondly, all taxes collected were accounted for from the ward level to the emirate level. Even though at the initial stage the emir and his lieutenants were allowed to retain 50% of the emirate's total revenue from taxes to meet their statutory needs, and pay the other 50% into the government treasury (the common fund of the protectorate), the Residents and DOs ensured that every penny was accounted for.

The third and perhaps most significant change was the placement, in 1909, of the traditional rulers on fixed salaries, paid from the *Bait-al-mal*, or public treasury. The salaries of some selected *hakimai* of Kano emirate in 1915 were as follows: Galadima £200, Wambai £240, Sarkin Bai £260, Sarkin Dawakin Tsakar Gida £360, Barde £160, Sarkin Rano £300, Sarkin Dutse £380, Sarkin Gaya £250, Sarkin Karaye £600.[87] The Emir of Kano earned £4,800, which was the same as what was earned by the Shehu of Borno, but £1,800 more than what was earned by the Emir of Katsina and £2,800 more than the salaries of the Emirs of Bauchi, Nupe, Gwandu and Zaria.[88] By 1926, the Emir of Kano was earning a basic salary of £6000 and allowances of £2,500. The Waziri then earned £1,200 the Madaki £1,200 and the Galadima £1,000.[89] In the absence of any record of how much was paid to the village and ward heads, we can safely and logically assume that they were respectively much lower than those of the lowest district head. Our assumption is based on the wide differential between the emir's total package of £8,500 and that of his immediate junior (the Waziri) of £1,200.

From all indications, the colonial government appeared concerned to prevent or forestall any loss of power or prestige that the traditional rulers might suffer as a result of the imposition of colonial rule. And since the colonial government had decided to rule through the traditional rulers, it was in fact necessary to arrest such a development. It was towards this end that the colonial government vested powers in the traditional rulers that were unknown in the pre-colonial era. Possibly, the colonial officers thought that the prestige, authority and dignity enjoyed by the traditional rulers stemmed from a monopoly of the legitimate use of the instruments of coercion, namely the *dogarai*, or emir's bodyguards, the courts and the prisons. They failed to realise that the prestige, dignity and authority of a traditional ruler in Kano, and in fact, many other African societies were related to how the ruler performed his socially expected roles. And those roles were not just what the colonial government conceived them to be.[90]

The colonial government's conception of a good and efficient traditional ruler was predicated on ability to maintain law and order, collect taxes as and when due and get their subjects to carry out all orders issued by the colonial government irrespective of how they felt about them.[91] To the Kano man on the other hand, the essential elements of good rulership were *adalci* defined as fairness, justice, or equity; moderation, empathy, and *imani,* literally faith, which is the first pillar of Islam. But in this context, it entails all that a true *mu'umin* or believer is enjoined to do. *Adalci* usually entails judging impartially among one's subjects. Empathy could entail generosity by the ruler to his needy subjects. For example waiving the tax for some subjects or a whole community whose predicament necessitated such benevolence. So also helping to buy a ram for the naming ceremony of a subject who, for some reasons, could not fulfill that social requirement. And even distributing presents to the poor and needy by agents of the emir.[92]

Obviously, then, to be able to meet the conditions for good leadership in the African context rulers needed large amounts of money. In the pre-colonial days, monies realized from taxation and sales of proceeds from slave-labor farms were used to meet those obligations. However, with the colonial policies on slavery and taxation which freed slaves and prohibited the retention of any portion of state revenue collected by the traditional rulers, and the placing of these officials on fixed salaries, which were meagre compared to what they formerly got, these traditional rulers found it increasingly difficult to meet those customary obligations of a good ruler. As Whitaker rightly observed, "the British, through the Indirect Rule system, aimed at promoting the prestige, status, influence, and bonds of traditional authority without at the same time increasing their legal and legitimate means of maintaining or promoting those characteristics."[93]

It was this dilemma of having to maintain a status without the legitimate means of doing so that forced a change in the relationship between the *sarakuna* and the *talakawa* in the following manner.

The authority of the traditional ruler as we noted earlier, hinged on his prestige and legitimacy which, in turn, were evaluated by how well he performed his socially expected roles as described above. The ruler rarely relied on coercion to exert compliance from the ruled. However, as the legitimate means to the effective performance of the ruler's socially expected roles diminished, so did his prestige and legitimacy. In the absence of any incentive from the ruler to make his subjects show respect to him through obedience, the ruler had two options left in order to continue to rule. The first, which went against the principles of indirect rule, and which some traditional rulers themselves might have found beneath their dignity was to explain their predicament to their subjects, by showing that a) they could not waive anyone's or any community's tax much as they might want to, without the approval of the British D.O., b) they could not afford the usual gifts to their subjects as custom required; and c) they could not continue to live the flamboyant lifestyles they were known for. But to take that option would be to negate the essence of the indirect rule policy, which was meant to keep the facade of authority of the traditional rulers, especially that of the emirs. The second option, which most traditional rulers chose, was to fail to explain the new dispensation to their subjects and proceed to exact compliance with their orders through coercion. In doing that, they found the British colonial administration a very reliable partner. This then was the beginning of the changed relationship between the *sarakuna* and the *talakawa.* An examination of how this relationship changed with specific reference to the methods of assessment and collection of taxes in the Kano Emirate may help put things in a proper perspective.

ASSESSMENT AND COLLECTION OF TAXES IN THE KANO EMIRATE UNDER COLONIAL RULE

We have noted in Lugard's speech that with the imposition of colonial rule, the emirs lost the right of taxation. That meant that in contrast to the past, neither the emir nor his *hakimai* had the power to determine how much tax was due from his emirate. That was the prerogative of the colonial rulers. The traditional rulers, on their part, were required to collect whatever amount the colonialists imposed on their people as soon as they were due. On that particular role of the traditional rulers, the colonial government was uncompromising.

Although apologists of colonialism have pointed to the existence of onerous taxes as a major bane of the Fulani administration,[94] what the British came to do later made saints of the emirs. For example, Polly Hill notes that on the eve of the colonial occupation of Kano a household was assessed at 4,000 cowries. But barely five years later, in 1908, the rate had been increased to 10,000 cowries.[95] After initially adhering to the pre-colonial practice whereby taxes were imposed on households, or production units, the colonial rulers abandoned it. Instead, they introduced male adult taxation. And by their definition, "adulthood... started from age ten to thirteen."[96] The effect of that decision was to increase the number of people liable to taxation. Not only was the actual number of taxable people increased, but the amount imposed was also increased without regard to ability to pay. The following table, containing the amount of taxes collected from nine emirates of Kano Province between 1903 and 1911, speaks volumes about colonial taxation policy:[97]

Fiscal Year	Amount Collected
1903-1904	£2,428
1904-1905	£7,149
1905-1906	£7,141
1906-1907	£13,442
1907-1908	£24,556
1908-1909	£51,842
1909-1910	£56,588
1910-1911	£69,659

By the 1928-29 fiscal year, Kano emirate alone collected £215,124 as general tax and £43,026 as *jangali*.[98] The arbitrary increase in taxes was matched with an equal determination on the part of the colonial rulers to deal ruthlessly with any traditional ruler who failed to meet his target. In 1914 alone, for example, 46 depositions were effected by the colonial rulers for tax-related problems.[99] Equally, those traditional rulers who were prompt in the collection of their taxes were rewarded with promotion, with bigger salaries, and in the case of potential emirs, with the office when it became available. Because the taxes imposed on the people were far in excess of what they could afford to pay, the previous practice whereby the well-to-do in the community offered to carry the extra burden of taxation on behalf of the poorer members of the community was discontinued. This was because in contrast to the past where what remained after everyone had taken what he could afford to pay was relatively small, in the new dispensation what remained was still too much for the few rich people to carry as an extra burden. But since the traditional rulers had a duty to collect those sums, the method of assessment and collection had to change. Under the new dispensation, the Resident would inform the emir how much was due from his emirate for the tax season. The emir then toured the districts, as before, to *fasa haraji* or break the tax and announce the *kudin goro* or flat rate. But instead of the traditional practice where the *dagaci* invited all the taxable adults of the village to an open space and brought some nuts of equal number as the amount due from the people of that particular area and got tax payers to distribute the tax burden amongst themselves, (taking into consideration the economic position of each member), now the *mai unguwa* and the *dagaci*, and in some instances the *hakimi* sat to assess the people.

Invariably the amounts imposed on the people were more than most of them could pay. But then the traditional rulers had a duty to the colonial government. In the circumstances in which they found themselves, either they sympathized with their subjects and invite the wrath of the colonial authorities, or they did the bidding of their bosses and lose the love and respect of their subjects. It was not an easy choice, but most traditional rulers opted for the latter. That generally characterized the relationship of the traditional rulers with their subjects for most of the colonial era. This development, among others, came to set the rulers apart from their subjects. Fear, not love or respect, came to characterize the relationship between the subject population and the rulers. The tax season came to be the most dreaded season in the emirate.

But that is not to say that the relationship between the *sarakuna* and the British colonialists was always cordial. For example, Emir Abbas, who was appointed by the British, barely tolerated them. It was no secret that Emir Abbas disliked the British colonialists and he extended that dislike to those of his district heads who identified with the colonialists. He was recorded to have had spies watching people who were suspected to be sympathetic to the British. He was also reported to have commissioned 100 mallams or Islamic scholars to be praying continuously for the end of British colonialism.[100]

It is significant to note that Emir Abbas died from an injury he sustained when the Resident for Kano kicked him in the ribs for daring to insult the King of England in reaction to an insult from the Resident.[101] Abbas' son, Abdullahi, also barely tolerated the British. For the twenty-seven years he ruled Kano, Emir Abdullahi Bayero vowed never to take a salary or accept any reward that could be seen as the proceeds of his participation in colonial rule.[102]

EMIRS AND POLITICS DURING COLONIAL RULE

When party politics was introduced in Northern Nigeria in 1950, two political parties emerged on the political scene. These were the Northern Elements Progressive Union, NEPU, founded on August 8, 1950, and the Northern People's Congress, NPC, founded on October 1, 1951.[103] These two political parties came to be identified with the two social classes of the North—the NEPU, representing the interest of the *talakawa* or commoners, and the NPC representing the *sarakuna* or aristocrats.

In its Declaration of Principles, issued two months after its founding, the NEPU made a strenuous attack upon the emirs and the NA system in Northern Nigeria. It alleged that the "shocking state of social order as at present existing in Northern Nigeria was due to the family compact rule of the so-called NA Administrations in their present autocratic form."[104] The NEPU further argued that all parties were but the expression of class interests and that there was a class struggle between the members of the "vicious circle of Native Authorities on the one hand, and the ordinary *talakawa* on the other."[105] NEPU, according to that Declaration, was to be dedicated to the struggle to emancipate the *talakawa* from domination by the privileged few who constituted members of the vicious circle of the Native Authorities.[106] NEPU's membership came essentially from the commoner class. Its founding fathers were equally from a commoner background.[107]

The NPC leadership, on the other hand, represented the aristocracy. Its objective was to prevent any radical break from the status quo. Even though it agreed on the need to reform the NA system, its philosophy was that the reform must be gradual and accommodative of the NAs. As the President-General of the party, Ahmadu Bello, the Sardauna of Sokoto and later Premier of Northern Nigeria emphasized in 1956:

> We believe in the institution of chiefs and as long as we are in power we shall ensure that the chiefs will have representation in the Regional Executive Council and that the House of Chiefs will continue to be part of our legislature... we believe that no lasting solution can be achieved without their fatherly, spiritual and moral support. Our attitude to chiefs and elders is one of respect and co-operation because we believe they have a very important part to play in the administrative, social and economic development of our people.[108]

Throughout the colonial period, the Northern Region House of Assembly was dominated by the NPC. Virtually all the members of the House of Chiefs were either full members or sympathizers of the NPC. Equally, a vast majority of the elected members belonged to the NPC. For most of the life of the Northern Assembly up to the collapse of the First Republic in 1966, the NPC, and by implication people of aristocratic background, dominated its membership. That dominance ensured the continued protection of the interests of the NA system.

But things did not always go smoothly between those who based their claim to authority solely on tradition, as exemplified in the persons of the N.A. functionaries, and those who based it on secular and elective authority as exemplified in the persons of the leadership of the Regional Government. The celebrated quarrel between Emir Muhammadu Sanusi of Kano and Premier Ahmadu Bello makes this clear.

EMIR MUHAMMADU SANUSI VERSUS PREMIER AHMADU BELLO

Muhammadu Sanusi was the Emir of Kano for ten years, from 1953 to 1963. With a long and glorious history, which predates the Fulani conquest in the early years of the 19th century, Kano was in fact the most important of all the Hausa kingdoms and later of the Emirates of the Sokoto Caliphate. Emir Sanusi believed in maintaining the powers and prestige that for centuries had been associated with the office of the emir and other related institutions in the emirate.

Ahmadu Bello, the Sardauna of Sokoto, was a great grandson of Shehu Usman Dan Fodio, the founder of the Sokoto Caliphate. Being a member of the Sokoto ruling family, the Sardauna had consistently acted in defence of traditional institutions. He was the leader of the NPC, which was identified as the party of the *sarakuna*. This same party, as we have noted, formed the first government of the self-governing Northern Region, within the colony of Nigeria and later within independent Nigeria. Considering that both the Sardauna and the Emir had a common interest in protecting and sustaining the *sarauta* institution in the North, what explains the rift between them in 1962-63, which led to the eventual abdication of Sanusi from the emirship?

54

To fully grasp the forces behind the rift between the NA as exemplified in the person of Emir Sanusi, and Regional Authority, as exemplified in the person of Sardauna Ahmadu Bello, we need to trace the relationship between Sanusi when he was Ciroma and Sardauna Ahmadu Bello before he became Premier.

When the winds of change began to blow up North from the South, the British colonialists realized that sooner rather than later, the Northerners, like their Southern counterparts, would begin to demand independence. In order to forestall the possibility of some unknown person emerging to lead the North (possibly from a Southern political party or a radical Northern party), the British decided to pick one Northerner and groom him to lead the North to independence. They saw Mallam Bello Dandago from Kano as the ideal candidate for the leadership of Northern Nigeria. But Sanusi who, as ciroma (heir apparent), was virtually emir because his aged father Emir Abdullahi Bayero was ill, influenced his father to advise the British against picking Bello Dandago. In advising against the choice of Bello Dandago, Emir Abdullahi Bayero argued that Sokoto and Gwandu, which enjoyed direct blood links with Shehu Usman Dan Fodio, could not recognize someone from a vassal emirate (as Kano theoretically was in relation to Sokoto) as their leader. Likewise, he added, Borno might not accept him. Instead, Emir Bayero suggested that whoever was to be chosen must be somebody who was going to be acceptable to all the emirates including Sokoto and Borno. He further suggested that the person should preferably come from the family of Shehu Usman Dan Fodio, the political and religious leader of all the emirates.[109] Ahmadu Bello was at that time the only member of the Shehu's family who had acquired enough Western education to be groomed to lead the North. That was how Ahmadu Bello came to lead the NPC, even though he was not a founding member of the party.[110] The Sardauna came to know about the role Sanusi had played in choosing him for the leadership of the North and that greatly endeared Sanusi to the Sardauna. Equally important in endearing Sanusi to the Sardauna was the role Sanusi played in saving the Sardauna from what was perceived as political victimization by Sultan Abubakar Siddique III of Sokoto, who jailed the Sardauna for alleged embezzlement of tax proceeds. Sanusi was reported to have contributed funds for the appeal of the case, which was won by the Sardauna.

In 1953, Emir Abdullahi Bayero died and Sanusi succeeded him as Emir. A year later, in 1954, Ahmadu Bello became leader of Government Business in the Colonial Government of Northern Nigeria. And in 1959 he became the Premier of self-governing Northern Nigeria. Throughout that period, the relationship between these two leaders could not have been better. But not too long after that rifts between the two leaders began to appear. The series of confrontations between the Sardauna and Emir Sanusi that began immediately after self-government was granted to Northern Nigeria in 1959, and which culminated in the forced resignation and exile of Emir Sanusi, have been comprehensively treated by Paden, Whitaker and Muffett.[111] At the risk of repeating some of these scholars' findings, I will summarize some of the more confrontational issues.

The first open encounter between the Sardauna and Emir Sanusi occurred in 1959 when, through protocol blunder, a seat was not reserved at the official Northern self-government celebration at Kaduna, for Emir Sanusi. On the Emir's arrival, a quick re-arrangement was made for his seating among the other dignitaries. But Emir Sanusi felt slighted by that action and he refused to stay for the celebration. No sooner had this incident cooled down than the Emir began to vehemently oppose some key pieces of legislation sponsored by the Sardauna government. Among these was the Provincial Administration Bill of 1962, which sought to introduce Provincial Commissioners for each of the thirteen Northern Provinces. According to the proposed legislation, the Provincial Commissioners were to be the political as well as administrative heads of their provinces. They were to be appointed from among members of the Regional House of Assembly and they were to be accountable to the Regional Government under the Sardauna at Kaduna. Emir Sanusi opposed that bill because he felt that nobody in Kano Province should be placed over him in official precedence. But despite Sanusi's opposition the bill was passed. Next, Emir Sanusi attacked a bill that proposed to transfer some functions of the NAs with regards to land matter to the Regional Government. Again, Emir Sanusi was not successful in stopping the bill from becoming a law.

Another area of confrontation between the Sardauna and Emir Sanusi was the way Emir Sanusi treated members of the Sardauna's cabinet when they went to Kano on official duty. Government ministers could not fly flags on their official cars in Kano because to do so was regarded as competing with the Emir, who alone flew a flag on his car in Kano. Furthermore, ministers had to prostrate themselves before the emir when they went to see him even on official matters. Emir Sanusi also disobeyed the Regional Government's order barring the use of sirens in Kaduna except for the Premier and the Governor. Anytime Emir Sanusi went to Kaduna he made sure that his siren was used from the gate of the city to his residence. The last straw appeared to have been Sanusi's behavior during the official visit to Kano of the Premier and his guest, the President of Niger Republic, Hammani Diori. A day before the visit protocol officials went to the palace and arranged how the reception of the Premier and the visiting Head of State was going to be conducted. It was agreed that when the two VIPs approach the palace, the Emir would come out and receive them at the gate of the palace and lead them inside. Palace officials and horses were lined up from the main road all the way to the gate of the palace. When the dignitaries arrived however, the Emir refused to come out and receive them. On at least three occasions, the Madaki pleaded with him to go out and receive the visitors, but he only nodded. After a very long delay, he finally rose up, went, and received them. Meanwhile, Hammani Diori saw the embarrassment written on the face of his host (the Premier) and he observed that in his country, no traditional ruler could do that to a government official, no matter how lowly the official was and expect to remain in office.

These behaviors of Emir Sanusi caused the Sardauna to decide to trim his sails. An opportunity was provided for the Sardauna when in late 1962 the Kano NA could not pay monthly salaries to its staff. Upon preliminary investigations, it was discovered that the NA had only £6,000 in its coffers whereas monthly salaries alone were £65,000. It was also found out that the Kano NA was indebted to the sum of over £500,000. The Sardauna government immediately appointed an ex-colonial officer, Mr. D.J.M. Muffett, as Sole Commissioner to inquire into the financial affairs of Kano NA. When Muffett submitted his Report in February 1963, most of the key Kano NA functionaries were indicted and relieved of their offices. The Emir was removed from his throne and banished to Azare. The Regional Government had thus proved its ascendancy over the powerful Kano NA. A new Emir, Muhammadu Inuwa Abbas, was appointed. The message of Sanusi's removal was clear enough not only for the new Emir of Kano, but other emirs as well. They either towed the line or were fired.

NOTES

1. On this legend and that of the founding of other Hausa states that came to be called the Hausa bakwai and the Banza bakwai, see, for example, Murray Last, "From Sultanate to Caliphate: Kano 1450-1800" in Barkindo, B., ed., *Studies in the History of Kano*, (Ibadan, Heinemann Educational Books, 1983); Dokaji, A., *Kano Ta Dabo Cigari*, (Zaria, Northern Nigerian Publishing Company, 1958, rev. 1978), H.R. Palmer, "The Kano Chronicle", in the *Journal of the Royal Anthropological Society* (1908).

2.   Some recent studies have questioned the suggestion that
     Gajemasu started the construction of the walls. See B.M.
     Barkindo, "The Gates of Kano City: A Historical
     Survey", in B.M. Barkindo, *op. cit.*
3.   Kano Chronicle, op. cit., p.111.
4.   The title sarki derived from a legend about Bayajida,
     Bagauda's grandfather, who is said to have arrived at
     Daura and put up in the house of an old woman.
     Bayajida requested his hostess to give him water to give
     to his horse. The old woman told Bayajida that there
     was no water in the house, and that a snake called Sarki,
     controlled the only well in the town. Sarki allowed the
     inhabitants of Daura to fetch water only once a week.
     Bayajida asked for the location of the well, collected a
     container from the old woman, went and beheaded the
     snake, and fetched the water. The queen of Daura was
     said to have been so pleased with Bayajida that she mar-
     ried him. Bayajida then came to be called "Makas Sarki"
     or the killer of Sarki. With time, "Makas" was dropped
     and he simply became "Sarki". For details of this legend,
     see Abubakar Dokaji, *op. cit.*, R. Palmer, "The Kano
     Chronicle," op. cit. among others.
5.   Fika, M.A., *The Kano Civil War and British Overrule*,
     (Ibadan, O.U.P., 1978), pp. 39-40.
6.   Murray Last, "From Sultanate to Caliphate: Kano 1450-
     1800" op. cit., also Abubakar Dokaji, op. cit. p.25.
7.   Murray Last, op cit.
8.   See for example Dokaji, A., *op. cit.*
9.   Op cit., p. 15. M.G. Smith argues that the Wangarawa
     arrived Kano during Muhammadu Rumfa's reign. See
     M.G. Smith, "The Kano Chronicle as History" in B.M.
     Barkindo, ed., *op. cit.*
10. The exact date of the reign of Sarki Muhammadu Rumfa
     is still a matter of contention. See M.G. Smith, *op cit.*
     Dokaji, for example, states that Rumfa reigned between
     1476 and 1513. Dokaji *op. cit.* pp. 19 and 24. Palmer, on
     the other hand suggests 1463-1499.

11. Kano Chronicle
12. al-Maghili, Sheikh Mohammed, *The Obligations of Princes: An Essay on Moslem Kingship,* tr. by T.H. Baldwin (Beyrouth, Liban, Imperial Catholique, 1932).
13. The average length of a public address of Emir Ado Bayero on any subject matter has been one to one-and-a-half typewritten pages, usually delivered in about five minutes. See the collection of speeches of the Emir in *Mai Martaba Sarkin Kano: Alhaji (Dr.) Ado Bayero,* (Northern Nigerian Historical Documentation Bureau, 1992).
14. Anania, D.L., Berthoud S., "L'Interieur de l'Afrique Occidentale d'apres Giovanni Lorenzo Anania (xvie siecle)", Cahiers d' Histoire Mondiale, xiv, 2, 1972. Cited in Murray Last, "From Sultanate to Caliphate" in B. Barkindo, ed., *op. cit.*
15. Dokaji, op. cit. p.26
16. Op cit., p. 27
17. ibid.
18. Op cit. p. 27.
19. Shehu Usman Dan Fodio, "Nur al-Bab", cited in Ibrahim Imam, *The Biography of Shehu Othman Danfodio,* (Zaria, Gaskiya Corp., 1966), p. 23.
20. See Appendix 1 for the full manifesto.
21. The title amir means "leader" and was conferred on all in whose hands the administration of the states of the caliphate was entrusted by Shehu Usman himself, or on his behalf. They were the representatives of the amirul 'mumineen in their domains. The head of the caliphate took on the title amirul 'mumineen or "leader of the faithful." He was also called Caliph, or representative of the Holy Prophet on earth. With the imposition of colonial rule, the Arabic word amir (leader) was anglicized to "emir." Technically, the amirs were also amirul 'mumineen in their own domains.
22. R.A. Adeleye, Power and Diplomacy in Northern Nigeria 1804-1906 (London, Longman, 1971), p.79.

23. Muhammad Bello in Infaqul Maisuri, cited in Sheikh Abubakar Gummi with Ismaila Tsiga, *Where I Stand* (Ibadan, Spectrum Books, 1994), p.89.
24. Writing here refers to the practice in most of the Muslim World where scholars write sections of the Holy Qur'an on a black slate to be washed with water and drank as remedy for various ailments.
25. Muhammad Bello had succeeded Shehu Usman Dan Fodio as Caliph following the death of the latter in 1817.
26. Although the Jihadists referred to the ruler as Amir, the vast majority of the people simply called the rulers by their Hausa title—Sarki.
27. That is the origin of the title Sarkin Bai (or sarkin baya, literally later emir) that the descendants of Mallam Dabo Danbazau bear until date.
28. Although the jihadists had earlier condemned monarchy, the Manifesto of the jihad (see Appendix 1) was conspicuously silent on the matter. Sheikh Abdullahi Bin Fodio, Shehu Usman Dan Fodio's venerable younger brother had reopened the issue after the jihad, insisting on the appointment of Amirs through consultation. Shehu Usman, perhaps being more elderly, more pragmatic and in full picture of the situation of the nascent Jama'at, spoke less about monarchy; and where he did so, he tried to suggest that a holistic approach was called for. As it turned out Shehu Usman was succeeded by his son Muhammad Bello. Bello's succession might have paved the way for monarchism in the emirates. On the debate between Shehu Usman and Abdullahi on hereditary succession see Ibraheem Sulaiman, *A Revolution in History: The Jihad of Usman Dan Fodio*, (London, Mansell Publishing Company, 1986), Ibrahim Sulaiman, *The Islamic State and the Challenge of History*, (London, Mansell Pub. Co., 1987), M. S. Zahraddeen, *Abd Allah ibn Fodio's Contribution to the Fulani Jihad in Nineteenth Century Hausaland*, unpublished Ph.D. dissertation, McGill University, 1976, and

Shehu Umar Abdullahi, *On The Search for a Viable Political Culture: Reflections on the Political Thought of Sheikh Abdullahi Dan Fodio* (Kaduna, NNN Commercial Press, 1984).

29. M.G. Smith, *Government in Zazzau: A Study of Government in the Hausa Chiefdom of Zaria in Northern Nigeria from 1800-1950*, (London, Oxford University press, 1960), p. 74. Such also was the fate of Sadiku of Katsina (1835-44) and Usman of Missau (1850-62). The former was deposed by Caliph Aliyu Babba (1847-59) and the latter by Caliph Ahmadu Atiku (1859-66).

30. Victor Low reports an instance where the congregation at a mosque refused to pray for an amir as an expression of widespread dissatisfaction with the amir. Cited in V. Low, *Three Nigerian Emirates: A Study in Oral History* (Evanston, Illinois, North-Western University Press), p. 33.

31. It should be noted that this announcement by the district head was just a formality as all the village heads and many of the subject population would have gone to the district headquarters when the amir went to break the tax, and heard the amir's announcement.

32. The *jakada*'s presence was not only to protect the interest of his overlord, the amir, but also the interest of the tax payers by ensuring that what the amir announced as the tax due from the district was what was actually shared out among the tax payers.

33. Not all the inhabitants of the villages were taxed. The conditions governing the imposition of tax on a person were basically three, namely, a) the person must be male, b) must be an adult (the definition of adult was left to the village and ward heads). But generally, an adult in Hausa society was and to some extent still is a married person), and c) the person must be able bodied. In actual fact most ward and village heads did not need to take a census of their wards or villages every year. As late as

1983, most ward heads I spoke to in Kano city knew the exact number of houses in their wards and the number and even names of the residents. See Ibrahim, O.F. *The Impact of the People's Redemption Party on Traditional Institutions in Kano State, 1979-1983*, Unpublished Msc. Thesis, Bayero University, Kano, 1983.

34. M. Perham, *Native Administration in Nigeria*, (London, Oxford University Press, 1937), p. 41.

35. Lady Lugard, *A Tropical Dependency: An Outline of the Ancient History of the Western Sudan with an Account of the Modern Settlement of Northern Nigeria*, (London, Frank Cass, 1964), p.442.

36. See W.N.M. Geary, *Nigeria Under British Rule* (London, Frank Cass, 1965; first published by Methuen and Co., 1927), pp. 7-8, and 203-205; Allan Burns, *History of Nigeria* (London, George Allen and Unwin, 1964, first Published 1929), pp. 167 and 230; C. Orr, op. cit., p.78.

37. Rex Niven, *Nigeria*, (New York, Frederick A. Praeger, 1967), p.13.

38. The difference between a colony and a protectorate is that natives of the colony were considered British subjects, whereas natives of protectorates were considered British protected persons. They did not have the same rights.

39. Charles Orr, *op. cit.*, W.N.M. Geary, *op. cit.* M. Perham, *op. cit.*, Lady Lugard, *op. cit.*

40. R. Robinson, J. Gallagher, with A. Denny, *Africa and the Victorians: The Official Mind of Imperialism*, 2nd. Ed. (London, Macmillan, 1981), p. 9.

41. K. Robinson and F. Madden, *Essays in Imperial Government*, (London, Basil Blackwell, 1963), p. 44.

42. Among the more prominent studies in this school were J.A. Hobson, *Imperialism: A Study*, (London, Allen and Unwin, 1938, 1st published 1902); K. Marx and F. Engels, *On Colonialism*, (London, Lawrence and

Wishart, 1960); V.I. Lenin, *Imperialism: The Highest Stage of Capitalism, A Popular Outline*, (Moscow, Progress Publishers, 1966, first published 1917). For an excellent annotated bibliography on the subject see Roger Brown and Bob Sutcliffe, eds., *Studies in the Theory of Imperialism*, (London, Longman, 1972), pp. 330-78.

43. J. Schumpeter, *Imperialism*, (Oxford, Blackwell and Co., 1951, first published 1919).

44. Prominent in this school were J. Schumpeter, in *op. cit.*; R. Koebner, *Empire*, (London, Cambridge University Press, 1961); Hans J. Morganthau, *Politics Among Nations: The Struggle for Power and Peace*, (New York, Alfred Knopf, 1960).

45. Ram Desai, narrates the following story widely believed in Africa to illustrate this point:

> "The missionaries came here and said, "let us pray," and we closed our eyes, and when we responded "Amen" at the end of the prayer, we found the Bible in our hands, but lo and behold, our land had gone into the hands of the missionaries."

Ram Desai, ed., *Christianity in Africa: As Seen by Africans* (Denver, A. Swallow, 1962), p. 17.

46. Curiously enough, most of these permissions were later claimed to be treaties. On the dubious role played by the missionaries in the colonisation of Africa see, for example, R. Desai, *op. cit.*; Robert I. Rotberg, *Christian Missionaries and the Creation of Northern Rhodesia 1880-1924*, (Princeton, Princeton University Press, 1965); M.D. Markowitz, *Cross and Sword: The Political Role of Christian Missions in the Belgian Congo 1908-1960*, (Stanford, Hoover Institution Press, 1973); H.B. Hansen, *Mission, Church and State in a Colonial Setting: Uganda 1890-1925*, (New York, Sant Martins Press, 1984).

47. I must point out that all religions and all ideologies believe in the superiority of their doctrines. To my knowledge, it is only Judaism among the major religions, which does not send out its members to seek new converts.
48. Tom Kemp, *Historical Patterns of Industrialization*, (New York, Longman, 1978), p. 9.
49. On the impact of industrialization on the political, economic, and social structure of British society, see Tom Kemp, *op. cit.*; David Thomson, *England in the Nineteenth Century*, (London, Penguin Books, 1950); Arnold Toynbee, *The Industrial Revolution*, (Boston, Beacon Press, 1968); Phillip A.M. Taylor, ed., *The Industrial Revolution in Britain: Triumph or Disaster*, (Boston, D.C. Heath and Co., 1958); Brian Tierney, ed., *Industrial Revolution in England: Blessing or Curse*, (New York, Random House, 1967).
50. From Plato through Augustine, Hobbes to de Tocqueville, Marx and later philosophers, one can hardly do justice to their writings without understanding the backgrounds from which they were writing.
51. H.T. Buckle, *A History of Civilization*, 2nd. Ed. (New York, Appleton and Co., 1910, first published in 1857).
52. W. Bagehot, *Physics and Politics: Thoughts on the Application of the Principles of Natural Selection and Inheritance to Political Society*, (New York, D. Appleton and Co., 1876).
53. J. Gobineau, *Essay on the Inequality of the Human Races*, tr. by Adrian Collins, (New York, H. Ferting, 1967).
54. Charles Darwin, *The Origin of Species*, (New York, Collier Macmillan Books, 1962, first published in 1852).
55. I must point out that Darwin himself did not make any claim about the superiority of one race over another. But his idea of the "survival of the fittest" among animal species was later employed by "scientists" to argue for inherent inequality of races.

56. Jules Harmand, "The Morality of Empire and the Policy of Association" in P.D. Curtain, ed., *Imperialism*, (New York, Walker and Co., 1971), pp. 294-95. Lady Lugard made a similar argument justifying the British conquest of Sokoto. See Lady Lugard, *Tropical Dependency, op. cit.* p. 440.

57. We shall not dwell on the differences among these methods. The important thing is that they all professed the same ends, i.e. civilizing the backward peoples of Africa and Asia. It is however, interesting to note that the particular policy adopted by each European power was determined, to a large extent, by its own political history. For example, the assimilation policy of the French was premised on the French belief (since the 1789 revolution) on political liberty and equality. Similarly, the British indirect rule was premised on some kind of monarchical paternalism.

58. Lord Lugard made this last point the title of his major work, *The Dual Mandate in British Tropical Africa* (London, William Blackwood, 1929).

59. For example, M. Perham in Native Administration in Nigeria, op. cit., p.87, cites H. Barth's report on the emirates of Northern Nigeria in the mid-19th century.

60. Islam being a complete way of life does not separate religious from secular leadership. Leadership should be in the service of God.

61. R.A. Adeleye, *Power and Diplomacy in Northern Nigeria 180-1906* (London, Longmans Group Limited, 1971), p.74.

62. See for example, the introductory chapter of M. Crowder and O. Ikime, eds., *West African Chiefs: Their Changing Status Under Colonial Rule and Independence* (Ile-Ife, University of Ife Press, 1970).

63. M.M. Tukur, *The Imposition of British Colonial Domination on the Sokoto Caliphate, Borno and Neighbouring States 1897-1914: A Reinterpretation of*

Colonial Sources, unpublished Ph.D., thesis, Ahmadu Bello University, Zaria, 1979.

64. M.M. Tukur, *op. cit.*, p.68
65. M.M. Tukur, *op. cit.*, p. 52.
66. Adeleye, *op. cit.*, p. 268, fn 48
67. Abubakar Dokaji, *op. cit.* pp 60-62, also Tukur, *op. cit.*, p.57.
68. See Abubakar Dokaji, *op .cit.* pp. 60-62. See also M.M. Tukur, Op. Cit., p. 57.
69. Tukur, M.M., *op. cit.*, p. 64.
70. *Op. cit.* p.60
71. Letter No. 125 in H.F. Blackwell, ed., *The Occupation of Hausaland 1900-1904, Being Translation of Arabic Letters Found in the House of the Waziri of Sokoto Buhari in 1903* (London, Frank Cass, 1969, 1st Published 1927).
72. Tukur, M.M., op. cit. p.61.
73. Dahiru Yahya, "The Legacy of the Emir of Kano Abdullahi Bayero, 1926-1953" A public lecture delivered under the auspices of Bayero University, Kano. Spring 1986. p. 5.
74. Dokaji, op. cit. p. 62, M.M. Tukur, op. cit. p. 62.
75. Dokaji, ibid.
76. There is a controversy over the use of the title of Sultan by the head of the Sokoto Caliphate. According to H.F. Blackwell, the title was used by Europeans to refer to the head of the Sokoto caliphate. The emirs addressed him as khalifa, which indicates both secular and spiritual authority. Blackwell, ed., op. cit. On the other hand, Murray Last argues that "the title given to the Amir al-mu'mineen were seldom flowery or eulogistic: rarely is the Amir al-mu'mineen even called khalifa." He further suggests that the Emir of Kano was addressed as Sultan by emirates like Gombe and Bauchi and in some correspondences even by Sokoto. Last, M, *The Sokoto Caliphate*, (London, Longmans, 1967), p. 196. What is

certain is that with colonialism his official title became Sultan.

77. Quoted from Lady Lugard, A Tropical Dependency, op. cit., pp. 450-52.

78. M. Crowder and O. Ikime have argued that "in a very real sense none of the chiefs who ruled under the French and the British were legitimate." See M. Crowder and O. Ikime eds., op. cit., p. xi.

79. Among the many verses in the Qur'an dealing with justice, (4:135) stands out. It says, "O ye who believe, stand out firmly for justice, as witnesses to Allah, even against yourselves, or your parents, or your kin, and whether it be against the rich or poor, for Allah can best protect both. Follow not the lusts (of your hearts), lest ye swerve, and if ye distort (justice) or decline to do justice, verily Allah is well acquainted with all that ye do." Other verses include 4:58; 5:29; 16:90; and 57:25. Islamic law stipulates amputation of the hand as punishment for theft, 100 strokes of the cane for fornication and 100 strokes of the cane plus stoning to death for adultery. While these sentences might appear harsh to non-Muslims, they were, in actual fact, rarely carried out because it was difficult to establish to the satisfaction of the shari'ah the commission of those unlawful acts. For example, for anybody to be pronounced guilty of adultery, that person must be sane, and the act must have been witnessed by four reliable witnesses who would testify to having seen the act being committed. In the alternative, the person is required to confess four times. Should he confess only three times and retract at the fourth, he cannot be found guilty. Some schools of Islamic legal thought insist that the four witnesses must have arrived at the scene of the act at different times. M. Perham once asked an alkali if he had ever sentenced somebody to death for adultery. The *alkali* told her that he had never, neither had his father nor grandfather who were *alkalai* before him. Asked why, he answered that it was most

difficult to establish guilt, unless there was confession by both parties. M. Perham, Native Administration in Nigeria, op. cit. p.93

80. A case in point was reported by Lord Lugard in his Political Memoranda that "the Oyo Province has accepted British suzerainty, and its loyal and enlightened ruler, the Alafin, is anxious to accept the same status as the paramount rulers of the North. The recent uprising of a portion of the Ibadan Bale-ship against the authority alike of the Alafin and of the British Raj, which was quickly suppressed by force, has deprived the subordinate districts of Ibadan of any claim to independence of the Alafin." Quoted in A.H.M. Kirk-Greene, *Principles of Native Administration in Nigeria, op. cit.*, p. 77.

81. The Satiru revolt near Sokoto, as well as the revolt of the people of Hadejia are two examples. In Kano Emir Abbas, who was appointed by the British, never fully gave them his support.

82. C.L. Temple, *Native Races and Their Rulers: Sketches and Studies of Official Life and Administrative Problems in Nigeria*, Second ed., (London, Frank Cass, 1968), p. 30.

83. It should be noted that districts were, in most cases, administrative designations and their boundaries were often redrawn to create more districts or to merge others.

84. Temple's Political Testimony. Quoted in A.H.M. Kirk-Greene, ed., *Principle of Native Administration in Nigeria: Selected Documents 1900-1947* (London, Oxford University Press, 1965), p. 57.

85. M.A. Fika, *The Kano Civil War and British Overrule 1882-1940, op. cit.*, p. 223.

86. It is interesting to note that colonial rule made emirs presidents of judicial councils that were supposed to be governed by the Islamic shari'ah, but did not make any effort to see to it that such emirs were knowledgeable in

the shari'ah. In the early years of the jihad, it was quite in order for emirs to be the presidents of their judicial councils, for, as with Kano, knowledge of Islam was the determinant factor in appointment to emirship. But by the beginning of the 20th century, pursuit of knowledge was undertaken only by those royals who had lost all hope of ever obtaining any office. See Dahiru Yahya, "The Legacy of the Emir of Kano Abdullahi Bayero, 1926-1953" op. cit., where he argues that "since Abdullahi Bayero's father, Muhammad Abbas, did not anticipate his eldest son Abdullahi Bayero, would secure any position in government, he put him on the path of scholarship."

87. Figures from M.A. Fika, Op. Cit., p. 233.
88. NAK/SNP/10/1/795/1913 Emirs and their Salaries list 1913.
89. M. Perham, *Native Administration in Nigeria, op. cit.*, p. 218. See also John Paden, *Religion and Political Culture in Kano*, (Los Angeles, University of California Press, 1973), p. 25.
90. On this point see C.S. Whitaker, Jr., *The Politics of Tradition: Continuity and Change in Northern Nigeria 1946-1966,* (Princeton, Princeton University Press, 1970), See also K. A. Busia, *The Position of the Chief in the Modern Political System of Ashanti,* (London, Oxford University Press, 1951).
91. See C.L.Temple, *Native Races and Their Rulers. Op. cit.*, especially the chapter titled "Anatomy of lying" pp. 103-122. See also D.A, Low, and R. Cranford Pratt, "Baganda Chief Negotiated Special Conditions for British Occupation 1900" in Wilfrey Cartey and Martin Kilson, eds., *The Africa Reader: African Reaction and Adaptation, Emergence of Masses, Formation of National Institutions,* (New York, Vintage Books, 1970); K.A. Busia, op. cit.

92. C.N.Ubah, *The Administration of Kano Emirate Under the British, 1900-1930,* unpublished Ph.D. Dissertation, university of Ibadan, 1973, p. 49.
93. C.S. Whitaker, Jr., op. cit., p. 218, Cf. Ronald Cohen, "The Analysis of Conflict in Hierarchical Systems: An Example from Kanuri Political Organization" in Anthropologica, Vol. 4, 31, 1962. A similar observation was made by Busia on the Ashanti chief. See also K.A. Busia, *The Position of the Chief, op. cit.* p.200
94. See Lady Lugard, op. cit. p. 401.
95. Polly Hill, *Population, Prosperity and Poverty: Rural Kano 1900-1970* (Cambridge, Cambridge University Press, 1977), p. 50.
96. M.I. Muhtar, *The Impact of British Colonial Domination on the Society and Economic Structure of the Society of Kano 1903-1950,* Unpublished MA Thesis, Ahmadu Bello University, Zaria, 1983.
97. Cited in Sule Bello *State and Economy in Kano 1894-1960: A Study of Colonial Domination*, Ph.D., ABU, 1982. p. 118.
98. NAK/KNPROF/236/1929
99. NAK/KNPROF/447/1914
100. M. M. Tukur, op. cit., 227.
101. As a result of that injury Emir Abbas could not return to Gidan Rumfa. He died at his Nassarawa palace. Hence the name Maje Nassarawa -the one who went to Nassarawa [and never returned]. Traditionally in Kano, emirs who died outside Gidan Rumfa are posthumously named after the places where they died. Another example is Abdullahi Maje Karofi, the father of Abbas.
102. Interview with Ibrahim Tahir, Talban Bauchi, Abuja, February 12, 1995.
103. The precursor to the NEPU was the Northern Elements Progressive Association, NEPA, founded in Kano in 1946, while the precursor to the Northern People's Congress was the Association of Northern People of Today, Jam'iyyar Mutanen Arewa A Yau, founded on

October 12, 1948, at Zaria. For details on the origins of northern political parties, see R.L. Sklar, *Nigerian Political Parties: Power in an Emergent African Nation* (Princeton, Princeton University Press, 1963). See also C.S. Whitaker, Jr.., *The Politics of Tradition: op.cit and B.J. Dudley, Parties and Politics in Northern Nigeria* (London, Frank Cass, 1968).

104. Sawaba Declaration: Northern Elements Progressive Union Declaration of Principles released in October 1950. Cited in A.D. Yahaya, The Native Authority System in Northern Nigeria 1950-1970, (Zaria, Ahmadu Bello University Press, 1980), appendix 4, p. 237.

105. Op. cit.

106. Op. cit.

107. The eight foundation members of NEPU were: Abba Maikwaru (Kano, Hausa), Bello Ijumu (Kabba, Yoruba), Maitama Sule (Kano, Hausa), Sani Darma (Kano, Hausa), Abdulqadir Danjaji (Kano Hausa), Ahmadu Bida (Bida, Nupe), Magaji Dambatta (Kano, Hausa), and Abba Kashiya (Kano, Hausa). Mallam Aminu joined them later.

108. Cited in C.S. Whitaker, Jr. The Politics of Tradition... op. cit., 398.

109. Perhaps the real reason for Sanusi's role in getting his father to advise against Bello Dandago was that he (Sanusi) was certain he was going to succeed his father as emir. Had he allowed Bello Dandago to be groomed to become leader of Northern Nigeria, then his (Sanusi's) own authority in Kano would have been undermined. It was primarily for this reason that Sanusi advised against Bello Dandago, or so many people believe.

110. On the founding members of the NPC, see Richard Sklar, *Nigerian Political Parties,* op. cit., pp. 88-101, 513-17, C.S. Whitaker, Jr., *The Politics of Tradition, op. cit.*, pp. 355-69, 384-91, and B.J. Dudley, *Parties and Politics in Northern Nigeria, op. cit.*, pp. 72-163. I am

grateful to Dan Masanin Kano Yusuf Maitama Sule and Justice Sanusi Ciroma Yusuf for some of the accounts narrated above.

111. The latest study and the most comprehensive with unequalled primary materials is J.N. Paden, *Ahmadu Bello, Sardauna of Sokoto: Values and Leadership in Nigeria* (Zaria, Alhudahuda Publishing Company, 1986), pp. 446-66, J.N. *Paden Religion and Political Culture in Kano,* (Princeton, Princeton University Press, 1973), pp. 266-72, C.S. Whitaker, Jr., *The Politics of Tradition: Continuity and Change in Northern Nigeria, 1946—1966,* op. cit., pp. 279—86, and D.J.M. Muffett, "Legitimacy and Deference in a Tradition-Oriented Society: Observation Arising from an Examination of some Aspects of a Case Study Associated with the Abdication of the Emir of Kano in 1963" in *African Studies Review,* 18: September 1975, pp. 101-115.

A PRBORN

GIDAN RUMFA ABOUT 1930

By 1926, when Abdullahi Bayero became the Emir of Kano, Gidan Rumfa had been radically transformed from what it had been on the eve of the British occupation. It was no more the political and economic nerve centre of the emirate. Even its legitimacy, which was predicated on Islam, had been considerably eroded.

In contrast to the pre-colonial days when the emir's court was the final place of authority, colonial rule had superimposed another kind of authority on that of the emir. Indeed, the emir needed approval to do a lot of things, including appointing his key titleholders. Economically, Gidan Rumfa had ceased to be the house of plenty that it had been. In the first place, the abolition of slavery had led to a drastic reduction in the output from the various royal farms spread across the emirate. Although the British colonial rulers allowed prisoners to work those farms, the yield was nowhere near what it had earlier been. Secondly, the decision of the British (discussed in the introduction) to rationalize taxation and place the emir and his lieutenants on salaries greatly reduced the disposable income of the palace. Whereas before colonial rule all proceeds (cash and kind) realized from taxation were brought to the palace to be disbursed as the emir saw fit, with most of them remaining in the palace, colonial rule monetized taxes and compelled the emir to account for every penny.

These developments naturally led to changes in social relations among the occupants of the palace. A number of the palace functionaries came to be placed on salaries too. The net effect of all those changes was some relaxation of the bond of servitude between the emir and his one-time slaves or servants.

One aspect of Gidan Rumfa that proved most resilient to all these changes was *fada* or palace culture. Perhaps, conscious of the waning power of the emir in the political and economic life of the emirate, deliberate efforts were made by Emir Abdullahi Bayero to give the institution some moral strength. Islam, which since the beginning of the British occupation had ceased to be the reason-for-being of the emirate, was given a new boost. Islamic education was emphasized. Apart from children who were traditionally required to attend Islamic schools and read the Holy Qur'an, married women of the palace were also encouraged to attend Islamic schools specially opened for them. Moral education was also given special attention.

Children of the palace were not distinguished by their parentage. The prince was not treated differently from the son of the servant or the royal slave. They attended the same schools, ate from the same pot, played on the same playground, and generally grew up respecting each other. Among the children, palace culture emphasized respect for elders.[1] When the emir was going to give the children some presents, for example, it was not to one of the princes that he gave the presents to share out, but to the oldest child among them, who could be the son of a slave or some servant.

Abdullahi Bayero was a very perceptive emir. He had foreseen the strategic role Western education was going to play in the new political system being fashioned out by the British. He had reasoned, early in his reign, that the future lay not so much in royalty but the acquisition of Western education. If Kano was to continue to be relevant in the emerging new dispensation—the Northern Region and Nigeria—Kano people needed to be encouraged to embrace Western education. By extension, if Gidan Rumfa was to continue to play a key role in the affairs of Kano, it should produce princes with Western education. Abdullahi Bayero then resolved that all his children of school age, male and female, would acquire Western education. He also ensured that all children resident in the palace were enrolled in the first Western education school[2] he opened in the palace in 1936.[3]

To encourage the children to stay in school, as well as the teachers to give their best, the Emir used to go and sit in some of the classes. He was also known to have taken lessons in English language and other subjects after the normal school hours.[4]

ANOTHER ADO IS BORN

About four years into his reign, on June 15, 1930, Emir Abdullahi Bayero was blessed with yet another baby boy, the eleventh to the Emir, and the second of three children to his mother.[5] He was named Ado, the Hausa version of Adam. That was the second time Abdullahi Bayero was naming his son Ado. His first son, who died at five, was the first to be given the name Ado.

Although Abdullahi Bayero seemed to love the name Ado, he never called the second Ado by that name, on any occasion except perhaps on the day he performed *khutba* informing the three-day-old baby of his name and on the seventh day when he formally announced the name to the public. For the rest of the twenty-three years that Ado lived with his father, Emir Abdullahi Bayero called his son Mallam. That was a singular honor the Emir bestowed on Ado. For Emir Abdullahi was not known to have called any of his other children by other than their given names. Many explanations have been put forward for Emir Abdullahi's decision not to call Ado by his name. One version is that *Pulaako* or Fulani culture inhibits parents from calling their first children by their given names.[6] And since the name Ado was that of Abdullahi's first child, the Emir observed that cultural inhibition. Another version, subscribed to by Ado's mother, Hajiya Hasiya, is that it was indicative of the special place Ado had in his father's heart. Right from birth, according to this source, Ado seemed to have endeared himself to his father, who took an exceptional interest in the boy. Within the bounds of palace culture, Emir Abdullahi Bayero did in fact shower his love on Ado. Both Ado and his mother believe that part of the reason for Emir Abdullahi's calling Ado Mallam, was a prayer or hope that the boy would someday grow up to exhibit the qualities of a mallam. A mallam in this case was not just somebody who was learned, one who knew right from wrong, or one who called people to the right path, but one who also practiced what he taught. In other words, one who lived by example. If those were the prayers of Emir Abdullahi, Allah seemed to have answered them early in Ado's life.

When Ado reached the age of seven, his father, the Emir, in keeping with palace custom, sent him to one of his slave-title holders called Maikano Zagi, to be brought up. It was while in the care of Maikano Zagi that Ado started exhibiting the characteristics of good leadership. He was honest, forthright, and a disciplinarian among his age mates. His reputation among his mates was such that the mere mention of his name was enough to elicit good behavior from them. So fearful of him were his erring mates that he was called "*Ado Dan Umma Dogarin Yan Sarki*," meaning "Ado the son of Umma the disciplinarian of princes."

From about the age of ten, Ado begun to have leadership positions thrust on him by his peers and he never failed to distinguish himself. In one instance when he and his friends were play-acting, Ado fell from a donkey and broke his hand. While his peers panicked and started running to seek help, Ado, in the tradition of his fathers and forefathers, even at that tender age, restrained himself from crying. His friends were amazed at that show of courage, and many of the elders of the palace could not hide their admiration for his valour.[7]

What Ado Bayero learned at home he practiced outside. At the Kano Middle School, where he was a student between 1942 and 1946, he never for once considered it beneath him, on account of his being a prince, to do the normal chores students were expected to do. While some princes were known to have at their beck and call many servants to do their own share of the chores for them, Ado Bayero was known to have physically swept the compound, and to have washed not only his own clothes, but sometimes also those of his seniors. In contrast to most other students from aristocratic (not even royal) backgrounds, Ado Bayero ate school meals. Alhaji Inuwa Wada, the Magajin Garin Kano and a teacher of Ado at the Kano Middle School, recalls vividly how Ado refused to allow his parentage to get to his head. He made friends from the ranks of both the rich and the poor, aristocrats as well as commoners. He was reputed to be the first Kano prince to cultivate the friendship of people from the other side of the city, namely the Hausa section.[8] Alhaji Muhammadu Aminu Sanusi, now Ciroman Kano, an age-mate, and nephew of Ado Bayero and his contemporary in primary and middle schools cannot remember even one instance when Ado had a quarrel with anyone. He was very patient.

Ado developed a habit around that time that has endured to this day, a habit he came to find especially useful as a legislator some sixteen years later. It was an unusual habit among children. At certain periods, he would keep away from his friends for days, not because he was angry with anyone or because he was overwhelmed with problems—at the age of ten, Ado could not have been hibernating to reflect on problems. Moreover, as a prince, both of whose parents were alive, and one who was his father's pet, Ado could not have been in want. The fact is that whenever he was asked why he went into hiding, he would answer that he simply wanted to be alone, and that was all the reason he could give. He did not give any justification for wanting to be alone, and luckily, none was demanded of him.

As Ado grew older, he came to find a justification for the habit he had developed from childhood. He came to reason that time, like life, is a trust from Allah. One therefore has a duty to manage it well and give to all that have claim to it. Time must be budgeted for one's creator, for one's means of livelihood, and for one's family and community, including friends. Time also has to be given to oneself. Keeping this trust means ensuring that all that have a claim on one's time get it, including oneself. One's own time could be used to reflect on matters that are essentially personal, or on matters of public interest. Such reflections might be carried out in solitude and perhaps through reading. What is essential is that one should be alone. When Ado kept away from friends at that time, therefore, he was, without necessarily knowing it, trying to ensure that play did not take an undue share of his time.

There was something about the way Ado comported himself, even as a youth, that made people who met him, not fail to respect him. He carried himself in a very dignified manner. He was self-confident without being self-conceited, proud but never snobbish, and dignified but not unapproachable. So manifest were these characteristics of Ado that when in 1952 he enrolled at the Zaria Clerical College, the nucleus of the present Institute of Administration of Ahmadu Bello University, the Principal, a Mr. M.C. Currey, surveyed the new students gathered in the assembly hall and pointing to Ado said, "this is your senior student." Significantly, neither Mr. Currey nor any of the other students, except the few who came from Kano, knew who Ado was.

The position of the senior student was one of great responsibility at that time. To him were entrusted all the things students needed for their comfort. These ranged from mattresses to soap and other amenities. Ado's self-denial endeared him to most of his colleagues and teachers. Unlike in the past where the senior students ensured that they had their fill of all provisions before distributing them to other students, Ado made it a point to take his share last. On many occasions, he had had to forego his own share of provisions. But never once was he heard to complain. He was always contented with the little he got.

At school and at home Ado never heard about a quarrel or some misunderstanding between his mates or relations without taking an initiative to reconcile the parties involved. He was known to have taken such initiatives not just with his younger siblings or juniors at school, but even with his elders and seniors. For that reason, among others, Ado was respected even by his elders, some of whom had children as old as Ado himself.[9]

MAKING HIS MARK

After graduation from the School for Arabic Studies, in 1947, at the age of 17, Ado decided it was time he paid his dues to his community. But unlike other princes, who went straight into the Native Authority system for some big office, Ado opted for something different. He joined the British Bank for West Africa (BBWA), now called First Bank of Nigeria. That was a radical break because at that time, given his background and education, Ado could have obtained a very big office in the NA system. In retrospect, working with the BBWA was a big blessing. It gave the young Ado a broad exposure that was to assist him in his later career. Unlike other Kano princes, and indeed Northerners in general, Ado opted to work with an institution the majority of whose workers came from other parts of Nigeria. Thus, even at that early age Ado was poised to learn about the different cultures within Nigeria. Working side by side with Igbos, Yorubas and people from other ethnic backgrounds at the BBWA must have contributed to Ado's appreciation of the complex nature of the evolving Nigerian State.

Another worthwhile experience Ado derived from working with the BBWA, and which was to stand him in good stead some fifteen years later, when he was ambassador in

Senegal, was the importance of proper book-keeping. As a bank clerk Ado saw how all accounts must be balanced daily before the workers could go home. A difference of £1 was enough to detain the affected workers for hours until the account was properly balanced. In other words, Ado came to realize early in his working career that every penny of public funds must be accounted for.

After a stint at the BBWA, Ado moved to the Kano Native Authority in 1949. While working with the Kano NA, he attended many clerical and administrative courses in both Nigeria and abroad. In 1952, he attended the Clerical Training College, Zaria. He also attended a course on Local Government in the United Kingdom. In 1953 he became the Chief Clerk of the Kano Town Council, a position he held until his appointment as Chief of Kano NA Police in 1956.

While still in the employ of the Kano Native Authority, as Chief Clerk of Kano Town Council, Ado contested and won elections on the ticket of the NPC to the Regional House of Assembly in Kaduna in 1954.[10] There again, Ado made an impressionable impact on the House. The contributions he made in the brief period (1955-1957) that he was in the House made him stand out as a very intelligent young man, who always did his homework thoroughly before speaking. On any issue on which he spoke, and there was hardly any on which he did not, he articulated his position with such confidence that his colleagues, especially the senior ones, were left wondering how such a newcomer could be so well informed on every issue, and so analytical in his presentation. Whether the issue before the House was economics or social welfare, finance or education, international politics or the Northernization policy, Ado's contributions were both well-researched and presented. Ado's leadership qualities were also recognized early in the Assembly when he became the first of the fifteen new members sworn in on March 2, 1955 to address the House and to thank it on behalf of his colleagues, for the welcome address given to them the previous day.[11]

After he had won the elections, Ado identified two factors that would help him make a success of his new mission as a legislator. The first was general and sometimes specialized knowledge about issues. That, he concluded, could best be derived from reading. Luckily for him, reading had been his hobby since childhood. As we noted earlier, he could keep to himself for days without feeling lonely. Equally, his education, both in Nigeria and abroad, had exposed him to most of the developmental issues the Assembly was going to be discussing. He then resolved to read as much as he could to be even better prepared.

The second factor in his success was a mastery of the Rules and Standing Orders of the House. These guide the operations of the House. While the first requirement portrays one as an authority on the issue being discussed, the second offers protection from any embarrassment resulting from falling foul of the rules of the game. Ado therefore made sure that by the time he was sworn in, he was fully conversant with the Rules and Standing Orders of the House. And it was a good thing he did, for while making his very first contribution to the House on March 3, 1955, about midway into the address, an older and respectable member of the House, Mallam Ibrahim Imam, interrupted his speech. He then charged Ado with impugning a member of the House. Knowing that he had not done or said anything that contravened the Rules, Ado was not at all rattled. The President of the House, Sir Rex Niven, intervened saying "The Honorable member [referring to Ibrahim Imam] would be very surprised if he spent an afternoon at Westminster. I think he can rely on me to pull up an Honorable member if he goes too far in a personal accusation."[12] With that, Ado Bayero continued his address.

That incident was significant in two respects. First, it showed that Ado Bayero, who was barely twenty-four hours old as a member of the House, was very well versed in its Rules and Standing Orders. Secondly, it showed that some of the older members were themselves not fully conversant with the Rules or were using their clout to intimidate other, especially newer, members from speaking their minds.

Another incident that showed Ado Bayero to be a serious member took place during a Question and Answer session on March 7, 1957. In March 1956, Ado Bayero had asked the Northern Region Minister of Health, Honorable Mr. G.U. Ohikere to state the number of maternity homes in the North and their locations. In his reply, the Honorable Minister had included Aro Agor, in Ilorin Division, among towns with that facility. But one year later, on March 7, 1957 to be precise, at the same Question and Answer session, Ado Bayero took on the Minister of Health thus:

Ado Abdullahi Bayero (Kano South):

Mr. Chairman, Sir, on the 8th of March 1956 I asked the Minister of Health about the number of maternity homes in the North and their whereabouts. In his reply, the Minister included Oro Agor, in Ilorin Division, among those particulars. I have information from that place that a maternity home has never been built there...

Hon. Mr. Ohikere (Minister of Health):

If it is the oral answer the member is talking about I said they were in Ilorin and Jos...

Ado Abdullahi Bayero:

Mr. Chairman, I said last year, not this year. I refer the Minister to his reply to Question 030 in column 281 of 1956 Hansard.
Mr. Chairman, I have information from that place that there is no maternity home in Oro Agor though people have been crying for one, so I would like the Minister to confirm whether there is really a maternity home in the town or not... Sir, it is very annoying to tell the people that they have got something which they have not got and which they are anxious to have![5]

When it is remembered that the Honorable Ado Bayero belonged to the same party as the Honorable Minister of Health, the seriousness with which he took his job may be better appreciated. Many a legislator would not take the trouble to verify claims made by a Minister, or where they stumbled on a piece of contrary information, they might not want to say anything that would embarrass their party.

A further examination of some of the contributions of the Honorable Ado Abdullahi Bayero on some of the issues discussed on the floor of the House might help shed some light on the argument we are trying to make. It will also indicate some matters of personal interest to him, and to which he has devoted his time since becoming Emir. Equally, it will show how most of the topical issues of contemporary politics—both domestic and international—are really not new, and that some forty years ago, the Honorable Ado Bayero had anticipated them and sought answers to them. We shall look at the opinion of Ado Bayero on six issues that are as relevant today as they were over forty years ago, when he expressed them. These are:

1. The question of peaceful co-existence among the heterogeneous people of Nigeria;
2. The increasing concern being expressed about the plight of rural areas;
3. The danger of states depending almost wholly on revenue allocated from the federation account;
4.   External borrowing to finance development projects;
5. The ratio between capital and recurrent expenditure in government spending and its impact on development; and finally;
6. The use of economic sanctions as instrument of foreign policy.

ON PEACEFUL CO-EXISTENCE

Hardly a day passes these days without Nigerians getting exhortations from their leaders—political, religious, and traditional—to learn to live with their fellow countrymen in peace. In recent years, especially since the crisis following the annulment of the June 12, 1993 Presidential elections, these leaders have made frequent appeals to their followers to exhibit a spirit of give-and-take in their relationship with their fellow countrymen. Going through the newspapers of this period, one would think that our leaders are only just realizing the importance of compromise, accommodation, and tolerance. But Ado Bayero has been preaching those values for over forty years in the public arena. In his contribution to the debate in the Northern House of Assembly on February 4, 1957, for instance, he said:

> ...We must try to compromise on many things. We must not say that we should have everything we want, because we do not get everything at once....[14]

ON THE PLIGHT OF RURAL AREAS

Until the dramatic fall in the price of oil in the late seventies, successive Nigerian governments paid scant attention to the rural areas. The federal, regional, and later state governments concentrated their expenditure on the urban areas. But things appear to be changing. For some time now, governments have been emphasizing the need for the incorporation of the rural economy into the national economy, through the provision of infrastructure and some of the basic necessities of life. The various governments are now arguing that since a majority of the population lives in the rural areas, we cannot rightly talk of development, if it does not reach the rural areas.

Again, Ado Bayero had realized that fact and had tried to impress it on his colleagues in the Regional Assembly as far back as 1957. In a contribution to the House on the subject Ado Bayero said:

> Mr. President, Sir, though elected from an urban area, I always take interest in the welfare of those in the rural areas. I want the government to give more attention to those people living in the countryside. ..."[15]

As he rightly stated, his constituency was urban. He therefore, had no obligation to make a case for rural areas. But that was the quintessential Ado. It was the interest of the generality of the people that he pursued, and not that of some 2,928 voters.[16]

Danger of Over-Dependence of States and Local Governments on Allocations from the Federation Account

In recent years, especially since the mid-1980's, concern has been expressed about the near complete dependence of most states and local governments on allocations from the federation account to be able to operate. In a number of states and local governments, receipts from the Federation Account constitute over 80% of their budget. That situation, it has been pointed out, does not augur well for development especially since the bulk of federal money comes from the sale of crude oil over whose price the government has no complete control. Efforts are nevertheless being made to correct the perceived anomaly.

But is that problem only now being realized? Forty-two years ago, Ado Bayero in his contribution to the debates in the House had said:

> Before going through the estimate and the speech made by the Financial Secretary, I came to the conclusion that something must be done if we are to continue to have stable financial position. A big percentage of our revenue comes from central funds, from Customs and Excise.... These are not stable... So I would like government to think over this program and think of other means of getting money.[17]

He did not stop at identifying the problem, but also suggested possible solutions thus:

> Government should find ways and means of taxing places of entertainment such as cinemas, bar and race meetings, where people with excessive [sic] incomes spend their money. ...[18]

87

ON EXTERNAL BORROWING TO
FINANCE DEVELOPMENT PROJECTS

It is now generally acknowledged that capital accumulation is a precondition of economic development. For poor Third World countries, borrowing is seen as one sure way of raising the needed capital. The issue today is not whether to borrow or not, but who is ready to lend the money.

But over forty years ago, when the matter came up in the Regional House, and some members had cautioned against borrowing, Ado had raised a Point of Information, where he made a very strong case for borrowing to finance development projects. Ado canvassed the very arguments that are being used by development economists today to convince people of the virtue of borrowing over forty years ago. He had argued, for example, that even the United Kingdom was borrowing money from the United States. At that particular time, he noted, UK was negotiating a loan of £500,000,000 from the US. Ado concluded thus:

There is nothing wrong with the government borrowing either within or without....If anyone thinks that borrowing is bad, then I think he is out of date....[19]

ON THE RATIO BETWEEN CAPITAL AND
RECURRENT EXPENDITURE OF GOVERNMENT

Budgets, whether of the nation, state, or local government, make provision for two kinds of expenditure: recurrent and capital. Recurrent expenditure is what is spent routinely and is expenditure that is consumptive. Capital expenditure, on the other hand, is expenditure incurred as a form of investment. It is incurred on the provision of infrastructure that facilitates the acquisition of more wealth. It therefore becomes obvious that for any economy to grow, its budget must give serious attention to capital votes. Contributing to the discussion on the Financial Secretary's Report for 1957,

Ado Bayero made the above observations and concluded that:

Agriculture is the main work of the common people of this Region; when we look at Head 246—Agriculture—the total of personal emoluments is £292,450, while the total of the other charges under the same Head shows £244,795 only. What we would have liked to see is less money spent on personal emoluments and more to assist farmers to produce more for consumption and export. ..."[20]

THE USE OF ECONOMIC SANCTIONS AS INSTRUMENT OF FOREIGN POLICY

Following the annulment of the Presidential elections held on June 12, 1993, limited economic sanctions were imposed on Nigeria by the nations of Europe, Canada, and the United States and that took many Nigerians by surprise. People realized that if the industrialized nations of the world decided not to trade with us, for whatever reason, we were doomed, because we were unprepared. Yet some forty years ago Honorable Member, Ado Bayero had foreseen that possibility, when he asked:

Consider what would happen if foreigners who made [sic] use of these products [our raw materials] were to boycott it [sic]. The result will be national economic collapse. ... [21]

Or consider the complaints by the raw-material-producing nations of the Third World that the Western Nations buy their raw materials cheaply but sell the products of those raw materials to them at exorbitant prices. Raw-material-producing nations complain that the industrialized nations dictate the prices of both the raw materials as well as the finished goods. But Ado Bayero had cautioned, over forty years ago that unless we put up factories to make use of those raw materials we would continue to be at the mercy of the industrialized nations who would always be able call our bluff.

Early in April 1957, while Ado Bayero was still working as Chief Clerk of the Kano City Council, his elder brother, Emir Sanusi, sent for him. The Emir was at his Wudil palace. Ado drove in the evening to the palace. There, the Emir informed Ado that they were considering appointing him the Kano NA Chief of Police, in succession to his elder brother, Muhammadu Kabir, who had been made a District Head. It was a very tough job, especially with the NEPU having its base in Kano. Luckily, Ado was given time to think over it. Ado Bayero gave a serious thought to the Emir's offer. He concluded that that office could make or mar him as a prince, depending on how he performed his role. After consultation with a few relations and confidantes, he agreed to take the challenge.

On his appointment as Kano NA Police Chief in April 1957, Ado Bayero decided to resign his seat in the Northern Region House of Assembly. In his letter of resignation to the President of the House, Ado Bayero said that his new office carried heavy responsibilities, and for that reason he would want to devote all his attention to the work. He resolved to abstain totally from politics and to sever all connections with all political parties for the whole of the period he held that office.[22]

Ado Bayero decided on his own to vacate the seat even though he was not obliged to vacate his Assembly seat in order to take up the Chief of Police job. Moreover, the legislative job was part-time and he could therefore have combined the two as many people did. From this, one could see a determination on his part to do a thorough job, without any inhibition. And a thorough job he certainly did, as Mahe Bashir Wali, a successor to Ado Bayero as Kano Police Chief, confirms. [23] According to Wali, Ado Bayero left a record as Kano NA Police Chief that has not been equalled by anyone who came before or after him. He noted that Ado Bayero lived by his word to be above partisan politics, a development that made the NPC government uncomfortable with him.

Wali worked as clerk in the NA police office at the time Ado Bayero was Police Chief, and later rose to become Kano NA Police Chief in 1964. He finally retired as the Deputy Inspector General of the Nigeria Police Force in 1989. He recalls that Ado Bayero assumed the office of Kano NA Police Chief with a clear idea of what he wanted to do. On assuming office, recalls Wali, Ado Bayero left no one in doubt that he was going to chart a new course for the Kano NA Police. He wanted to build a police force that was loved and respected by the people, a police force that the people saw as friends, helpers and protectors not what he inherited, a group who were feared, hated, and perceived as extortionists by the people. To achieve that goal, the Police Chief employed two strategies. The first was a complete review of the NA Police Code. With his exposure to various police codes, in the course of his many courses in Nigeria and England, Ado Bayero was quick in noting the need for a review of the NA Police Code. The new code sought to educate the officers, individually and collectively, on the role of police officers. It emphasized the need for them to cultivate the friendship and trust of the people. It also emphasized the need for them to be independent and not to allow themselves to be used by the powers-that-be, to settle scores. It therefore guaranteed them security from political and other pressures. Equally, the new code emphasized discipline. The new Police Chief took a personal interest in establishing a disciplined force. He seriously reprimanded any constable who committed any act that fell short of the expectations of his officers. In his reorganization of the NA police, Ado Bayero opened its gates to women. Thus, for the first time, the Kano NA police had a policewoman.[24]

Ado Bayero's principled handling of the NA police in very difficult times and under intense political pressures endeared him to many of the NEPU leaders in Kano. It must be noted that it was not that Ado Bayero went out of his way to protect NEPU members and leaders even when they had committed offenses. What he simply did was to make sure that nobody was penalized without a just cause. He put a stop to the prevalent practice whereby ordinary people or prominent members of the opposition party, NEPU, were arrested and detained on the orders of some powerful people in the society, only to be released after a day or two without any charges brought against them. That, in itself, was a big relief to the NEPU leaders and members, as most of the arrests of their members ended up not getting to the courts, especially when the party began to use lawyers to defend its members. As Alhaji Tanko Yakasai, a one-time General Secretary of the NEPU observed, "the hostility that the NA police directed at the NEPU changed with Ado's assumption of office." Yakasai recalls an incident to buttress his position. He said that some time in the late 1950s when Ado Bayero was the Kano NA Police Chief, Alhaji Ibrahim Musa Gashash was attacked as he was driving from Dandali Quarters, through Tudun Nufawa to Fagge. He went and lodged a complaint with the NA Police. Yakasai was one of those accused, together with Tijjani Na Abba, Uba Na Alkassim, Aminu Tiya, and others, of instigating the attack. Instead of signing their arrest warrant, as had been the practice, Ado invited them to come to the police station. When they came, they were taken to the Emir's court where the matter was treated as a civil case. According to Yakasai, had Ado Bayero not been the police chief, they would have been convicted. Yakasai also recalls that as the Hausa editor of the *Daily Comet*, he published a story that angered the authorities. They directed that he be arrested. But Ado Bayero did not comply with their wishes. Instead, he asked to be shown where that publication infringed the laws of the land; and that was how the matter ended.[25]

While this conduct of Ado Bayero may today appear very normal, and indeed what is expected of any good police officer, in those days it seemed very revolutionary. It will seem even more so when it is remembered that the nucleus of the NA police was the *dogarai*, or the emir's bodyguards. These men were essentially recruited from the emir's slaves. To these people, there was no distinction between the state and the emir; the laws of the state were the emirs' laws, and any violation of those laws was viewed as a personal affront to the emir. Hence, the viciousness with which these law enforcement agents visited persons perceived to have broken the law.

A number of developments, discussed in the next chapter, led to Ado's appointment as Nigeria's ambassador to Senegal in late 1962. There again, Ado sought to excel, and he did so in at least three areas. First was the administration of the chancery in Dakar. He believed that much of his success as an ambassador would depend on how disciplined his staff were and how much co-operation he got from them. He therefore set out early on his assumption of duty to underscore the importance of discipline and teamwork among the workers. He appealed to the staff to see the chancery as a small family. He called for honesty and dedication to duty. He particularly emphasized the need for financial probity at all times, but allowed everyone to do his or her work to the best of his or her ability. The only caution was that everyone should always make sure that he or she did not do anything that would dent the image of the chancery, whether in the host country or at home. In return, he ensured that every member of staff got all his or her legitimate entitlements without any delay.

On one occasion when some member of staff erred, the Ambassador had called him into his office and spoke to him at length. He did not apply punitive measures and he did not discuss the matter with anyone. That strategy worked as the officer, who was notorious for that kind of offense, never committed the same mistake again up to the time Ambassador Bayero left the post. Ambassador Bayero's style of administration won for him a lot of respect among the chancery staff. Meanwhile in Lagos, the Prime Minister, Alhaji Abubakar Tafawa Balewa, was inundated with reports of rifts among top diplomats in Nigerian missions abroad. The reports were so disturbing that the Prime Minister dispatched the Deputy

Permanent Secretary in the Ministry of External Affairs, Mr. Joe Iyala, on a fact-finding tour of all Nigerian missions abroad. On his return, Mr. Iyala wrote a very comprehensive report and submitted it to the Prime Minister. In the report, Mr. Iyala singled out Dakar for special commendation. He noted that it was only in Senegal that the ambassador and all his key officers got on very well. He also noted the very family-like atmosphere in the embassy. As a result of that Report, Prime Minister Abubakar Tafawa Balewa called the Premier of the North, Sardauna Ahmadu Bello, and thanked him for recommending Ado Bayero to him as an ambassador.[26]

The second area in which Ado excelled was in cultivating the friendship of the head of state of his host country. In diplomacy, that has inestimable advantage. It gives your country the ear of the highest authority in your host country. Although protocol may require that procedure be followed, where a strong personal friendship has been established, protocol does give way to informality, even in state matters.

Ambassador Bayero was thirty-two years old when he went to Senegal. In age, he was the youngest ambassador in Dakar. President Leopold Sedar Senghor was at that time fifty-seven. He was a philosopher, an intellectual, a teacher,[27] and he wanted people to see him as such. He wanted the Senegalese to learn English. He could speak it himself and he always wanted to speak in English especially in public. That was one reason why he took an interest in Ambassador Ado Bayero. A second reason was that as a philosopher and teacher he wanted to impart knowledge. He therefore loved people who sought knowledge from him, especially young people to whom he could pass on his philosophy. Ado Bayero, as we noted earlier, was always hungry for knowledge. He was either reading books or reflecting on issues. So when he met President Senghor, the philosopher-author of Negritude, Ado Bayero was a willing student. Senghor, for his part, found the young ambassador very intelligent and interesting to chat with, often asking probing questions. Soon enough, Senghor began to invite Ambassador Bayero to the State House, in Dakar, for chats over tea or coffee.

At the official level, Senghor saw an opportunity to solve his own domestic political problem, by establishing a very cordial relationship with Nigeria. He had some problems with Sheikh Ibrahim Niass, the leader of the Tijjaniya brotherhood in West Africa, which had resulted in the vast majority of the population of Kaolack, Niass' birthplace in Senegal, rejecting Senghor's party, the Union Progressite Senegalaise (UPS). As a politician, he could not afford to ignore such an important group. Senghor knew that next to Kaolack, Sheikh Niass' largest followers were in Northern Nigeria. He therefore reasoned that by cultivating a good relationship with Nigeria, especially with Ambassador Ado Bayero, whose father, Emir Abdullahi Bayero, was a good friend of Sheikh Niass; he would be laying the basis for reconciliation with the people of Kaolack.[28] With these considerations therefore, President Senghor's house was always open to Ambassador Bayero.

The final area in which Ado excelled was when he decided, on his own, to enroll for a course in French so that he would not need anyone to translate or interpret anything for him. That decision was instructive. Ambassadors were not required to understand the language of their host country. Within the embassy, there was always an officer whose job was to translate all documents into the official language of the country of the ambassador so that he could read and act on them. Many people who had reached the post of ambassador would never dream of going to the classroom to take language lessons, especially when their promotion was not tied to attending such a course.

Years later, when the civil war broke out in Nigeria and Emir Ado Bayero's diplomatic skills were sought, that personal friendship he had cultivated with President Senghor was to prove of immense value to Nigeria, as we shall discuss in chapter five.

NOTES

1.   For a beautiful though brief account of the culture of respect in Gidan Rumfa see Ruqayyatu A. Rufa'i, *Gidan Rumfa: The Kano Palace* (Kano, Triumph Publishing Company, 1995), p. 135-37.

2.   The first school in Kano was opened in 1908, at Gidan Dan Hausa. It was meant for the princes. But since the emirs in the North initially perceived Western education as one way to mislead their people from their religion, they hid their own children and sent sons of slaves or servants. It was Emir Abdullahi Bayero who changed that practice.

3.   The first classroom for western education in Gidan Rumfa was opened at the house of Idi Majasiddi in the northern section of the palace. Alkali Husaini Sufi, *Mu San Kammu*, (Kano, Mai-Nasara Press, 1993), p. 185.

4.   Alkali Husaini Sufi reports that Emir Abdullahi Bayero and Wali Suleiman took lessons from Mallam Garba Karaye, then teacher at Cikin Gida Primary School. *Mu San Kammu* op. cit., p. 187.

5.   Emir Abdullahi Bayero had 26 male and 39 female children. For their names see Ibrahim Ado Kurawa, Sullubawan Dabo (Kano, Kurawa Publishing Company, 1990).

6.   Apart from names of first sons, mention is also avoided of the names of parents, in-laws, and ruling or immediate past emirs. Abdullahi ibn Abbas, for example, was given the name Bayero, Fulani word for the second son, which Abdullahi Maje Karofi was to Amir Dabo, to shield the name Abdullahi in deference to late Emir of Kano Abdullahi Maje Karofi, the father of Abbas. Zawiya, S., Sadauki, T., *Jigatau Dan Bayero: Sir Muhammadu Sanusi*, (Kano, Zawiya ent. 1991), p. 32.

7.   Interview with Alhaji Lawal Hussain, a childhood friend and confidant of the Emir. Kaduna, December 4, 1993.

8.   Kano city is administratively divided into four sections: North, South, East and West, each comprising tens of

wards. Kano North is inhabited by predominantly the Hausa, the original settlers of Kano, and who are basically traders, while Kano South is predominantly inhabited by the Fulani, who constitute the administrative cadre of the emirate since the jihad.

9. The then Emir, Muhammadu Sanusi, who was 25 years older than Ado, and one of whose sons, Muhammadu Aminu Sanusi, was an age-mate of Ado, had always treated Ado as if he was much older than he actually was.

10. Unlike successive constitutions from 1979, the Constitution of that time allowed NA employees to participate in partisan politics.

11. The others sworn in on the same day were: Mr. K.P. Maddocks, Ag. Civil Secretary; Hon. Aliyu Turaki, Mallams Abubakar, Ibrahim Gusau, Sarkin Duguri, Fate Das, Idris Tafida, Muhammed Sani, Maiwada Kano, Ado Sanusi, Uba Ringim, Sani Ungogo, Umar Madaki, Umar Audi. Source: NRL HA Debates 3-3-55. (Kaduna Government Printer).

12. Northern House of Assembly Debates, February-March, 1955. Government Printer Kaduna.

13. NHA Debates, February-March 1957. Government Printer Kaduna.

14. NHA Debates 1st session, February-March 1957. Government printer, Kaduna.

15. Ibid.

16. In the elections of 15/11/56, Ado Bayero (NPC) got 2928 votes to Babba Dan Agundi's (NEPU) 499 and Ali Abdallah's (independent) 74 to emerge winner of the City South Constituency. Other results were City East Alhaji Ahmadu Dantata (NPC) 2119, Aminu Kano (NEPU) 1776; City West Ibrahim Musa Gashash (NPC) 3252, Sani Darma (NEPU) 1229, Waje Haruna Kassim (NPC) 2026, Tanko Yakasai (NEPU) 1773. Source: Telegram from the Resident of Kano to Northern House

of Assembly Clerk, Kaduna, dated 11/16/56. MP253/s.2/76A NAK.

17. NHA Debates 1st Session Feb-March 1957.
18. Ibid.
19. Ibid.
20. Ibid.
21. Ibid.
22. The letter of resignation written in Ado's own hand-writing was addressed to the Clerk of the House and dated 31st may 1957. Original in Ado Bayero PF. NAK/kanprof/403.
23. Mahe Bashir was the third Police Chief after Ado Bayero. The first was Usaini Galadanci, followed by Sani Gwarzo. Mahe was appointed by Ado Bayero in late 1964. The same Ado Bayero appointed Mahe to the office of Walin Kano after the latter had retired from the Nigeria Police Force.
24. Wamban Kano Alhaji Abbas Sanusi, in Fatima Rabi'u, *Sarkin Kano Ado Bayero: Tarihin Rayuwarsa Tun Daga Haihuwa Zuwa Yau* (n.p. 1994), p.117.
25. Interview with Alhaji Salihu Abubakar Tanko Yakasai, April 12, 1997, Kano.
26. I am grateful to His Royal Highness the Emir of Daura, Alhaji Muhammadu Bashar, for first bringing this information to my attention, and Mai Girma Ciroman Kano Alhaji Muhammadu Aminu Sanusi, for detailed discussion on it. Emir Muhammad Bashar was at that time (1963) a Minister of the Regional Government under the Sardauna. Ciroman Kano Alhaji M.A. Sanusi, C.O.N., joined the Foreign Service in 1957, served in various posts, including the first head of Foreign Intelligence, Ambassador to Canada, Belgium and the EEC, and the Republic of China. He finally retired as Permanent Secretary, Ministry of External Affairs in 1978. Ciroma Muhammadu Aminu Sanusi died on May 8, 2000.

27. *Africa Year Book of 1974*, A *Daily Times* of Nigeria Publication has described Senghor as "a poet and philosopher of international stature... the ideal philosopher-ruler envisaged by Plato, the Greek philosopher."

28. It is believed in Kano that the relationship between Emir Abdullahi Bayero and Sheikh Niass was such that the Sheikh made a special supplication to Allah for the Emir. The Sheikh had prayed to Allah to protect the Emir and his offsprings who shoulder the burden of emirship. The Sheikh had also prayed that should any person do anything meant to disgrace or ridicule Emir Abdullahi or his sons, that person should have a taste of what he had done to them in this world before the final judgement. Kano people are quick in citing the fate of first, Premier Ahmadu Bello, who was assassinated along with one of his wives barely three years after he had dethroned Emir Sanusi; Muhammadu Abubakar Rimi, who lost his position and was jailed barely two years after he had boasted that dethroning the Emir of Kano was an easier task for him to accomplish than removing a cap from his head; and Generals Buhari and Idiagbon, who found themselves detained for many years, barely one year after they had restricted the Emir's movement to within Kano City for half a year.

FROM  PRINCE TO KING

ADO BAYERO *SHI NE* SARKI

"Ina mai tambari? A buga. Ado Bayero shi ne Sarki."
("Where is the tambourine drummer? Beat it. Ado Bayero is
the [new] Emir.") With that proclamation by the Kano
Provincial Secretary, St. E.D. Nelson, popularly called Zaki
by the people of Kano, on Friday October 11, 1963 Ado
Bayero became the 13th Emir of Kano and the 56th in the line
of Kano kings since Bagauda in 999 AD.

The prelude to that proclamation had begun barely
twenty-four hours earlier. The Madaki of Kano, the late
Alhaji Shehu Ahmad, had set the process in motion on
October 10, when he invited the three other kingmakers of
Kano Emirate to his Yola residence in Kano city. The three,
the late Alhaji Bello Barwa, the Makama; the late Alhaji
Bello Dandago, the Sarkin Dawaki Mai Tuta; and Alhaji
Muhtari Adnan, the Sarkin Bai, gathered at Yola just before
Maghrib. When they had said the Maghrib prayer, the Madaki
informed them that they were wanted at the Residency in
Nassarawa. Nothing more was said by either the Madaki or
any of the other three invitees until they got to the Residency,
which today houses the Kano State Government House, along
State Road.

They were ushered into the Residency, where they
awaited the arrival of the Provincial Secretary for Kano
Province. He did not keep his guests waiting for long. St.
E.D. Nelson came down from his one-story house. After the

usual exchange of greetings, he went straight to the business of the evening. They were gathered there that evening, according to St. Nelson, to choose a successor for the late Muhammadu Inuwa to the throne of Kano. He then handed to the Madaki, being the leader of the council of kingmakers, a note containing guidelines on eligibility for the office. Not that the kingmakers were not aware of them. It was more of an act of protocol than spelling out any rigid criteria.

The guidelines listed four main attributes that the king-makers were required to take into consideration in making their choice. First was the candidate's character. The man chosen must be of known honesty and integrity, faithful to his trust and an upholder of righteousness and truth. Secondly, he must be someone who respects the law. He must be one who, in the words of the administrative oath, "will do his duty without fear or favor, affection or ill will." Thirdly, he must be a man of proven ability with long experience of adminis-tration; one who could not only control the destiny of his people but would also listen to advice and criticism; and would moreover act not alone but in concert with his Council in a true spirit of co-operation, for the highest benefit of the people. Fourthly, he must be a man whom the generality of the people would willingly accept as their ruler.[1]

Having done that, St. Nelson took his leave of the com-mittee to come back after they had reached a decision. The Madaki led the deliberations. He began, in the tradition of Muslims, with prayers to Almighty Allah to guide them in what they were gathered there to do. He then started the assignment with a review of the role of traditional rulers in a rapidly changing polity, the need to strike a balance between modernity and tradition, and the need to save the institution from the vagaries of partisan politics. One after another, he reviewed the credentials of the numerous eligible princes. In his opinion, he said, Ambassador Ado Bayero should be the Emir. Not one voice of dissent was raised. All the others agreed that was the best choice. So the committee sent for St. Nelson, who on his arrival asked if a decision had been reached and the Madaki answered in the affirmative. The Provincial Secretary asked who their choice was, to which the Madaki replied "Ado Bayero." He quickly added "But he is not in the country. He is the nation's ambassador in Senegal." St. Nelson turned to the other members and asked if that was a unanimous decision, to which each one of them answered "yes." He then said, *"To Madaki. Daidai ne. Wannan zabenku,"* ("OK Madaki. This is your choice.") He then promised to relay the decision to the authorities in Kaduna, adding that he would revert to them as soon as he had heard from the government. The meeting was then adjourned.

The kingmakers did not have long to wait, for early the following morning the Madaki was contacted to assemble his councillors once again, although this time they were to meet at the palace at nine in the morning. Other dignitaries were invited too. At precisely 10.00 a.m. the Resident drove into the palace. He addressed the dignitaries telling them of the kingmakers' choice and the Regional Government's approval. From that moment, he said, Ado Bayero was the Emir of Kano. He added that the Federal government had already been informed, and the Emir would be home as soon as possible.[2]

A New Homecoming

The telegram to Ambassador Ado Bayero was very specific. "Proceed to Lagos for consultation." While still wondering what the cause of the urgency in the telegram might be, he received a telephone call from London. Alhaji Abdulmalik Attah, the Nigerian High Commissioner to London, had called to convey his condolences to Ambassador Ado Bayero over the news of the death of his uncle, Emir Muhammadu Inuwa. On his way to Lagos, Ado Bayero decided to stopover in Kano to offer and receive condolences as is customary. Hardly did he know that he was stepping on to Kano soil for the very first time as its Emir.

When the British Caledonian airplane that brought Ambassador Ado Bayero to Kano on Monday October 14 landed at about 5 p.m., Ado had not learned of his selection as the new Emir. The first hint was when he was climbing down the stairs of the airplane. One of the local staff of the airline, on recognizing him, clenched his fist and said *"Allah Ya kara maka imani"*; literally "May Allah increase your faith." Although that prayer was a form of salutation exclusively reserved for emirs, it did not occur to Ambassador Ado Bayero that he had already become Emir. Incidentally, the airline official did not repeat it. But more signs began to appear when, after he had submitted his passport for immigration formalities, the immigration officer, upon looking at the name and photograph on the diplomatic passport, raised his head and looked at the ambassador. Without even stamping the passport, he returned it to Ado, his hand trembling. By now Ambassador Ado Bayero had begun to feel uncomfortable. He picked up his hand luggage, which was all he had, and proceeded to go out through the arrival hall. Just then, somebody in the crowd waiting to receive overseas passengers, rushed out and immediately prostrated before Ado Bayero, saying *"Ranka ya dede* [sic]"; "May you live long." Ado Bayero was baffled. "What are you doing Mike?" Ado asked his friend, Michael Agbamuche. "Have you not heard it?" the latter replied. "You are the new Emir of Kano. It was announced on the radio."

Ado Bayero could not believe his ears. He instantly began to recall the actions of the airline official and the immigration officer. By now, a few people had noticed the new Emir. He began to feel embarrassed, attired as he was, in a three-piece suit. He asked Agbamuche, if he had a car. Agbamuche replied in the affirmative. Ado Bayero then said, "Please get me out of here fast."

Given the news he had just received, and in view of the way he was dressed, Ado Bayero found it difficult to go into the city. So they drove to Agbamuche's house at No. 11A New Road, Sabongari. There, Ado Bayero borrowed some traditional, though not Hausa clothes from his friend, Mike. It was a three-piece *babbar riga, wando, and jamfa*, and a cap to match which amounts to a complete traditional Hausa out-fit. But the difference was that the set was made not of bro-cade, or plain material, but *atamfa*, which in Hausaland is reserved for women. Yet, Ado Bayero still felt it was better than appearing in a suit. His friend, Mike, dropped him at the residence of the Kano Provincial Commissioner, Alhaji Aliyu Magajin Garin Sokoto.

The Provincial Commissioner was surprised to see Ambassador Ado Bayero in Kano. On hearing that Ado Bayero was coming straight from London, he told Ado that he was supposed to go to Lagos as Alhaji Abubakar Tafawa Balewa, the Federal Prime Minister, was expecting him. Together, they rushed to the airport. But they missed the last flight and they had to go back to the Provincial Commissioner's residence. There, the Provincial Commissioner telephoned the Premier of Northern Nigeria, Alhaji Sir Ahmadu Bello, the Sardaunan Sokoto, and informed him that Ambassador Ado Bayero had arrived Kano.

The Sardauna, who was a distant cousin and traditional playmate of Ado Bayero, was afraid that Ado Bayero would decline to be emir. To forestall that he had discussed with the Prime Minister, Abubakar Tafawa Balewa and the two had agreed that the news of Ado's selection as emir should be kept a secret from him and he was to be advised to pro-ceed from Europe to Lagos. It was arranged that as soon as he had landed in Lagos he would be flown to Kaduna where the Premier would break the news to him and cajole him, if necessary, into accepting the offer.

Ambassador Ado Bayero and the Sardauna exchanged some pleasantries over the phone and the Premier was relieved to know that he did not have much cajoling to do. The Provincial Commissioner was directed to arrange for Ado Bayero to be in Kaduna that night.

After the telephone conversation, Ambassador Ado Bayero thought he needed some befitting clothes with which to go to Kaduna. He then borrowed the Provincial Commissioner's car, and drove incognito straight into the walled city. Ado Bayero parked the car at Kofar Kudu, a few hundred meters away from the main entrance to the palace. He then walked past the city hall to his personal house in Kabara quarters, some few hundred meters to the Northwest of the palace. As soon as the women in the house saw him, they broke into joyous ululation. Ado Bayero appealed to them not to make any noise, as he did not want anyone to know he was in town. He quickly went into his room, brought out some traditional clothes, and walked out of the house.

Ado Bayero made various efforts not to attract attention to himself, waiting until it was dark before coming into the city, parking his car some distance away from his house, and even appearing in Yoruba traditional attire. Yet, as soon as he had parked the car, Mallam Garba, who had taught Ado Arabic at the School for Arabic Studies, recognized him. Without uttering a word, he followed Ado Bayero, at some distance, to the house. He waited until Ado came out and followed him back to the car. Just when Ado Bayero had opened the door of the car and was about to enter, Mallam Garba saluted him, and prayed for him. He told Ado Bayero that he had recognized him as soon as he parked the car, and that he had followed him to the house and back. Ado Bayero thanked him for the prayers and quickly entered the car and drove off.

That night they set out for Kaduna, where they spent two days with the Premier and other members of the Northern Region Government. Ado was congratulated by members of the Northern Region Cabinet, members of the Northern Region House of Chiefs and other top government functionaries.

THE SELECTION OF A KING

To the Emir and the Sarkin Bai, Alhaji Muhtari Adnan, the only surviving member of the Kingmakers' Council that chose him in 1963, as well as to the people of Kano, Alhaji Ado Bayero was simply Allah's choice. The odds against him were just too great. In the first place, he was unschooled in the intrigues of palace politics. Secondly, he had never held any traditional title, one of the indices by which a candidate's administrative capability could be adjudged. The only office he had held within the traditional set-up was the Wakilin Doka, chief of the Native Authority Police. That, strictly speaking, cannot be compared with being a district head, for example, or membership of the Emir's Council where, through the contributions one makes at meetings, or the actions one takes as district head, one could make an impact on the kingmakers. Or even more significantly, by being a district head one could be in a position to bestow favors, build a large following and thereby lay claim to acceptability.

The other factor militating against Ado Bayero was his absence from the scene of the political struggles during its most crucial days. He was in far away Switzerland attending a course in French language when his uncle, the Emir of Kano, Muhammadu Inuwa died. It is pertinent to note that in Kano, as in all the emirates of the former Sokoto Caliphate, no delay is allowed in the process of choosing a new emir whenever the position becomes vacant. The reason is that Islam prohibits self-canvassing or lobbying for public offices.[3] It is reasoned that delays in filling existing vacancies might create an auspicious environment for people interested in those offices to do what is religiously prohibited, human nature being what it is.

The despatch with which vacancies are filled is, therefore, to save eligible people from the temptation to do what is prohibited by their religion as well as to make things easier for the kingmakers. Before colonial rule, the kingmakers' council regularly reviewed the position of the eligible princes. At any given time, the council had up to three princes, listed in preferential order, who could succeed a dead or deposed emir and that information was kept in strict confidence. Upon their conquest of the emirates, the British colonial rulers maintained that practice. The only difference was that during their time the appraisal was not done by the kingmakers' council, but by the European Resident, District Officer, or Assistant District Officer, depending on the grade of the emir. They opened a secret file titled: "Emirs and their Probable Successors." In the entry for 1916 for instance, the following appears:[4]

Office	Successor	Remarks
Emir of Kano	1. Wambai [Usmanu]	Emir's elder brother; if an immediate successor necessary.
	2. Santuraki	Emir's nephew.
	3. Umaru	Emir's younger brother
	4. Dan Iya Abdulqadir	Emir's son; rather too young; if the emir lives a few years longer, would be a very probable choice.[5]
Emir of Yauri	1. Mu'allayidi (Ubandoman Bakundi)	Emir's brother
	2. Haruna Tukur (*Hakimin* Wurkunu)	Emir's brother
	3. Sidi (Dangaladima)	He is next in order of succession. See 1915 Conf. Report on chiefs.
Etsu Nupe	1. Yerima	Vide conference file (A member of Masaba family should be appointed)
Sultan of Sokoto		Too early to say.
Emir of Zaria	1. Dangaladima	Madaki or Makamakarami is not recommended. See Conf. Rep. A change of dynasty will be beneficial
	2. Magaji	
	3. Dallatu	
	4. Danmadami	
	5. Wali	
	6.Turaki Babba	

Although they appraised likely successors, the colonial rulers still allowed the traditional kingmakers to follow the traditional method of choosing the successor. Where the choice of the traditional kingmakers coincided with that of the colonial rulers, that choice was upheld. But where it did not, the appraisal of the colonial rulers determined who became emir.

Thirdly, in a society that had much deference for age, Ado Bayero, at thirty-three, did not appear to stand a good chance against many of the other contenders, some of whom were old enough to be his father.[6] Thus, when the race started, he was already handicapped. But these seeming disadvantages turned out to be his trump cards.

If the institution of traditional rulership is to be insulated from the vagaries of partisan politics, reasoned the kingmakers, it needed at the helm of its affairs somebody who had not been tainted already. They recognized that nobody who was holding a traditional office at that time could claim to be non-partisan.[7] Indeed, apart from Ado Bayero himself, who was in far away Switzerland, and Aminu Sanusi, who held the title of Ciroma and was in the Foreign Service in Lagos, all the other princes who were considered for the office were bona fide members of the NPC.

What appeared to have brightened the prospects of Ado Bayero for the office, in spite of the obvious handicaps he had, including his age (he is reputed to be the youngest Emir of Kano after Ibrahim Dabo)[8] were his performance as the Kano NA Police Chief. Other factors were a series of developments within the Kano Emirate beginning with the institution of the Muffett Commission of Enquiry into the Finances of the Kano NA by the Northern Regional Government in 1962, and the resultant abdication of the throne by Emir Muhammadu Sanusi.

We noted that when party politics was introduced into Northern Nigeria in the early fifties, the colonial government allowed traditional rulers to actively participate in it. In fact, they encouraged the traditional rulers to support the NPC against the NEPU and other smaller parties. Either because they saw the NPC as their party or because they wanted to please the British administrators, emirs embarked on massive recruitment of membership for the NPC. Many incentives were given to NPC members or sympathizers, while members or sympathizers of the other parties were victimized. The emirs appeared to be competing among themselves for who would produce the emirate with the least opposition to the NPC. In the pursuit of that objective, all instruments at the disposal of the emirs were used. The NA police was used to arbitrarily arrest NEPU members and supporters, and the emirs' and alkali courts were used to jail them under the flimsiest excuse. Indeed, so common was the arrest and jailing of NEPU members and supporters in Kano in the 1950s and early 1960s that one's membership of or support for the party was not considered complete unless one had served a jail term, or had been detained at a police station on account of his or her political views.

Although until he became the Kano NA police Chief, Ado Bayero was a member of the Northern House of Assembly on the ticket of the NPC, he did not share the view of most NPC leaders and NA officials that members of the opposition party must be persecuted until they renounced their membership. As Chief of the Kano NA police from 1957 to 1962, Ado Bayero resolved to tame the system he inherited. He took personal interest in all cases that were political in nature and insisted on personally interviewing all suspects before their cases were sent to the alkali courts. In most cases, he discovered that the suspects had been arrested on trumped-up charges and he promptly released them. Sidi Ali recalls some instances where Ado Bayero, as NA Police Chief, came to the rescue of NEPU supporters, to the chagrin of his bosses. He narrates how a NEPU member was arrested at Jahun and brought all the way to Kano in chains. Upon enquiring what the offense of the man was, he was told that the man had abused the Emir. Ado Bayero thereupon directed that the man be unchained, adding, "The emir is my father. I forgive him." He gave the man five shillings to pay for his transport back to Jahun. A second case was where somebody was arrested by an NA police constable at Ringim and brought to Kano. When asked what the man's offense was, the constable told the Police Chief that the man was wearing a NEPU badge. Ado Bayero was reported to have removed the badge from the accused and put it on his own chest. He then asked the constable to arrest him.[9]

There was also an instance where Emir Sanusi directed that Shehu Satatima and Tanko Yakasai, two NEPU leaders, should be arrested over the role they had allegedly played in the selection of market leaders. Ado Bayero sent word to them to go into hiding. But what really put him on a collision course with the NPC leadership was the case of a man who was brought from Ringim accused of killing an NPC member. In the past, the NA police would have charged the man at an alkali court with murder, a capital offense. But Ado Bayero opposed that course of action and transferred the case to the Nigerian Police Force. The accused was charged, tried, and found guilty of manslaughter, which attracted a jail term.

The last straw appears to have been his refusal to co-operate with Mr. D.J.M. Muffett, the Sole Commissioner appointed to investigate the finances of the Kano Native Authority. It is reported that early on his arrival to assume duty, Muffett approached the NA Police Chief, Ado Bayero, for assistance. Ado Bayero pointedly told Muffett, "I cannot assist you to destroy my brother. I'd help you in your investigations if you had not already made up your mind [on the outcome of your investigations]."[10] Within seven days of that encounter, Ado Bayero was offered an ambassadorial post. He did not ask for the post, and wondered why the offer was being made to him. As is customary the offer was made through the emir. Ado Bayero then discussed with his elder brother, the emir and sought his advice. Emir Sanusi gave his blessing. Thereafter, Ado Bayero accepted the offer and set out for Dakar.

These incidents did not go unnoticed by the people of Kano and especially the kingmakers. They portrayed Ado

Bayero as someone who was just, sympathetic, honest, sincere, loyal, and above all independent-minded. These were the qualities that the people of Kano needed in their new emir after their traumatic experience with the deposition of Sanusi. To most Kano people the NPC government at Kaduna had been unfair to Emir Muhammadu Sanusi, who was known to have spent most of his time and energy trying to make his emirate a safe NPC haven. That feeling partly explains the decision of the NEPU leadership to direct its members and supporters not to co-operate with Muffett, even though they were the worst victims of Emir Sanusi's persecutions.

HOLDING AND CONTROLLING THE NEW REINS

Exactly one week after he had been proclaimed Emir, Alhaji Ado Bayero was sworn in at the Provincial Commissioner's Lodge. The oath of allegiance was administered by the Chief Imam of Kano, Mallam Dalhatu, with the three Federal and Regional ministers from Kano in attendance.[11] It was, strictly speaking, a local affair. That ceremony was to be followed four months later, on February 27 1964, by an elaborate ceremony of presentation of staff of office to the Emir at Kofar Mata, just outside the eastern walls of the old city. Sir Kashim Ibrahim, the Governor of Northern Nigeria, read the statute confirming the emirship on Alhaji Ado Bayero and presented him with the staff of office. The audience numbered tens of thousands of people. Among the dignitaries who graced the occasion were the Premier of Northern Nigeria, Alhaji Sir Ahmadu Bello, Sardaunan Sokoto, his cabinet members as well as ministers and members of the diplomatic corps from Lagos. There were also Alhaji Sir Abubakar III the Sultan of Sokoto, the Emir of Gwandu Alhaji Haruna Rashid, and other traditional rulers from other parts of the country. Among those from the south was Prince Sijuade who represented his father, the Ooni of Ife, and who was later to become the Ooni of Ife and one of the Emir's closest friends.

Ironically, some of the main considerations that had made Ado Bayero the ideal choice for the office of Emir in October 1963 were later to become problems for him in his early days in office. We noted that Ado Bayero never held any traditional title or office before he became Emir. That, in effect, implied that even though a prince, and therefore one presumed to be familiar with palace protocol, he had not fully imbibed most of the values and mores associated with that protocol.[12] These are values that are acquired through proximity to the palace and constant practice.

In the first place, Emir Ado Bayero was faced with the problem of how to relate with his friends of many years' standing. Many of them now could not just visit him as before, not because the Emir was too busy to see them, but because whenever they visit him he would treat them as before and they felt embarrassed that the Emir should be that humble. He could see some determination on their part not to do anything that would be considered a breach of protocol, especially as the palace officials and titleholders did not approve of the Emir humbling himself before his subjects.[13]

Secondly, as someone reputed to be fair and firm, Ado Bayero was used to saying his mind. But he was to learn that as the Emir, diplomacy should be his watchword. He learned to keep his feelings to himself. Whereas he could instantly make a commitment to Adamu Gaya in 1945, or Babba Dan Agundi in 1959, as Emir he would only say "we shall look into the request."[14] Thirdly, he found that he was virtually imprisoned in the palace. He could not, like before, go and watch a film at any of the cinema houses in Kano, or go for a stroll or take a drive around town. He could not do any of the many other things he was used to doing without the Makama, the Madaki, the Sarkin Bai, or one of the other elder district heads politely telling him that that was not the way his ancestors did things. On some occasions the objection to the Emir doing something came, not from the district heads, but the palace officials, including slaves, many of whom live and die for the institution.[15]

Even if he had reservations about some of these restrictions, the new Emir did not show them. He abided by whatever words of wisdom the elders advised, and he has never regretted that. But many years later, he embarked on a deliberate strategy to modify some of this protocol, taking extra care to ensure that the institution is not in any way undermined. He reasoned that the institution must be made to move with the times, or it would become a relic.[16]

At the political level, Emir Ado Bayero had two initial problems to contend with. The first was how to neutralize the pockets of opposition to his appointment, and the second was how to relate to the growing movement in the emirate opposed to the Regional Government in Kaduna, especially following the forced resignation of Muhammadu Sanusi as Emir. The successful way in which he tackled these two problems set him out, early in his reign, as an able crisis manager.

In the first instance, a few titleholders whose preferred choice for the office of Emir had not been successful were afraid that the new Emir was going to deprive them of their titles, demote them or sanction them in some way for not supporting him. That fear was not completely unjustified, as it had been the practice that new emirs appointed or promoted their own loyalists, usually their own sons or full brothers, to positions of trust. But Emir Ado Bayero did neither. As far as he was concerned, he had competed with no one, and therefore did not recognize some people as being for him and others against him. Every titleholder was allowed to retain his title and to perform his duties.

That singular decision of the Emir endeared him to many. It demonstrated, more than anything else did, his determination to run an inclusive administration, where everybody truly belonged, and where the Emir was seen to be the "father of all his people." In fact, it took nearly thirty years after he had become Emir, for Ado Bayero to agree to give any of his sons a traditional title.[17]

Next, following the forced resignation of Muhammadu Sanusi as Emir earlier in the year, Kano people had buried their political differences and had come out in solidarity with the deposed Emir. They interpreted the treatment of their Emir as an insult to Kano and its people. Even the NEPU, with its strongly anti-traditionalist position, temporarily identified with ex-Emir Sanusi. A new political party, the Kano People's Party, KPP, emerged in Kano at that time, dedicated to the return of the exiled Emir to Kano, or at least the appointment of his son, Ado Sanusi, the Dan Iyan Kano, as Emir. This was at a time when Muhammadu Inuwa was already Emir.

As Emir, Muhammadu Sanusi was known to have vigorously championed the cause of Kano before the Regional Government, and he was particularly concerned about the siting of economic and industrial projects in Kano. In his first year in office, 1954, he took up the case of Kano at the Regional Assembly thus:

> We wish to complain to the Government that of the amount of money allocated to the various provinces for development works, Kano does not get a fair share.... We consider this unfair....[18]

Given his influence with the Regional Government, various interests in Kano—industrial, commercial, bureaucratic—saw in Emir Sanusi everything that the Kano people needed to ensure that their interests were taken care of at the regional level. It was not surprising therefore that these same interests found in his deposition the catalyst needed to bring them together to pursue what they defined as "Kano's interest" as opposed to the "Northern interest." This development accentuated an already latent Kano sub-nationalism, which gained expression in the demand for the excision of Kano Province from the Northern Region to constitute a separate Kano State. So strong was this sub-nationalism that a movement, the Kano State Movement, was formed to pursue that demand.

Emir Ado Bayero found himself in a very difficult position on these two issues. He could not support the KPP in their declared goal of returning ex-Emir Sanusi, then in exile at Azare, to Kano or appointing his son, Dan Iya Ado, as Emir. Neither could he openly support the demand for the creation of a separate Kano State, since the Regional Government, to which he was accountable, was seriously against it. But Emir Ado Bayero had to find a way out. He decided to tackle first the more serious problem, the demand for the return of ex-Emir Sanusi. We noted that throughout the reign of Muhammadu Inuwa, the KPP had been demanding the return of ex-Emir Sanusi. That, in effect, meant that the party and by implication its members and supporters, did not confer legitimacy on Muhammadu Inuwa's emirship. If that development was allowed to continue, Emir Ado's own legitimacy was also going to be questioned by the same group. Emir Ado Bayero felt that must not be allowed to happen. But he also believed that diplomacy and not force was a better instrument for bringing about a lasting peace. He therefore decided to pursue the path of diplomacy. First, as we noted, he allayed the fears of pro-Sanusi activists, including those holding titles, about any reprisals from him. He sent out signals that he was ready to work with everyone irrespective of his past allegiance. His closeness to his elder brother, ex-Emir Sanusi, was played up. He also emphasized the need for people to bury their differences for the good of the emirate.

That approach worked magic, for in late November, just one month after his accession to the throne, the Secretary General and the Deputy President of the KPP, Mallams Balarabe Hamza and Muhammadu Sule respectively, announced the dissolution of the party. The two also called on Kano people to co-operate with Emir Ado Bayero for the progress of Kano.[19] Perhaps just as important in securing the sympathies of the KPP for the Emir were his personal reputation and the passage of time. It will be recalled that as Kano Police Chief Ado Bayero was so fair and firm that he was even suspected to be sympathetic to the NEPU. That reputation and the respect NEPU members had for him contributed to the softening of attitudes within the KPP, which comprised many NEPU stalwarts. Furthermore, the fact that Ado Bayero did not directly succeed Sanusi made him less open to accusation of having played a part in the deposition of Sanusi. Indeed, Ado was in far away Senegal, as ambassador, when Sanusi was deposed.

The second problem was more difficult to deal with, as it pitched the Emir between showing loyalty to the Regional Government and giving effective leadership to his own people. Was he to openly support his own people in their quest for what was obviously in the interest of his emirate? Or was he to support the government that had appointed him and could also depose him? Emir Ado Bayero suddenly found himself in the shoes of his grandfather, Muhammadu Abbas, and his father, Abdullahi Bayero. The only difference was that Emirs Muhammadu Abbas and Abdullahi Bayero were dealing with colonial powers whereas Emir Ado Bayero was dealing with an indigenous political power.

Kano, as we have noted, has prided itself in being the industrial, commercial, and economic nerve centre of the North. Kano Province alone contributed to the regional purse more than what six provinces put together contributed. The people of Kano believed that with their fertile land, population, enterprise and industrial and economic base, they could develop faster on their own than within the Northern Region. Indeed, there was a general belief in Kano that the Northern Regional Government was sabotaging Kano's economic progress.[20]Any suggestion of excising any part of the North to constitute a separate state was anathema to the NPC government at Kaduna. It would undermine the NPC's slogan of "One North One People" to which the Sardauna was fiercely committed.

By July 1965, the Kano State Movement was transformed into a political party. The objective was to contest and win all the elective seats in Kano, and use those platforms at the Regional and National level to pursue their quest for a separate state within the Federal Republic. Given the popularity of their cause, prominent Kano sons, including top NPC leaders, were believed to have lent the Kano State Movement

their support.[21] Through dialogue, and the active involve-
ment of people such as Alhaji Shehu Ahmed, the Madakin
Kano, and Speaker of the Northern Regional Assembly, who
was respected by both the Emir and the Sardauna, Ado
Bayero succeeded in winning the sympathy of the leaders of
the Movement as well as the understanding of the
Government at Kaduna. Although the situation was deterio-
rating by the day, it did not get to the point where the Emir
would have been required to choose between Kaduna and
Kano before the military struck in January 1966.

NOTES

1.   KanProf: 8455
2.   Interview with Alhaji Muhtari Adnan, the Sarkin Bai
      of Kano and District Head of Dambatta. It is pertinent
      to note that Sarkin Bai Muhtari Adnan is the only living
      member of the Kingmaker Council that deliberated and
      recommended Ado Bayero for the office of Emir of
      Kano in 1963. The account narrated here contrasts with
      John Paden's suggestion that, at the meeting of the king-
      makers, a consensus could not be reached on any one
      candidate for the emirship and that the Madaki and the
      Makama supported Tafida Muhammadu Usman, that
      the Sarkin Dawaki Mai Tuta supported Wambai
      Abubakar Sanusi, and that the Sarkin Bai supported Dan
      Iya Abbas Sanusi. See John Paden, *Religion and
      Political Culture in Kano*, op. cit., p. 237. The account
      of the Sarkin Bai, I believe, is more reliable for three rea-
      sons. Firstly, he participated in the selection process.
      Secondly, Paden does not give us the source of his infor-
      mation. And finally, while Paden claims that "the selec-
      tion process took about two weeks and in the end the
      kingmaker council could not agree on anyone," the
      records show that Emir Muhammadu Inuwa died on
      Tuesday October 8, 1963 and Ado Bayero was con-

firmed Emir on October 11, 1963, a difference of three days. He was sworn-in on Friday October 18, 1963. See NAK/acc/7 and the *Nigerian Citizen* newspaper of 10/19/63, p.1.

3. The Prophet Muhammad (S.A.W.) was reported to have replied to some people who went and requested him to appoint them to some position of authority thus: "We do not appoint to this position one who asks for it nor anyone who is covetous for the same." Hadith 4490 cited in Sahih Muslim, tr. by Abdulhamid Siddiqi, (Beirut, Dar Al Arabia, 1971), Volume Three, p. 1014.

4. NAK/SNP/6/5/1916.

5. It is interesting to note that as a result of the constant review of the Confidential Reports, by 1919 when Emir Abbas died, Dan Iya Abdulqadir, who had in 1916 been rated very high, did not even feature among the serious contenders, who were Usman and Abdullahi Bayero.

6. Of the seven princes named by Paden as contenders for the office, Ibrahim Cigari, the Dan Lawan and District Head of Zakirai was 55 and Muhammadu Usman, the Tafida and District Head of Ringim was 63. Paden Ibid.., p. 235.

7. The exception was Alhaji Muhammadu Aminu Sanusi, who held the title of Ciroman Kano. Aminu had given his father, Emir Sanusi, a condition for accepting the office of Ciroma. And that condition was that he was only going to take the title but not the functions that go with it. Aminu did not want his career in the Foreign Service cut short.

8. Ibrahim Dabo, the second Fulani emir, and the founder of the Dabo dynasty in Kano ascended the throne at the age of 28 years.

9. Sidi H. Ali, *Alhaji Ado Bayero: Symbol of Royal Justice, Wisdom, and Patience*, (n.p. 1988), p. 112. For detailed discussion of the injustices meted out to NEPU members and supporters in the 1950's in Northern Nigeria, see R. Sklar, *Nigerian Political Parties: Power in an*

Emergent African Nation, (Enugu, NOK Publishers, 1983), Billy Dudley, *Nigerian Political Parties*, op. cit., C.S. Whitaker, *The Politics of Tradition: op. cit.*

10. In retrospect, Ado Bayero was right, for 15 years later, Muffett was to admit that ""Its [government] conviction both that it was necessary for it to act, and that it was able to, arose first from the fact that the emir had lost the support of the Kano people, and, secondarily, that the government could not afford, the repetitive calls on it to bail out Kano financially..."" See D.J.M. Muffett "Legitimacy and Deference in a Tradition Oriented Society: Observations Arising From an Examination of some Aspects of a Case Study Associated with the Abdication of the Emir of Kano in 1963" in *African Studies Review,* op. cit.

11. The ministers were Alhaji Yusuf Maitama Sule, Federal Minister of Mines and Power, Alhaji Sule Gaya, Sarkin Fada, Regional Minister for Local Government and Alhaji Umaru Babura, Sarkin Fulanin Ja'idanawa, Regional Minister for Social Welfare and Co-operatives.

12. Emir Ado Bayero himself overestimated his familiarity with palace protocol when in a reply to a question after he had been sworn in said: "After all, I have only been an ambassador for a few months whereas I have been with the Kano Native Authority all my life." *Nigerian Citizen*, 10/19/63, p.1. But in an interview with the editor of the *Nigerian Citizen* five months later, Emir Ado Bayero was to admit that his mode of life had changed drastically from what it used to be. *Nigerian Citizen*, 3/11/64, p.1.

13. The celebrated case of Emir Abbas is till told among the royal servants to deter any emir from humbling himself.

According to palace sources, Abbas had a childhood friend who was very wealthy, but not of aristocratic birth. After Abbas had become Emir, his friend continued to pay him visits at the palace. The friend however, did not observe palace protocol especially in his relationship with the emir. He would ride into the palace without notice and the emir would grant him audience. Sometimes he would stay very long thereby depriving

others of the opportunity to see the emir. When the palace officials expressed their concern about the breach of protocol, the
emir simply ignored them. They decided to deal with the situation. One evening, the head of the emir's bodyguard called
all the servants in the palace and directed that when the emir
comes out the following morning, no one should sing his
praise, pick his robe as it falls from his shoulders, say any of
the dozens of praises that are always said, or blow the *algaita*.
The maids were also warned not to sing the emir's praise when
he came out of his section of the palace. The head of the bodyguard and a few of his staff then went to the *Mai Babban Daki,
the emir's mother,* and narrated their problem with the emir to
her. They then told her that they had devised their own strategy of dealing with the matter. The following morning the
emir came out and was surprised to find that no one was
singing his praises among the maids in the palace. He did not
react. He moved towards the court. Again, the servants stood
still, with none of them helping him with his overflowing
gown. He went and sat down on his throne without anyone
singing his praises. He then realized that the situation was serious. But he did not know what was actually wrong. After a
short stay, he stood up; asked for his horse and rode to his
mother. He narrated his experience that morning to her. After
he had finished, she advised him on the need to observe palace
protocol, hinting at the way he was treating his friend. The
emir thereafter left for the palace. Shortly after that, the friend
rode into the palace. As usual, he went straight to the emir. To
his surprise, the emir directed his servants to bundle the man
out of the palace. As soon as that directive was given the whole
palace broke into a festive mood, the servants singing the
praises of the emir, the maids breaking into joyous ululation
and the drummers beating their drums as never before.

14. See chapter Ten for details of how he committed himself to Adamu Gaya and Babba Dan Agundi in the 1946
and 1959 respectively.
15. Barely three months in office, Emir Ado Bayero admitted to the editor of Nigerian Citizen that his mode of

life had changed drastically. *Nigerian Citizen*, 1/26/64,
p.8. Royal slaves and servants are the greatest defenders of the institution as exemplified in the case of Emir
Abbas in footnote 13 above.

16. See chapter Ten for details.
17. Perhaps the temptation or pressure to give his sons titles
would have been greater if the Emir had older children
at the time he became Emir. In 1963, when Ado Bayero
became Emir, his eldest son, Muhammadu Sanusi, who
is called Lamido, in deference to Emir Sanusi, was less
than ten years old. In 1989, Lamido was given the title
of Dan Ruwata, later promoted to Tafida and is now
Sarkin Dawakin Tsakar Gida. Three other sons of the
Emir have since been given titles. These are Aminu as
Turaki, Nasir as Tafida and Ahmad as Dan Ruwata.
18. NHC Debates, September 14, 1954, p. 29.
19. Nigerian Citizen, 11/27/63, p. 2. Incidentally, the
President of the KPP, Mallam Bello Dankano, was
police orderly to Ado Bayero when the latter was police
chief.
20. Paden, J.N., *Religion and Political Culture in Kano, op.
cit.* p. 219.
21. Paden gives the names of Bello Dandago, the Sarkin
Dawaki Mai Tuta of Kano; Alhaji Inuwa Wada, the
Magajin Garin Kano and Federal Minister of Works;
and Alhaji Yusuf Maitama Sule, the Dan Masanin Kano
and Federal Minister of Mines and Power as some of
those who supported the Movement. Op. cit., p. 331 fn.

Emir Ado Bayero acknowledging cheers from his subjects on his return from medical treatment abroad in April 2000.

Emir Ado Bayero receives tumultous welcome from his subjects as he returns to Kano after receiving medical attention abroad.

Hajija Hasiye Bayero, Emir Ado Bayero's mother.
She kept her pact with her son.

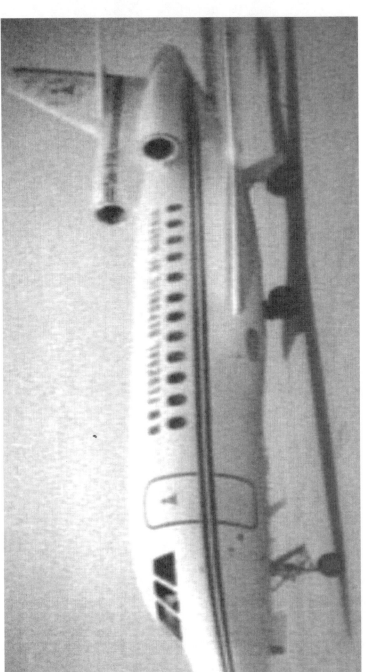

The presidential plane that brought back Emir Ado Bayero to Kano after receiving medical treatment abroad.

Emir Ado Bayero

*Emir of Kano (1920 - 1953) and late father of Emir Ado Bayero,
Alhaji Abdullahi Bayero — a perceptive Emir.*

Emir Ado Bayero

As Chancellor of University of Maiduguri, Emir Ado Bayero hands the diploma of Honorary Doctorate Degree to Vice President Atibu Abubakar at a Special Conferment Ceremony in June 2000

In a handshake with Governor Abdullahi Wase of Kano State after the Eid prayer. Directly behind the Emir is Sheikh Isyaku Rabi'u

A man of many seasons: Emir Ado Bayero welcoming Colonel Sani Bello when the latter arrived to assume duty as governor of Kano State in August 1975.

Emir Ado Bayero receiving visiting Zimbabwean President Robert Mugabe in the company of President Ibrahim Babangida at the Palace in 1989.

Emir Ado Bayero in full regalia, stepping out of the Palace.

Emir Ado Bayero being congratulated by General Shehu Y'Adua at his installation as Chancellor of the University of Ibadan, April 27, 1976.

Three of the Emir's titled sons, (L-R,) Sarkin Dawakin Tsakar Gida, Tafida and Turaki, at the conferment of an honorary Doctorate Degree on the Emir by the Bayero University Kano in 1994.

Emir Ado Bayero with former Head of State, General Muhammadu Buhari (immediate right), Wali Mahe Bahsir (far right back row) Governor Dominic Oneya (immediate left front row) and Mallam Yahaya Gusau (far left back row) when the Petroleum Trust Fund Board of Trustees paid him a courtesy call in 1997.

Emir Ado Bayero with other traditional rulers, (left to right)) Olu of Warri, Ooni of Ife, Emir Ado Bayero, Obi of Onitsha, and Esama of Benin

The Emir of Kano, Alhaji Ado Bayero, recently undertook a familiarization tour of private hospitals in Kano. This pictures shows the Emir being shown around the Maimuna Allah-Ray Medical Center during the visit.

Picture by Sadiiku Alhaji Aliyu-Kano

Role Reversal: Emir Ado Bayero plays host to his erstwhile host President Sedar Senghor at the Palace. Emir Ado Bayero was Nigeria's Ambassador to SEnegal when he was chosen to become Emir - 1963.

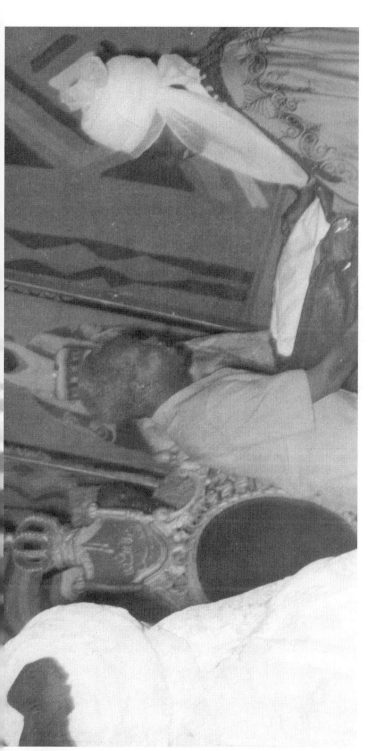

No staate or official visit to Nigeria is complete without a visit to the Royal Court of Kano. Here, President Julius Nyerere of Tanzania receives a gift from Emir Ado Bayero at the Palace in November 1976.

Emir Ado Bayero presenting a gift to Saint E.D. Nelson as the latter bade Nigeria farewell on May 25, 1982.

The Emir of Kano, Alhaji Ado A. Bayero, visits the Moral Re-Armament Conference Center in Caux, Switzerland. Here, he meets with Vijitha Yapa from Ceylon, Peter Thwaites from Australia, Nils-Erik Saarnbrink from Sweden, and John Gibbins from England outside Mountain House. (August 1968)

The Pro-Chancellor of the University of Maidugari, Emir Ado Bayero helps Nigeria's Vice-President Atiba Abubakar put on the academic cap at the special convocation to award the beepee an honorary doctorate degree in law, June 2000.

Kano people welcoming their Emir from a 2-month medical treatment abroad, early 2000.

Here ae some of the royal lancers on horseback at the installation of the Emir of Kano.

Emir Ado Bayero being congratulated by General Shehu Y'Adua at his installation as Chancellor of the University of Ibadan on April 27, 1976.

THE FIRY COUP

THE DAWN OF KHAKI ERA

Given the soured relationship between Kano and Kaduna, manifested in the founding of the Kano People's Party, KPP, and the Kano State Movement, KSM, which were vigorously demanding a separate Kano State, the news of a military coup d'etat that toppled the Kaduna Regional government on January 15, 1966 was generally well received among the opposition groups in Kano. But that was before those groups had learned of the lives that had been cut short and even worse the pattern of killings of both military and civilian leaders. Even though there was formidable opposition to the Sardauna and the NPC in Kano, Jos, Zaria and some other parts of the North, few people would agree that the Sardauna and the peace-loving Abubakar Tafawa Balewa deserved the brutal killings meted out to them by the soldiers. And much worse, it was later established that the coup had been led by predominantly Igbo officers and that it was mainly military officers of Northern origin as well as their politician counterparts who were killed.

The Igbos resident in Kano and other parts of the North were quick in openly identifying with the new military rulers. They set out to ridicule the assassinated Sardauna and other Northern leaders by producing, displaying and dragging in the streets enlarged photographs of the bullet-ridden body of the

Sardauna. So blatant were the Igbos in ridiculing the Northerners that the new military government had to promulgate a decree empowering law officers to "arrest anyone who displays or publishes the photograph of any person living or dead in a manner likely to provoke any section or community."

When General Johnson Thomas Umunna Aguiyi-Ironsi seized power from the majors who had planned and executed the coup, his first few appointments did not help to allay the fears of Northerners about a planned Igbo domination. Virtually all his key advisers were Igbo. Before long, the import of the new military regime's policies began to sink in and those Northerners who had initially rejoiced at the news of the coup realised how foolish they had been. Not surprisingly, therefore, when the North rose up against the Igbos in May 1966, it was Kano, Zaria, Jos and other towns with a record of established opposition to the NPC; and having given initial support to the coup, who were the most ferocious in attacking the Igbos.[1]

January 15, 1966 was a Saturday. It coincided with the 25th day of the holy month of Ramadan, 1385 after Hijra. The usual morning recitation from the Holy Qur'an was going on at the palace with the Emir in attendance, when St. Nelson drove in. On sighting the Provincial Secretary's car, the Emir knew instinctively that something was amiss; for St. Nelson knew that for the whole of the month of Ramadan the Emir reserved that time of the day for readings from the Holy Qur'an.

St. Nelson walked into the palace and the Emir went in and met him. St. Nelson looked disturbed. He apologised to the Emir for coming at that time of the morning, 8. A.m. but added that his mission was important and could not wait. He then informed the Emir that the British High Commissioner had called and informed him that there had been a military coup early that morning and that the Premier, Sir Ahmadu Bello, had been killed. The Emir remained silent. He tried hard not to betray his emotions. His mind quickly went back to the previous night: the Sardauna had phoned him at about 8 p.m. and told him that he had information that some officers of the Nigerian Army were planning to topple the government and assassinate him. The Emir had advised that immediate steps be taken to foil the coup plan by ordering the immediate arrest of the suspects, and even more urgently that the Sardauna should take steps to ensure his own safety by keeping away from his official residence. But the Sardauna would do neither. He believed in destiny, which cannot be changed. After all, Islam, which he came to champion in the North, teaches that even before one is born, the Almighty Allah has charted his destiny, which includes his fortune, his life span, his works, and whether he will be among the wretched or the happy ones.[2] Nothing one does can change what Allah has already destined. But neither the Emir nor the Sardauna knew the end was that close.

After St. Nelson had left, the Emir invited some of his councilors and mallams and briefed them about the sad news that St. Nelson had brought to him. They prayed for the repose of the soul of the Sardauna. They also prayed for peace in the country. The Emir sat down, wondering what the coup portended for the nation.

ENCOUNTER WITH A FRIEND

At about 11 a.m. the secretary to the Kano Provincial Commissioner, PC, Alhaji Usman Liman, Sarkin Musawa, telephoned the Emir's secretary and told him that soldiers had gone to the PC's residence and arrested him and that they were on their way to the palace. On hearing that, the Emir immediately directed that the court be adjourned and everyone was advised to go home. No reason was given for the unusual behavior, but the palace officials ensured that everyone heeded the advice to leave. The Emir then sat waiting for the soldiers. As soon as the people had left, two military vehicles pulled in to the palace. A captain, leading the team, walked up to the Emir, saluted him and said, "Your Highness,

I am very sorry, I regret to say that you are under arrest, and you are asked to follow me." The Emir did not argue nor ask any question. He simply said, "OK, let's go." He then stood up and followed the captain to the vehicles. There was a third vehicle, belonging to the Provincial Commissioner. The Emir was directed to join the PC, Sarkin Musawa, who was seated in the back seat of his official car. Two drunk-looking soldiers were in the front seat with guns pointed at the Emir and the PC. The two military vehicles escorted them to the army barracks.

Upon seeing them, Lieutenant Colonel Chukwuemeka Odumegwu Ojukwu, the Battalion Commander in Kano, came out of his office and greeted the Emir. He apologised that he should have gone to the palace himself to brief the Emir about developments, but that even he was not in the proper picture of what was happening. That was why he had been on the phone all day trying to reach Lagos or Kaduna. Together, the three walked into Ojukwu's office. After they had sat down Ojukwu resumed talking, saying that there seemed to be some confusion as there was no report from either Lagos or Kaduna. Then he added that he suspected that the Sardauna had been killed. He asked the Emir for his support to ensure that peace prevailed in Kano. Ojukwu then requested permission for himself to call the Emir on phone if necessary. He already had the Emir's telephone numbers. The Emir granted the request. Then turning to Sarkin Musawa, Ojukwu directed him to go and remove all his personal belongings from the official residence of the PC with immediate effect.

Just at that time, the Madaki of Kano, Alhaji Shehu Ahmad, and other Emirate Council members arrived at the barracks. As soon as their presence was announced to Ojukwu, he told the Emir and the PC that the meeting was over and that they could leave. All three of them stood up and walked to the door of Ojukwu's office. The Emir noticed that the military vehicles that had escorted them to the barracks were not there. Although there were some other vehicles, brought by his councilors, the Emir insisted that he be taken back to the palace in the same way in which he had been brought, with a military escort, since after all, he had been brought to the barracks under arrest. Ojukwu denied ever having directed the arrest of the Emir, explaining that it was over-zealousness on the part of the young officer.

When the military vehicles came, Ojukwu asked the Captain if he, Ojukwu, had directed the captain to go and arrest the Emir of Kano. The captain stood at attention, in silence. He was then directed by Ojukwu to take the Emir back to the palace. Just when they were about to leave, Ojukwu asked the Emir if he needed any military protection at the palace. The Emir replied in the negative.

The Emir's reason for insisting that he be taken back to the palace in the same way in which he had been brought out of it, was to assure the people who might have seen or heard that he had been taken away that he had been brought back safely. That way, no room was going to be left for speculation as to the fate of their Emir.

The following morning, Sunday January 16, Ojukwu came to the palace. He told the Emir that he had come to update him about developments and to ask for his assistance to calm the nerves of the people. The Emir asked Ojukwu in what way he could be of assistance, and Ojukwu said that he would want the Emir to make a radio broadcast to the people appealing for calm. The Emir told Ojukwu that he did not think that he should make any broadcast; but Ojukwu insisted that it was necessary. He added that to avoid further bloodshed, everything should be done to discourage the people from taking the laws into their own hands. The Emir then agreed to make a broadcast provided Ojukwu himself prepared the speech. They drove to the broadcasting house, where Ojukwu wrote down the speech, which the Emir translated and read out in Hausa. It was a very brief speech, which appealed to the people for calm, and asked them not to do anything that would worsen the already tense situation. The

Emir added that people should leave everything to Allah, who is the best protector.

DAYS OF ANXIETY

The days following the coup saw much confusion in Kaduna. There was no government. Even though Major Hassan Usman Katsina had been appointed Governor of the North, the machinery of government could not be easily assembled again. Some of the top civil servants just boycotted their offices. In the absence of the political class, Governor Hassan Katsina began his tenure by calling a meeting of Northern traditional rulers at Kaduna. All the key traditional rulers convened for the meeting presided over by the Governor, with some permanent secretaries, Ahmed Joda, Ahmed Talib, Yahaya Gusau, Ibrahim Dasuki and others in attendance. The first meeting deliberated over developments in the country since the coup, and offered prayers for the repose of the soul of the Sardauna and all those killed in the coup and for peace in the country. At that inaugural meeting, no mention was made of the ethnic nature of the coup. The emphasis was on the need for the traditional rulers to ensure peace in their respective domains.

About a week later, another meeting was called, also at Kaduna. It was at that meeting that it was formally announced to the traditional rulers that the Federal Prime Minister, Alhaji Abubakar Tafawa Balewa, had been killed. About two days to that meeting, Lieutenant Colonel Yakubu Gowon, then Chief of Army Staff, had visited the Emir at night. He told the Emir he had come to brief him about developments in the country. In the course of their discussion the Emir asked Gowon about his colleagues who were said to be missing, namely Brigadier Zakaria Maimalari, Colonel Kur Muhammed, Lieutenant Colonel James Pam, Lieutenant Colonel Abogo Largema and others. Gowon sadly told the Emir that they had been confirmed dead.

The Kaduna meetings came to be held more regularly and for longer duration, and became almost a weekly affair. In some weeks, the meeting lasted three or more days. By the end of March, a certain general perception had developed among both the common people of the North as well as the elite that the policies being introduced by the new military government were designed to retard the progress of the region. That perception of the administration was not helped by the behavior of the Igbos resident and working in the North, who taunted the Northerners saying that they had been kicked out of power and that it was an Igbo government ruling Nigeria.

When these concerns began to feature in the meetings of the traditional rulers, the Federal Government felt disturbed by it. At one of the meetings, a senior military officer was sent by General Ironsi, the Supreme Commander, as the Head of State was then addressed, to deliver a veiled threat to the traditional rulers. The officer told them that the Supreme Commander had information that they were against the government and policies of the Supreme Military Council. They were warned against disloyalty to the government of the day.

The meeting instructed the officer to go and tell General Ironsi that the people of the North were apprehensive of some of the policies introduced by the Supreme Military Council. They added that they suspected that the appointment of the Nwokedi Commission to "Study and Report on the Administrative Structure of the country" was a ruse, as the SMC had already taken a decision to abolish the federal structure of government and replace it with a unitary system.[3] They cautioned seriously against any such move, as the North would not accept unitarianism at that stage of its development.

Whether the officer delivered the message to his Commander-in-Chief or not, General Ironsi on May 24 signed into law Decree 34 of 1966, known as the Unification Decree, which actualized exactly what the Northern leaders had cautioned against. The federal system was abolished and the four regions decreed out of existence. The National Government was to legislate for the whole country, while the public services were to be unified. There were to be groups of provinces with prefectorates to be headed by prefects, who were going to be appointed by the Supreme Commander. Although Decree 34 was to take immediate effect, the Governors of the regions were allowed to continue to function, this time as governors of groups of provinces, not regional governors. It was an interim measure pending the take-off of the unitary state.

THE UNIFICATION DECREE AND ITS AFTERMATH

Northern leaders had serious reservations about Decree 34. Federalism, as far as they were concerned, was non-negotiable. Virtually every important group in the region felt threatened by unitarianism. The traditional rulers, the custodians of the culture of their people, felt that the sense of identity that federalism gives each culture would be eroded in a unitary set-up. The suggestion by the Supreme Commander that traditional rulers would be rotated, like civil servants or soldiers, did not help matters.[4] The political class—Party leaders and employees, legislators, members of the executive, political appointees in regional parastatals, and others—in the Region feared they were going to be put out of work and the civil servants also felt threatened. In the absence of a regional service, they would have to compete with the more educated Southerners for the few positions in the national civil service. Northern students were equally aggrieved with the Decree. They saw their prospects of automatically securing jobs on graduation diminished as a result of the unification. Both the civil servants and the students reasoned that the prefects, who were to be appointed, being administrative officers, would have to have a minimum qualification of a university degree. At that time, the whole North could not boast of more than a few hundred graduates. In contrast, the East, West and Mid-West Regions had tens of thousands of graduates; In fact, they had surplus graduates looking for jobs. Incidentally, the University of Nigeria, Nsukka, produced its first set of graduates that year.[5] There was every indication that the graduate unemployment problem in the South was going to be aggravated. Hence, the Northerners felt that Decree 34 was carefully designed and promulgated to pave the way for Southerners, particularly Igbos, to come and fill all the proposed offices of prefects as well as other administrative jobs in the North.

It should be noted that generally Northerners, irrespective of class and political persuasion, were united in their belief in the virtue of the Northernization policy that the deposed regional government was pursuing. Northernization, like Westernization and Easternization before it, was a policy whereby the government embarked on a deliberate and calculated strategy to fill all vacancies in the Northern civil service and its parastatals with Northerners. Where there were not enough Northerners with the requisite education, training, or experience, preference was given to expatriates. In the absence of expatriates, Nigerians from other regions would be recruited. That policy was vehemently criticized by Nigerians from the South, especially those from the East. They argued that the North treated other Nigerians as though they were second-class citizens in their own country;[6] that even Europeans or Ghanaians were treated better than they, who were Nigerians were. The argument was further made that since the North needed manpower to develop, and the South had it in surplus, it was in the national interest that the North should tap the surplus resources of the South for even development.

The leaders of the North, on the other hand, argued that the preference for expatriates over other Nigerians was informed by practical reality. In the first place, once a Southerner was recruited, he or she could not be asked to go when a Northerner became available for the job, but the contract of a European or a Ghanaian employee need not be renewed at expiration. As soon as the North had produced a qualified person for any position an expatriate was holding, that expatriate's services could be dispensed with without any furor. Secondly, the leaders of the North believed that when a Southerner held an important position in government or a parastatal, any available vacancy was filled by people from his family, hometown, or region. Southerners holding important positions in the Northern civil service or parastatals were not known to have encouraged Northerners to enter the service. In fact, some Northern leaders even alleged that where a Northerner and a Southerner with the same qualifications and experience applied for the same job, and the interview was conducted by a Nigerian senior officer from the South, the applicant from the North was sure to lose the position. Finally, the regional government argued that as a government, its obligation was to its citizens. If the Southern regional governments had an unemployment problem, it was not the duty of the Northern government to provide jobs for their people and thereby, transfer their problems to the North.

The release on May 24, 1966 of decree 34 otherwise known as the Unification Decree, enraged the people of the North. It confirmed their worst fears that the Southerners, especially the Igbos, were set to dominate them, having killed their important political and military leaders. They set out to give vent to their anger by targeting Federal Government establishments that were mainly staffed by Igbos for torching and vandalization. The Nigerian Railways Corporation, the Electricity Corporation of Nigeria and the Post and Telecommunications Department were the worst hit. Ordinary Igbos, who had been taunting Northerners in the markets and on the streets, were also, targeted, and many of them were killed in the major towns of the North. After two days of bloody rioting in major towns from May 29 onwards, with the rioters calling for "*a ware*" or the secession of the North from the federation, the situation was brought under control. The traditional rulers made constant appeals to the people to stop the riot. Thus, Emir Ado Bayero addressed his people over the radio urging, appealing and pleading for restraint. The broadcast was aired almost every hour during those two days. Virtually all the traditional rulers of the North did the same. Nevertheless, the Ironsi government believed that it was the traditional rulers who were instigating their people to oppose the government. To take care of the recalcitrance of the traditional rulers Ironsi invited them to Ibadan for a meeting on July 28. It was rumored in the North that the government had planned to eliminate those traditional rulers whom it suspected to be against it. Ado Bayero was said to be one of the Emirs marked out for elimination by the government.[7]

The cry for the secession of the North from the federation was not limited to the civilian population. Even senior military officers called for the dissolution of the federation. Although the leaders of the January 15 coup, particularly Majors Emmanuel Ifeajuna and Chukwuma Kaduna Nzeogwu were reputed to be detribalized officers, and that they had wanted the victims of the coup to be truly national in spread, the fact was that in the actual execution of the coup the North was the worst hit both in terms of the number of casualties and their status in the polity. Aside from the political leaders already noted, all military officers but one, of the rank of Lieutenant Colonel and above from the North, were eliminated.[8] It was not just the elimination of these officers, but also the brutal and callous manner of their elimination that aroused the anger of the surviving officers and men of the armed forces from the North. Zakaria Maimalari, for example, was reportedly shot in cold blood by Igbo officers who had only a few hours earlier joined him in merriment at his wedding party, while James Pam was invited out by his immediate subordinate, Anuforo, an Igbo officer, and shot right in the presence of his wife and children. These gory acts were not helped by Ironsi's decision not to court-martial the planners and executors of the coup. Ironsi's failure to bring to book those "mutineers," (which was how he described them) after they had killed their senior officers, made the remaining Northern officers, including Murtala Mohammed, resolve to strike.[9]

The Ibadan meeting was very tense. The Northern traditional rulers, as a group, were meeting with the Supreme Commander for the first time since he became Head of State. They knew that he suspected them or some of them, of disloyalty as his national broadcast of June 1, indicated. But they were also resolved to tell him what they believed was the position of the North. The meeting began with the Supreme Commander lecturing the traditional rulers on the significance of reciting the national anthem at the beginning and end of each important event. He then went on to say that:

> It is regrettable, indeed painful, to recall that some traditional rulers pitched their fortunes with one or the other of those warring camps and so did much to bring the institution of chieftaincy into ridicule and contempt....

Continuing, General Ironsi stated:

> In my view, every Nigerian should regard theObong of Calabar as his Obong, the Ovie of Oghara as his Ovie, the Emir of Argungu as his emir, the Ooni of Ife as his ooni, the Obi of Onitsha as his obi, and the Oba of Lagos as his oba...

That statement was interpreted by the traditional rulers, especially those from the North, as a confirmation of the rumor circulating in the North at that time that with the unification of the country, traditional rulers were going to be subject to postings from one emirate or kingdom to another just like civil servants or military commanders. The traditional rulers, especially those from the North felt very uncomfortable with that statement. No contributions or comments were taken before the meeting adjourned, to be reconvened the following morning. Later in the evening, a cocktail party was held for the dignitaries.

While the cocktail party was going on in the Government House, some soldiers who felt aggrieved with what had been happening since January were busy perfecting their own plans to strike. These were mainly soldiers from the North, some of whom had earlier called for secession. Late that night, they struck, killing the Head of State, General Ironsi and his host, the Governor of the Western group of provinces, Colonel Adekunle Fajuyi. After more than twenty-four hours of confusion, the military came out with a statement announcing Lieutenant Colonel Yakubu Gowon as the new Head of State and Commander-in-Chief of the Armed Forces. The traditional rulers dispersed to their various domains to await the policies of the new government.

THE COUNTER-COUP OF JULY 1966

The counter-coup of July 1966, planned and executed as it were by some of the remnants of Northern officers in the army, mostly junior officers, sent shivers down the spines of many Igbo officers and civilians. It was seen as having been deliberately planned and executed to avenge the first coup. That, coupled with the events of late May in major Northern cities, made the Igbos ask how safe they were going to be in a new Nigeria headed by a Northern officer. Added to that general feeling among the Igbos was the belief of Lieutenant-Colonel Ojukwu, who had become the military governor of the Eastern group of provinces, that Lieutenant-Colonel Gowon, not being his senior in the army, could not be his Commander-in-Chief. Indeed, that was not the first time that Lieutenant-Colonel Ojukwu would take on Lieutenant-Colonel Gowon on a matter of seniority in the Army. When Lieutenant-Colonel Gowon, then Adjutant-General of the Army, received information that Ojukwu had arrested the Emir of Kano on the day of the first coup, and had also declared martial law in Kano, he had called Ojukwu and demanded to know who had authorized him to take those steps. Ojukwu had replied to Gowon that he did not take his orders from Gowon, but from his Brigade Commander. Gowon had retorted that under normal circumstances that was correct, but he reminded Ojukwu that the times were not normal and so he, Ojukwu, should take orders from him. Ojukwu never did.[10] In fact, Ojukwu was to say with pride twenty-six years later, that he was one of the few officers that the Nigerian Army had produced who had never served under an officer junior to him.[11]

The ethnic violence of May had led to a large exodus of people of Eastern origin from the North. Although the trend was abated and most of them had returned to the North after assurances from traditional rulers, the governors of both the Northern and Eastern group of provinces and the Supreme Commander himself, the counter-coup of July caused panic among the Easterners once again. The Northerners, particularly those who had felt most aggrieved by the actions of the Igbos when Ironsi was in power, set out to vent their anger on the Igbos. The result was the death of a number of them. Efforts were made, and with some success, by the authorities to bring the situation under control; but the damage had been done. When the news of the killing of Igbos in Kano reached the East some Hausas living in Port Harcourt and the Imo River area were attacked and killed on September 23 in retaliation. The British Broadcasting Corporation, BBC, carried the news of the killing of Hausas in its bulletin of October 4, Radio Cotonou carried it the following day, and the media in the North did not help matters with the radio stations beginning a continuous relay of the Radio Cotonou story. The regional government also issued press releases amplifying the news.

The *New Nigerian* newspaper, while reporting the attack on the Igbos in the North, also carried stories about the fate of Northerners in the East. In one such story titled "Pathetic Story of a Refugee Girl from the East" the October 15, 1966 issue of the paper carried a photograph of a Northern girl called Gambo Umoru. Miss Umoru, 14, was given ample space on page 6 to narrate her experience at the hands of Igbos at Enugu. According to Miss Umoru:

> I and my parents with some other worshippers were saying our prayers in the evening at a mosque in Enugu on that fateful day

when some unknown rascals set fire on the mosque.... After the fire, my parents were nowhere to be seen. I ran to the house and got five pounds from where my dad kept his money and set out on a journey to an unknown destination.

Miss Umoru was said to have reported herself to the Central Police Station Broad Street, Lagos. Yet another story titled "Northerners from East Tell their Story" in the same newspaper of October 5, 1966 narrated how some 400 Northerners evacuated from the East in a specially chartered plane went through hell at the hands of the Igbos, as "even policemen of Eastern origin who tried to protect us were killed."

The net effect of all those stories was to make Igbos targets for elimination virtually throughout the Northern Region. They fought back in self-defense, sometimes killing some of their attackers or Northerners who happened to be caught in their midst.

It was in that situation that Lieutenant-Colonel Ojukwu advised that all Nigerians of Eastern origin should go back to the East and that the Northern government should guarantee their safe passage. Similarly, Northerners resident in the East should leave the territory, as his government could not guarantee their safety. The return of the Easterners to the East and the stories they narrated about their horrendous experiences raised passions among their brethren, leading many people to ask if they would not be better off in an independent state. This was because there was hardly any household especially in Igboland that did not have at least one of its members working in the North, as a civil servant, company employee, trader, transporter or artisan. So when these stories were narrated – and they were narrated with such vividness—one could not fail to feel deeply about the loss. And for those who had lost relations, especially those who had narrowly escaped being killed themselves, the experience kept haunting them.

At the military level too, great distrust had crept in. The spirit of camaraderie characteristic of soldiers was sorely lacking. It was against that background that Ojukwu began to prepare for secession. It took him ten months from August 1, 1966, when Gowon was declared Head of State and Commander-in-

Chief of the Armed Forces, to May 30, 1967, three days after Gowon had announced the break-up of the federation into twelve states, to announce the secession of the former Eastern Region and the creation of the Republic of Biafra.

After thirty ensuing months of civil war, during which period Emir Ado Bayero strove hard to bring about peace with some measure of success, Ojukwu's rebellion was crushed, and Nigeria was re-united.

NOTES

1. The ethnic violence against the Igbos started in Kano a few days after Decree 34 had been released. From there, it spread to other towns in the North. See Daily Times June 1, 1966, p. 1.
2. The fifth hadith of Al-Nawawi in *The Selected Traditions of Al-Nawawi*, tr. by M.O.A. Abdul (Lagos, Islamic Publications Bureau, 1982).
3. The Commission was established on February 12, 1966.
4. General Ironsi was not categorical on this matter as his address to the traditional rulers at the Ibadan Conference reproduced below indicates. But since a rumor had been circulating about that for some time, Ironsi's statement, along that line, seemed to have lent credence to the rumor.
5. 470 graduates were released into the Nigerian labor market in June 1966 from the University of Nigeria Nsukka. See Daily Times June 22, 1966, p. 3.
6. Barely 24 hours after assassinating the Sardauna, Major C.K. Nzeogwu told top civil servants of the Northern Region that he had killed the Sardauna among other reasons for his Northernization policy. See John Paden, *Ahmadu Bello Sardauna of Sokoto: Values and Leadership in Nigeria*, op. cit., p. 664.
7. Ironsi's broadcast to the nation on June 1, 1966 specifically singled out Kano and Kaduna as areas where rumors about

his person were currently circulating. The full text of the address read:

"I have been informed of rumors about my person currently cir culating in some areas of the Northern group of provinces, par ticularly Kaduna and Kano....

"I am therefore taking this opportunity to make it clear per sonally through this broadcast to the nation that there is no truth whatsoever in these rumors...

"The Public should realize that rumors of this kind or any other disquieting nature are deliberately calculated to create unrest in the country and destroy the efforts at present being pursued with sincerity and by well-meaning Nigerians for national recon struction...

It was to avoid the situation now developing that I specifi cally instructed, a few days ago, that the general public should be alerted to the dangers of allowing themselves to be worked up into a state of disaffection which would lead to serious distur bances in different parts of the country...

"I warn all those involved in the present campaigns of vicious rumor-mongering to put a stop to this dangerous practice...

Daily Times June 2, 1966, p. 18.

8. These were Brigadier Zakaria Maimalari, Colonel Kur Mohammed, Lt. Col. Abogo Largema, and Colonel James Pam. The exception was Lt. Col Yakubu Gowon. The only Igbo officer killed was Lt. Col. A Unegbe, who had refused to participate in the January 15, 1966 coup.

9. Murtala Muhammed was particularly grieved by the killing of Brigadier Zakaria Maimalari on January 15. Exactly one week after Maimalari's assassination, on January 22, Muhammed was blessed with his first baby boy. He named the boy Zakaria, in memory of the officer he so much respected.

10. Interview with General Yakubu Gowon, May 26, 1997.

11. *Newswatch* Magazine, September 28, 1992, p.13.

THE VEASON

CHANCELLOR UNIVERSITY OF NIGERIA

While tension was still high between the East and the rest of Nigeria, particularly the North, Lieutenant-Colonel C.O. Ojukwu, Governor of the Eastern Region, and Visitor to the Eastern Region-owned University of Nigeria, Nsukka, UNN, offered the Emir of Kano, Alhaji Ado Bayero, the office of the Chancellor of that university. At the time the offer was made, March 8, 1966, Dr. Nnamdi Azikiwe was the Chancellor. The Emir gave the offer a serious thought. First, he reasoned that UNN was the brainchild of Dr. Azikiwe and he deserved the honor to continue as its Chancellor. Secondly, the Emir suspected that Ojukwu wanted to remove Zik for some reason he did not want to make public.[1] For these two reasons, the Emir seriously considered turning down Ojukwu's offer. But, as with all his other decisions, Ado Bayero looked beyond the personalities involved. It was the survival of the nation that was at stake. The Emir reasoned that at a time when there was mounting tension between Igbos and Northerners, a time when a majority of Northerners felt that Igbos were set to dominate them, having killed their political and military leaders, he needed to do something to ease tensions. He also needed to disabuse the minds of his people about their perception of some Igbo grand design against them, considering the fact that their political and military leaders had been killed. Accepting the offer, he reasoned, would send an important symbolic message not just to the Northerners, but to other Nigerians as well. And so, popular opinion in Kano and the North in general notwithstanding, he wrote to Ojukwu on April 5, 1966 accepting the offer.

The installation ceremony was fixed for June 25. Ado Bayero looked forward to that date. He wanted to take his message for peace and unity into Igboland. He had for years, and especially since January 1966, harped on that to his own people. There were some home truths he could not say to the Igbos on his own soil. Such things as their insensitivity to the feelings of their hosts, as demonstrated when they openly boasted that the national government was Igbo-controlled. Or how they were taunting Hausas about the assassination of the Sardauna and Abubakar Tafawa Balewa. These were things that had alienated the Hausas from the Igbos. Such advice, coming from the Emir while in Kano could have incited the Hausas; but now, on Igbo soil, he intended to be as frank as possible. He intended to tell the Igbo leadership, so that they could get the message across to their people in the North, some of the grievances of Northerners against them.

In the meantime, the Emir continued to use his good offices to ensure that the latent anger of the people of the North did not explode. He succeeded until May 23, when General Ironsi announced the promulgation of Decree 34, otherwise known as the Unification Decree. That was the last straw. The message of that Decree, as understood by the Northerners was that the Igbos were truly set to dominate them. As shown above, the Northerners' reaction was swift; all over the North Igbos became targets of mob action.

The traditional rulers and the government moved fast and restored order. By June 2, when the three-day region-wide uprising was effectively crushed many Igbos and some Northerners had lost their lives, many more had been maimed and their properties plundered, and many of the Igbos who had survived the uprising decided to move back "home." There thus began the first exodus of Nigerians from their region of residence by choice to their region of origin by destiny. Although a series of appeals were made to the Igbos to return to the North, the basis of mutual trust had been severely undermined.

It was in that pervading atmosphere of distrust that Emir Ado Bayero set out from Kano to attend the ceremony of his installation as the second Chancellor of the University of Nigeria at Nsukka on June 25, 1966. Many people had advised him against going to the East at that time. He was advised to request for a postponement of the ceremony so as to allow time to heal the wounds of the May uprising. But Emir Ado Bayero could not understand why he should be appealing to Igbos to return to the North and assuring them of their safety when he could not go to the East. Peace, he concluded, does not just happen. It is sought: consciously, actively, resolutely, and steadfastly, and it requires understanding. He needed to go to the East to dialogue with the leaders, especially the intellectual community there. It was only through proper understanding a nd respect of the aspirations and fears of each group that lasting peace could be established.

So, as Ojukwu and Gowon were trading accusations, Ado Bayero went to the East twice in his capacity as the Chancellor of UNN. On both occasions, the Emir chose to stay not at Nsukka, the University town, but at Enugu, where he was the guest of his friend, Ojukwu. The two spent hours talking about how to avert the looming crisis

A Safe Haven for All

It will be recalled that in the May uprising in the North, the Emir made several appeals to the people not to take the law into their own hands, and to a large extent, the appeal was heeded as normalcy was restored within three days. But the second uprising occasioned by the information that some Hausas had been killed in Port Harcourt was more difficult to contain. In his determined effort to save the situation, Emir

Ado Bayero was accused by his own people of being insensitive to their feelings and over-protective of Igbos. The accusations were levelled against the Emir because he literally turned the 50-acre palace into a safe haven for Igbos. Any Igbo who came to the palace was given full protection. Indeed, the Emir did not wait for frightened Igbos to come to the palace; he went out of his way to seek them and give them protection.

One of the most graphic examples of the Emir's efforts was the case of Chief Michael Agbamuche who, thirty years later became the Attorney-General and Minister of Justice of Nigeria.[2] Mr. Michael Agbamuche was an Igbo from what is now Delta State of Nigeria. He had come to settle in Kano in the 1950s and had established a very successful law practice in the Sabongari area. As a lawyer, he had been very impressed with the way Ado Bayero, then Chief of the Native Authority Police, ran his department. He had watched with admiration how the young NA Police Chief had introduced significant reforms in the NA police. Ado Bayero likewise admired Agbamuche for his learning. Although Agbamuche was some ten years older than Ado Bayero, they held each other in mutual respect, and the two soon became friends.

According to Chief Agbamuche, he returned home from court one afternoon in August 1966 and his telephone rang. It was the secretary to the Emir of Kano. He told Mr. Agbamuche that the Emir wanted him to come to the palace immediately. Agbamuche rushed to the palace. There, the Emir told Agbamuche that they had information that some people were after him and that his life was in danger. "You must not sleep in your house tonight" the Emir said. Agbamuche, who had only a few weeks earlier acquired a shotgun, thanked the Emir and his councilors for their concern for his safety, but boasted that he was going to sleep in his house and that his attackers would be most welcome. Thirty years after that incident Agbamuche vividly recalls the Emir's reaction to his statement.[3] The Emir said, "Mike, even if you succeed in killing nine out of ten, and you are eventually killed, we would have lost you." Agbamuche was also advised that it might be safer for him to leave Kano until his safety was assured. He was offered a place to sleep in the palace and early the following morning at 4.00 a.m. he was driven to the airport to catch the London-Lagos flight that made stopovers at Kano. To Agbamuche's pleasant surprise the emir handed him a round-trip ticket reading Kano-Lagos-Benin-Lagos-Kano, saying that as soon as it was safe, he should return to Kano. That was not the only surprise. As if the Emir knew that Agbamuche had only £30 on him, the Emir also gave him £250.

On his arrival at Lagos, Agbamuche telephoned his house in Kano and indeed, the Emir's fears were confirmed. The house had been raided that night, at about 2 a.m., but Agbamuche was inside the impregnable Gidan Rumfa, as the guest of the chief occupant, the Emir.

Many years later, Agbamuche was to learn that the people sent after him went to the Federal Club in Kano looking for him. He was there, but because they did not know him, they were on the lookout for his car, the make, model, and registration number of which those who sent them had given them. When they did not see the car, they had asked a few people around the club about him. Their appearance raised suspicion among the people they asked. The people therefore told them that Agbamuche had not come that night. Early the following morning, the people passed the information to the District Head of Waje who, in turn, passed it to the Emir.

Another occasion on which the Emir saved Agbamuche's life was during the civil war. When the federal troops captured Warri, Agbamuche was one of many civilians arraigned before the Umuegbu Tribunal on charges of conspiracy against the Federal Government. In his defense before the Chairman of the Tribunal, Agbamuche brought out a hand-written letter the Emir had sent to him. In it, the Emir expressed regret for the incident that had led to Agbamuche's departure from Kano. He also told Agbamuche that his house and everything inside is safe and asked how he was doing at home. He ended by saying that he prayed that sooner or later normalcy would be restored and that Mike would return to Kano to resume his practice. According to Agbamuche, he gave the Chairman of the Tribunal the letter to read. After he had read it, Agbamuche said, "with the Emir of Kano as my friend, how can I be against the Federal Government? Who is more federal than the Emir of Kano?" The tribunal chairman released him there and then.

Another important Igbo man who credits Emir Ado Bayero with saving his life is Chukwuemeka Odumegwu Ojukwu. But for the Emir of Kano, according to Ojukwu he would have been dead over thirty years ago. Ojukwu recalls the incident as if it happened only yesterday.[4] Ojukwu had been a friend of Ado Bayero even before Ado became Emir. With Ojukwu as Battalion Commander in Kano, and Ado Bayero as Emir, their friendship grew. They shared and did a lot of things in common. So close were they that even when they bought private cars, they agreed on the registration numbers that they were going to have. While Lieutenant-Colonel Ojukwu had KA 2000, Emir Ado Bayero had KAB 2000. Ojukwu used to pay the Emir private visits and the Emir used to reciprocate those visits. It was while the Emir was on one of those visits to Ojukwu one very hot afternoon that Ojukwu complained about the heat in Kano and particularly his house. According to Ojukwu, even if the Emir had heard the complaint he did not react to it.

A few weeks later, the Emir returned to Ojukwu's house. He invited Ojukwu to join him on a ride without telling him where they were going. They drove around town for some time before heading towards the Nassarawa Government Reservation Area, GRA. They pulled up in front of a certain compound in the GRA, which was full of trees, shrubs, and various plants. They got out from their car and went inside the house. It was really cool; the tall trees providing ample protection from the scorching heat of the sun. Emir Ado Bayero asked Ojukwu whether the house was cool enough for him. Ojukwu could not believe his ears. He immediately moved most of his personal effects into that house. Since army headquarters had not formally given him permission to move out of his official residence, many people including his soldiers were not aware that he had moved to the GRA. He saw people at the office and in the official residence, but in his private time, he was in the GRA.

He kept that schedule until the military struck in January 1966. In the ensuing crisis his official residence was attacked and a grenade thrown into it shattering everything inside. Luckily for Ojukwu, he was fast asleep in the house provided for him by his friend the Emir. The perpetrators of that act did not know that, of course.

IN SEARCH OF PEACE

The declaration of the birth of the Republic of Biafra by Lt. Col. Ojukwu on May 30, 1967, three days after the announcement by General Gowon of the creation of twelve states from the former four regions, posed a fresh challenge to Emir Ado Bayero. The die had been cast. All diplomatic efforts to get the two sides to abandon the path of carnage had failed. Each side wanted the other to concede to its demands: the East wanted to be left to have full control over its security and economy, while the rest of Nigeria wanted the East to be treated as an integral part of Nigeria. For nearly a year, round table conferences within and outside Nigeria had not been able to produce an acceptable solution. Both now resorted to might to determine who was right.

Once war had been declared against Biafra, and young men from Kano and other parts of Nigeria were being conscripted to go to the battlefront, Emir Ado Bayero's latitude to preach peace was seriously circumscribed. He could not in the day appeal to able-bodied men to come forward and enlist in order to protect the unity and territorial integrity of their fatherland, and in the night preach peace, which is the direct opposite of war. In a war situation, total commitment, especially of the leaders of society, is crucial. But how was he to show total commitment? By appearing hawkish and advising General Yakubu Gowon to stop being soft on Ojukwu? Or by urging Gowon to declare an all-out war against the rebels?

General Gowon was not disposed, at least in the initial stages of the secession, to either of the two suggestions. But more importantly, the Emir himself, like Gowon, did not want the war to sow the seeds of hatred between the two sides. If soldiers had to fight for a known cause, they should by all means be supported; but they should not be encouraged to visit mayhem on defenseless civilians in the name of prosecuting a war. He also reasoned that the longer the war lasted, the more misery it would bring to the people, and more remote would be the prospects of early reconciliation.

Ado Bayero was quick in realizing that the strategy adopted by the Biafrans to prosecute the war would not allow the Federal side, despite its relative advantage in arms and ammunition as well as armed soldiers, to easily crush the rebellion. From the beginning, the Biafrans identified two battle fronts: the actual ground over which the tanks were to roll, and the mind of the international community where moral, financial, and military support needed to be sought. They had reckoned, early in their planning that in an all-out war, Biafra would be overrun in a matter of weeks. What they therefore needed was international support, first to restrain the Federal side from embarking on an all-out war, and second to provide them with military supplies to enable them to keep the Nigerians at bay. Thus was created one of the most effective war propaganda machines in the history of Africa.

Decades before Ted Turner came up with his Cable News Network, CNN, that shrank the world into the television screen, the Biafrans had found a way of getting horrifying pictures of starving children, emaciated nursing mothers, and devastated infrastructure on to the pages of many influential newspapers and magazines in Europe and America. They had also established strong lobbies in virtually all of Europe and America. Their message was a simple one: a predominantly Muslim Federal side was bent on annihilating the Christian population of the East. The pictures, some of which were real, while many more were photo tricks, were allowed to speak for the suffering Igbo nation. The Biafran propaganda worked magic in a number of countries in Africa and Europe, especially those with predominantly Christian populations. In Africa, Ivory Coast, and Gabon, two former French colonies recognized Biafra. So did Zambia and Tanzania—two partners of Nigeria in the Commonwealth.[5] The Benin Republic and Cameroon, also Francophone states and Nigeria's neighbors to the west and east respectively, did not give Nigeria the support it had taken for granted. In Europe, Portugal, Spain and France supported Biafra. There were other states under intense domestic pressure to recognize and support Biafra, and this support and recognition translated into the pouring of arms and ammunition into Biafra. That, in turn, meant many more years of killing, maiming, and suffering for the mass of the people on either side.

Ado Bayero felt that the situation must not be allowed to continue. Everything must be done to let the world know the truth about the war. Nigeria must counter that propaganda war and let the world know that the war was not religious. The world should be made to know that although the Nigerian Head of State was from the North, and that his first name, Yakubu, was the Muslim version of Jacob, he was not a Muslim, but a faithful Christian. Indeed his father was a church pastor. Likewise the Vice-chairman of the Federal Executive Council, Chief Obafemi Awolowo, a Yoruba from the Southwest, was a devout Christian and so indeed were most of the key figures in the federal government.

The federal government, at about the same time, also realized the need to reach out to the international community. It needed to consolidate the support of its traditional allies, win the support of the neutral states, and try to influence the policies of those states that had already recognized Biafra.

SHUTTLE DIPLOMACY

General Gowon found Emir Ado Bayero most helpful in pursuing these foreign policy objectives. Ado Bayero proved particularly helpful in dealing with the neutral and unfriendly states. One of the first assignments he undertook in that regard was to Senegal. An influential member of the Economic Organization of the Francophone States, Senegal's opinion, and especially that of its president, Leopold Sedar Senghor, was much respected in Paris and the capitals of most of French-speaking Africa. Unlike Gabon and the Ivory Coast, which recognized Biafra in line with their metropolitan master's (France) covert policies, Senegal did not accord official recognition to Biafra.[6] So Ado Bayero started from there. He was on a familiar turf, having served as Nigeria's ambassador in Dakar some four years earlier and cultivated the friendship of President Senghor. Late in 1968, Emir Ado Bayero flew to Senegal where his "teacher" received him. Emir Ado Bayero took pains to explain to President Senghor the situation in Nigeria. He emphasized that the war was not a religious war, and listed for him the entire key figures in the Federal Government indicating their religious affiliation by their names and offices. It was a hard sell, because quite apart from Senghor's natural sympathy for fellow- Christians, he believed in the right of people to self-determination. If the people of Eastern Nigeria did not want to be part of the federation, because they felt they were going to be better off on their own, why must they be compelled to do otherwise? It was also believed in Nigeria that Senegal felt threatened by Nigeria's size. With a dismembered Nigeria, Senegal was likely to become the principal sub-regional power in West Africa. That prospect was believed to have been part of what informed France's decision to support Biafra.

Ado Bayero's mission was to get President Senghor to use his influence to dissuade France and her other ex-colonies from supporting Biafra. Senghor was to educate them on the realities of the Nigerian civil war. More importantly, if Senghor could, through President Felix Houphouet-Boigny or President Albert Bernard Bongo (who later converted to Islam and took the name Omar Bongo) of Gabon, or even France, talk to Ojukwu on the futility of war, he would be doing a great service to humanity. Before he left Dakar, Ado Bayero succeeded in getting some assurances from Senghor that he would see what he could do. He did, indeed, keep his word although not much came out of his efforts.

Not long after his return home, Ado Bayero set off again, this time to the Arab states of North Africa and the Middle East. He visited Morocco, where he met with King Hassan II, and later went to Saudi Arabia and Egypt. Egypt proved helpful. So did a number of Arab states, and also the Soviet Union and its allies. The traditional supplier of arms to Nigeria— Britain—was not supplying enough. For a number of reasons, including domestic pressures, the political leaders had initially been compelled to limit their supplies.[7]

Ado Bayero continued to seek ways of ending the war, while at the same time trying to garner support for the Federal Government. He spoke about it at every international forum he attended, especially at the annual meetings of the Swiss-based Foundation for Moral Re-Armament (MRA) in Caux, Switzerland.

It was after one of such Moral Re-Armament Conferences in 1969 that Ado Bayero felt a great conviction that he must go and personally meet Ojukwu and talk to him. He felt that not all the efforts he and others had been making through third parties were yielding the desired result; perhaps because the message was not getting to Ojukwu in the language he would appreciate. He was convinced that a one-to-one talk with Ojukwu would make him see the irrationality of hanging on to confrontation. Ojukwu needed to be made to sit down alone and in silence to ponder over the motive of the confrontation and the cost to humanity. Once he was resolved to go, Ado Bayero called General Gowon on the phone and intimated him about his intention. Gowon was uncomfortable with the suggestion, especially given the Federal Government's experience with a Katsina officer who was killed by the Biafrans. But the Emir was a strong believer in moral re-armament and nothing would stop him. First, he flew to France and from there to Gabon and into Biafra incognito. He went in the night, had a meeting with Ojukwu that lasted some hours, and left that same night. Ado Bayero was convinced that at that time, in late 1969, Ojukwu had become boxed into a hole by his lieutenants. Ojukwu, as far as the Emir could tell, was willing to make peace. But after a meeting with his lieutenants he was apparently over-ruled. The Emir left for France, then Switzerland and then back home. Not long after that, Ojukwu fled to the Ivory Coast, ending his dream of a Republic of Biafra.

THE RETURN OF THE IGBOS

On January 15, 1970, at a ceremony in Lagos, Colonel Phillip Effiong, the officer Ojukwu left in charge of Biafra as he fled, signed documents acknowledging Biafra's formal and unconditional surrender to the Federal Government. On his part, General Gowon announced a policy of "No Victor, No Vanquished." He also announced the Federal Government's resolve to embark on the 3Rs—Reconciliation, Rehabilitation and Reconstruction.

No sooner had these policies been announced than the Igbos who had hearkened to Ojukwu's call in 1966 and 1967 to return to the East began to hasten back to their old bases. In the North, and especially in Kano, they were very well received. The Emir had addressed the people over the radio, at the end of the war, saying, "*Alhamdu Lillahi*, (Praise be to Allah) the war is over." He reminded the people of the Head of State's policy of "No Victor, No Vanquished" and appealed to Kano people to reintegrate the Igbos, who would soon be returning, into the social and economic life of the state.

When the Igbos fled from Kano on the eve of the war, many of them had left their properties—landed, industrial, and vehicular—behind. Some of those properties, especially the houses, were viciously vandalized during and after the disturbances that led to their departure. Some Hausas began to take advantage of the flight of the Igbos by declaring the properties they left behind *ghanima* or war booty. In other words, the Igbos had been conquered and whatever they left behind was for their conquerors. Indeed, some people had gone into the Sabongari and helped themselves to many movable properties. When information reached the Emir about what was happening to Igbo property he immediately stepped in. He went to the broadcasting house and made a public appeal to the people not to tamper with the property of the fleeing Igbos. That broadcast was carried repeatedly on radio Kano. The state government, on the advice of the Emir, set up a committee that was given the responsibility of identifying all abandoned properties and their owners.

To ease its work, the committee created two sub-committees—one for landed properties and another for industrial and vehicular properties. A register of abandoned landed properties was opened with the assistance of the Kano NA, which had the records of all Certificates of Occupancy of the Waje and Sabongari areas. Another register for all industrial, vehicular, and other properties was also opened. All those people who had appropriated abandoned properties were made to return them to the two sub-committees. After all the abandoned properties had been registered, the committee asked interested persons to formally apply for caretaker positions for any of the abandoned properties. To qualify to be given a house as a caretaker, the applicant had to identify an abandoned house and submit an estimate of the amount of money that would be needed to renovate and make it habitable. The committee would then verify the costing. The applicant would also show proof that he had the money to effect the repairs within an agreed time, and he had to agree to pay all rents collected to the committee. In return, he was given an agreed percentage of the rent as his commission. Subsequently, the committee refunded him the money for any repair work for which it gave prior approval and which it certified done to its satisfaction. Meanwhile, the initial money he invested in the repairs was regarded as a fixed deposit that was to be returned to him at the expiration of the contract. Industrial properties, like printing presses, block-making machines, metalworking machines etc., were also given to caretakers who operated them and made returns to the committee.[8]

At the end of the war, Emir Ado Bayero called on the committee to have its books ready as the rightful owners of the properties were coming back for them. As the Emir said, those properties were *amana*. "*Amana* is a trust and Allah *Subhanahu Wa Ta'ala* has said, "O ye who believe, Betray not the trust of Allah and His Apostle, Nor misappropriate knowingly things entrusted to you (Q8: 27)." In another verse, Allah says, "Allah Has commanded you to render back your trusts to those to whom they are due, and when ye judge between man and man that ye judge with justice, Verily how excellent is the teaching which He giveth you, For Allah is He Who heareth and seeth all things (Q4:58)." Also quoting the Hadith, the Emir had said, "The signs of the hypocrite are three: whenever he speaks he tells a lie, and whenever he promises he breaks his promise, and whenever he is entrusted he betrays the trust."[9] Emir Ado Bayero reminded the people that the right of ownership is held sacred in Islam, and that Islam does not discriminate among people on account of religious belief, when it comes to the sanctity of private property. The Ulama also added their voices to what the Emir had been preaching. They noted that there are two levels of amana. The individual level and the societal level. At the individual level, they said, it takes discipline, honesty, selflessness, fear of Allah, and great moral courage to always keep *amana*. For a society or community, in addition to the above qualities, its leaders must also be ready to apply sanctions upon individual members of the larger society to ensure conformity with those qualities.

As a result of the work of the two sub-committees and the exhortations of the Emir, many Igbos were given a pleasant surprise on their return. First of all, once it was established that they were the legitimate owners or heirs to the owners (if the owners had died during the war) of any property, they did not have any problem getting them back. Secondly, in most cases they found the houses in very good shape, sometimes better than they had left them. Finally, the rent realized from the property was given to the owners. With the rents collected, many Igbos began a new life and before long, many of them had become very wealthy in Kano.

Indeed, the re-integration of the Igbos did not start with their return to Kano. It began immediately after the war and especially after the Emir's broadcast to his people. At the end of the war many Igbos who had joined the Biafran army decided to go back to civilian life, but they did not know where to begin. They had lost their businesses, their industries, their capital, and all. They needed money to pay the school fees of their children, to repair their damaged homes, to begin a new life. Unlike their brethren who had all their investments in the East and had lost much of it to the war, the Igbos who had left properties in Kano, took advantage of the Emir's address and immediately sent emissaries to Kano requesting financial assistance either to pay the school fees of their children, or to take care of some urgent domestic needs. Once it was established that an applicant had landed or industrial property that was in the care of either or both of the sub-committees, the main committee advanced some money to him or her through the emissary pending his or her arrival to formalize the re-possession of his or her properties.

Although the civil war was said to have been a war mainly between the North and the Igbos, at the end of the war, the reception the Igbos got from the Northerners, especially Kano, was unlike anything they received anywhere else including parts of the East. For example, whereas the Igbos were given back their properties immediately on their return to Kano, and as we saw with accumulated rents, in Port Harcourt the Igboman never really succeeded in getting back his property even when he had produced all the documents to prove that the property was legally his. Many an Igbo had returned to Port Harcourt after the war and tried to claim his house only to spend huge amounts of money on litigation without getting the property back. In some instances, the Igbo returnee who had insisted on getting back his property had been eliminated. Indeed, the fact that abandoned properties never became an issue in the North, whereas to this day it is a sensitive issue in the East, speaks volumes of the efforts of Northern leaders, especially Emir Ado Bayero, to protect the properties of their Igbo brethren.

Even more significant than returning abandoned properties to the Igbos was the way many Hausas treated Igbo children. Some Igbo parents who realized that it was too late for them to escape safely from the North through the Middle Belt to the East with their children, decided to entrust their children to the care of their Hausa friends and neighbors. Most of these children were only ten years old or younger. Many of the new parents gave their adopted children common names among the Hausa, in addition to taking their surnames. They also introduced them to Islam; and since they had been born in the North, and were growing up there, they had no problem with the language. It was therefore not too difficult for them to be fully assimilated. To this day, in many parts of the North, there are a number of people who are ethnically Igbo but culturally Hausa. Quite a number of them have come to occupy key leadership positions in their adopted states. They are not discriminated against, and in fact they do not even claim to be Igbos, not because they do not know their roots, but, as one of them explained, it would be "the height of ungratefulness to abandon a family that had saved your life, fully accepted you and taken care of you, simply because the trouble is over."[10] Many Igbo parents who had fled never managed to come back. But even those who did return did not insist on their children being returned to their homes. They were quite pleased with the way they saw them being brought up. Of course, some were not happy with the conversion of their children to Islam, and their bearing Hausa names, but they also realized that those developments had their own advantages. With their Western education, the Igbo-Hausas stood a good chance of occupying important positions in the governments of their adopted states, and while in those positions they could be expected to protect the interest of their ethnic brothers, blood being said to be thicker than water.

CONTAINING RELIGIOUS AND ETHNIC CRISES

Another area in which Emir Ado Bayero's impact has been greatly felt is in containing religious and ethnic crises within his domain. Since the early 1980s when the Nigerian economy began to face difficulties, there has arisen in the urban areas a large number of unemployed or underemployed people. In Kano and other cities that had for a long time attracted ambitious able-bodied men from the rural areas and other surrounding cities and even neighboring countries, the downturn in the economy made for the rise of increasing frustration among this group. This is a group that appears disenchanted with the state for its failure to provide opportunities for its members to realize their goals. And every now and then, in the last twenty years, members of this group look for the slightest excuse to vent their anger on other groups who are wrongly perceived as the cause of their plight. In most cases, this group, even though a number of them do not come from Kano or its environs, are jealous of other Nigerians particularly from the Southern parts of the country who have also come to Kano in search of the proverbial golden fleece but who, unlike the Hausa migrants were actually making it. Thus, the economic success of the Southern migrants is a continuous source of envy to the migrants from the North. And for this reason, the latter group looks for the slightest excuse to make their Southern compatriots feel unwelcome in Kano. The expression of this feeling in the last twenty years has taken two forms: religious and ethnic crisis.

The long presence of settlers from other parts of the country in Kano has led to the rise of a significant population of

Christians in the state capital. Even long before colonial rule, Kano has respected the rights of non-Muslims resident in its territory to practice their religion. Indeed, the introduction of the Sabongari wards during colonial rule was to ensure that settlers from the Southern parts of Nigeria and from other West African colonies who were predominantly Christians were not restricted in their religious and other cultural practices. Due to the city's very strong Islamic tradition, living in the old walled city would have entailed just that.

In 1985, the peace and harmony that had for long characterized relationship between Kano's predominantly Muslim population and its minority Christians was seriously threatened. This came about as a result of a decision by the leadership of the Anglican church in Kano to pull down its over fifty-year-old church and put up in its place a more modern and bigger edifice. Incidentally, the old church happened to be right in front of Kano's second Juma'at mosque built sometime in 1970. When the news of that decision reached the Muslim community, its members resolved not to allow that to happen. It appeared that for as long as the Anglican church remained the small, inconspicuous edifice it had hitherto been, the Muslims tolerated its presence in front of the mosque. But when it was suggested that the church was going to be as big as, if not bigger than the mosque, the Muslims would not accept it. Tension filled the whole town. Then the Emir stepped in. He invited the religious leaders, both Muslims and Christians. It was not easy persuading the Christian leadership to abandon a piece of land that they had for over fifty years possessed legally simply because some Muslims could not tolerate the presence of a church near a mosque. Rationally, he understood the Christian leadership's adamant position on the matter. But as the leader of Kano, he needed to ensure that lasting peace prevailed. Prominent Kano Christians among them the late Ambassador John Mamman Garba and Justice Haruna Dandaura who have a lot of respect for the Emir understood the difficult position of the Emir and appealed to their colleagues to concede to the emir's request to move to an alternative site.[11] After the crisis had been settled, Emir Ado Bayero sought audience with the leadership of the Christian community in Kano and apologized to them for what happened and thanked them for their understanding and co-operation.[12]

On another occasion in 1991, the Christian community in Kano invited a renowned European evangelist Reinhard Bournke for a special crusade. About a week before his arrival, hundreds of thousands of posters were on all walls in Kano. No part of Kano was spared those posters, including the old city, which prided itself on being the custodian of the Kano culture. But a new dimension was added to the preparation to receive Bournke when about three days to his arrival hundreds of thousands of flyers were released to mostly youth specially invited from other states of the North to go and distribute. The flyers were printed in English, Arabic, Ajami, or Hausa in Arabic script and Hausa in English letters. The idea was to reach out to every person who could read. These youth, both male and female, took thousands of these flyers into the two main markets in Kano—Kurmi and Sabongari—and into the homes of Muslims. According to reports, they gave the flyers to everybody they saw, whether Muslim or Christian. Where Muslims had refused to collect the flyers, these overzealous youth were reported to have dropped them in their shops or the doorsteps of their homes. These activities of the Christians enraged the Muslims so much that on the day Bournke was to arrive Kano, the Muslims decided to go on rampage. Many churches were razed to the ground. Emir Ado Bayero stepped in. In a radio and televised broadcast, he criticized those who committed the arson in the name of Islam saying that what they did was against the teachings of Islam. He pointed out that Islam, as a religion of peace did not encourage indiscipline. He also criticized the Christians for their insensitivity and the reckless manner their youths went about distributing the flyers. Later during the day, he went round the city including the Sabongari area appealing for calm. He called both groups to order and normalcy was restored.

NOTES

1. Dr. Nnamdi Azikiwe, the President of Nigeria, was away in England when the military struck on January 15, 1966. By the time he returned to Nigeria, on February 25, 1966, Lt. Col. Ojukwu had been appointed Military Governor of Eastern Nigeria. Zik moved straight to the East. His first public reaction to the overthrow of the government of which he was the President was made fifty days after his return, on April 15, 1966, at Nsukka. In that reaction, Zik welcomed the military take-over, and accused the old regime of corruption, and nepotism. See New Nigerian of 16/4/66, p.1 "Zik Welcomes New Regime: Says Old one was Corrupt and Nepotic." It is difficult to establish Zik's motive for making that statement, as I could not get to interview him before he passed away on May 11, 1996. That statement, unfortunately, appeared to lend credence to the ethnic conspiracy theory that began to circulate after the coup. Apart from the one-sided killings, Zik's absence from the country at the time of the coup was used to justify the allegation that it was an ethnic plot. It is equally likely that Zik, who had moved to the East, was under pressure from his people to identify with the new government, hence that public reaction.
2. Chief Michael Agbamuche died in April 1998.
3. Interview with Chief Michael Agbamuche, Abuja, November 18, 1996.
4. Interview with Chief C.O. Ojukwu, Abuja, March 2, 1997.
5. The recognition of Biafra by Gabon and Ivory Coast had a more serious security implication for Nigeria than that of Zambia and Tanzania. Gabon and Ivory Coast

could be used (and they were actually used) as transit points for deliveries to Biafra as both countries are under two hours from Nigeria by air. Tanzania and Zambia's recognition, on the other hand, was more of a diplomatic loss, given their distance, at least six hours from Nigeria.

6.   For obvious reasons Leopold Sedar Senghor could not give recognition to Biafra. Senegal's population was predominantly Muslim, even though President Senghor was a Catholic. Biafra's portrayal of the war as a religious war made it politically suicidal for him to support it, much as he might have sympathized with the Biafran cause. Moreover, as we noted in chapter two, he needed Nigeria's friendship.

7.   Major-General Joe Garba noted that many years after the war, when he met James Callaghan, the British Foreign Secretary during the war years and complained that Britain let Nigeria down during the war, the Foreign Secretary told him that he thought they had done rather well considering the pressure on them to recognize and aid Biafra. Joe Garba, *Revolution in Nigeria: Another View*, (London, Africa Journal Limited, 1982), p.116.

8.   The management of the industrial properties exposed some Kano people, for the first time, to handling industrial machines. One of Kano's prominent printers and block makers of today, Alhaji Nasiru Ahali learned the two trades when he won the care-taker-ship of an abandoned printing press and a block-making machine.

9.   Sahih al-Bukhari

10. Interview with an Igbo-Hausa. The interviewee has requested anonymity.

11. For details see O.F. Ibrahim, "Religion and Politics in the Transition: A View from the North" in Diamond, L., et al eds., *Transition Without End: The Babangida Years*, (Colorado, Lynne Rienner, 1987).

12. Interview with Justice Haruna Dandaura, Abuja, June 30, 1999.

THE REVOLUTIONARY YEARS 1966-1979

THE MILITARY AND TRADITIONAL AUTHORITY REFORMS

From his ascession to the throne of Kano in 1963 to the collapse of the First Republic, Emir Ado Bayero ruled Kano Emirate. As the head of the Kano Native Authority, NA, the Emir exercised executive, legislative, and indeed judicial powers over a population of over four million. The Northern Region government graded his court "A Unlimited." That, in effect, meant that the Emir's court had the status of unlimited jurisdiction in all cases—civil as well as criminal. It could pass the death sentence, though this was subject to confirmation by the Regional government. The Emir, also through the NA, appointed the judges of the thirty other *alkali* courts in the NA.[1] The promotion and discipline of the judges were, in the final analysis, the prerogative of the Emir.

As the chief executive of the Kano NA, the Emir presided over meetings at which by-laws were made for the good governance of the Native Authority area. He also determined how much tax was to be collected in the year and then shared the tax burden among the districts in his NA. Furthermore, through his representatives at the grassroots—the district, village and ward heads—he determined how much each taxable adult would pay and went ahead and collected the same when due. All public land was held in trust by him and he or his representatives allocated parcels to individuals and groups

for residential, commercial, industrial, farming and other purposes, as they saw fit. Finally, as the head of the NA, he had
full responsibility for the maintenance of law and order,
peace, and the security of lives and property. To fulfill those
obligations he had, in addition to the judiciary, the Native
Authority Police, and the prisons under him.

That was how powerful Emir Ado Bayero was on the eve
of the first military incursion into politics in January 1966.
But thirteen years of military rule changed all that. By the
time the military finally left the political scene in October
1979, they had succeeded in effecting fundamental socio-
political reforms that completely changed the position of the
once all-powerful emirs of Northern Nigeria into mere fig-
ureheads.

It is ironic that the most revolutionary changes that
stripped the emirs of every constitutional power that they
had enjoyed were introduced by the military, an institution
that has generally been believed to be very dependent on
them to govern. It is argued that when the military strikes, one
of the first measures it takes is to proscribe political parties
and other political structures like parliaments and the executive council. The professional politicians are held at bay
and the traditional rulers come to assume the functions of
the proscribed political parties. They mobilize grassroots support for the military governments' programs. The military
governments also rely on them to act as link between the
government and the people and vice versa. Yet, it was during
the period of military rule that the traditional rulers in the
North "lost out." What happened? Were the reforms carried
out behind their backs? Did they just wake up and find that
changes were being effected, and that it was too late to
protest? Or did they protest, but to no avail? How did Emir
Ado Bayero see the changes, and what were his reactions? In
the final analysis, how did Emir Ado Bayero perceive those
changes and their implications for the long-term survival of
the institution?

For the six months that he was in power, General Aguiyi Ironsi distanced his administration from the politicians who had been toppled. That left him with only the traditional rulers as a link with the masses of the people. As expected, the traditional rulers enjoyed the new prominence they were getting.[2] But the Ironsi regime did not last long. When General Gowon became the Commander-in-Chief, he decided to court the politicians as well as the traditional rulers. He embarked on wide-ranging consultations with various opinion leaders and interests in the country on the way forward for the nation. Among the opinion leaders he consulted in the North were leaders of the proscribed opposition parties, notably the NEPU and the United Middle Belt Congress, UMBC. In fact, the President of the NEPU, Mallam Aminu Kano was appointed a member of Gowon's cabinet, while Tanko Yakasai, also a leader of the NEPU, was appointed to the first cabinet of Kano State, headed by Deputy Police Commissioner Alhaji Audu Bako. Joseph Tarka, the leader of the UMBC was also in Gowon's cabinet. These people, among others, used their proximity to the government to highlight the ills of the NA system, as it existed at that time.

General Gowon, in the face of the national crisis, sought to introduce reforms that would take care of the grievances of the masses of the people especially in the North, where the democratic space was most constricted. But Gowon was cautious of embarking on any adventure that could alienate the powerful traditional rulers from his government. He reasoned that it would help if he was able to carry some of the important traditional rulers along before he introduced the reforms. He thought of discussing the matter with the Emir of Kano. But then Emir Ado Bayero personified the very system that was to be reformed. He presided over the most powerful NA in the country, and as such could not be expected to easily give in to the disempowerment of that system. Yet, Emir Ado Bayero was also the most exposed of all the emirs and chiefs. He had been educated in Nigeria and in England. He had twice submitted himself to the test of the popular will, and on both occasions, he had enjoyed a landslide victory. He had represented Nigeria at the highest diplomatic level in Dakar, as Ambassador; and he had seen, on his wide travels, how socio-political reforms had paved the way for socio-economic development in other countries. These personal characteristics, Gowon thought, would help to lessen his task of persuading Emir Ado Bayero to support the reforms.

The meeting with Emir Ado Bayero was unusually brief, given the importance Gowon attached to the subject matter. Gowon had expected to make a strong case for the reforms, perhaps giving personal guarantees to protect some of the interests of the emirs. But he found out that that was not necessary. Emir Ado Bayero clearly understood the need for reforms, as a means of moving forward. All he advised was that the reforms should be gradual, so that there would be no serious dislocation in the society. Furthermore, he advised that it would be helpful if some of the emirs were apprised of the government's plans, and perhaps asked for their suggestions. Gowon agreed that the reform should be introduced in stages. He also agreed that each region (and later state) should be allowed to introduce its own reforms taking into consideration the socio-cultural peculiarities of the state. Finally, Gowon agreed that Emir Ado Bayero should go out and intimate his brother emirs about the proposed reforms.

Thus in a series of reforms between 1967 and 1971, the Federal Military Government appropriated to itself exclusive control over the police and the prisons, while the judiciary was placed within the concurrent jurisdiction of the State and Federal governments. This move involved the simultaneous abolition of the Native Authority Police and the Native Authority Prison Departments. The Emir's Judicial Council and, with it, his judicial authority were supplanted by the Kano State Area Courts Edict of 1967. That Edict submerged the powers of the Alkali courts into the Area Courts of the State Judiciary, which was headed by the State Chief Judge—an appointee of the State Government. The loss of power over the police, prisons, and the judiciary deprived the Emir of the most important outward manifestations of his authority.

Other measures undertaken by the military regime that appeared to have had an adverse effect on the emirate system were the series of Local Government Reforms of 1968, 1972, and 1976. Under the 1968 Local Government Reform, the term Native Authority (NA) was replaced with Local Government Authority (L.G.A.), which referred essentially to the same territorial administration. Kano State thus came to comprise four LGAs, namely Kano, Kazaure, Hadejia and Gumel. In furtherance of that reform, the State Government zoned the state into eight administrative areas. Kano LGA had five of these, while each of the other three LGAs had one. The State Government appointed zonal administrative officers for each of the administrative areas. They were made the accounting officers for the LGAs to which they were posted. That automatically meant that the emirs were no longer the chief executives of the LGAs. In Kazaure, Hadejia and Gumel LGAs the Zonal Administrative Officers became the accounting officers of their LGAs. In the case of Kano LGA, with five zones, the Zonal Administrative Officers were the accounting officers of the districts that made up their zones. All of them reported directly to the Secretary to the State Government. Their role was to act as links between the people at the grassroots and the State Government— explaining government policies to the masses and informing government of the views and needs of the masses of the people. By that action, in effect, one of the major functions of the district, village, and ward heads was formally vested in the government-appointed administrative officers.

While the Gowon administration shied away from introducing a national local government reform, preferring to leave each state to introduce the reforms it could contain, the Murtala-Obasanjo regime that came to power on July 29, 1975 made it clear from its inception that a major re-organization of the local government system throughout the country was part of its transition program. True to its word, a major national reform of the local government system was undertaken in 1976 and General Olusegun Obasanjo credits Emir Ado Bayero for the significant role he played in that process.

FURTHER REFORMS

Upon assuming office as the Chief of Staff Supreme Headquarters in the Murtala-Obasanjo government, Obasanjo whose office was responsible for state administration, including all the reforms, invited Emir Ado Bayero to Dodan Barracks, Lagos, the seat of the Federal Government, to discuss the proposed national reform of the local government system. General Obasanjo constituted a small committee comprising Emir Ado Bayero, the Etsu Nupe, Alhaji Umaru Sanda Ndayako and Mallam Yaya Abubakar, at that time the Permanent Secretary, Political Division of the Cabinet Office, Lagos, to examine proposals submitted to the Federal Government and make recommendations. After many weeks of study and deliberations, the committee submitted its report to Obasanjo. The report endorsed virtually all the recommendations for the democratization of the local government system. Obasanjo was pleased to find that the committee made recommendations that were even more far-reaching than were contained in the proposal submitted to it. An enlarged meeting of traditional rulers and other interest groups was held where Obasanjo, who had by now succeeded Murtala Muhammed after the latter was assassinated in an abortive coup on February 13, 1976, acknowledged the contributions of people like Emir Ado Bayero in the process leading to the formulation of the new policy. According to Obasanjo, Emir Ado Bayero's role in mobilizing support for the reform among his colleagues was instrumental to the success of the program. [3]

When it came into force, the reform made it possible for the first time in the North for chairmen of the councils to be selected from among the elected men.[4] The council, which comprised elected and nominated members in the proportion of 74 percent to 26 percent respectively, listed three candidates in order of preference, which was then sent to the state governor through the emirate council. The Emir could change the order of preference, but he could not include a name that was not originally there. Approval was then sought from the Governor. The supervisory councilors were also elected by members of the council, even though their confirmation did not require the governor's approval. These largely elected councils were given most of the functions and powers that the NAs had been exercising up to that time, while the state government took over the rest.

With the usurpation of virtually all the powers of the NA by the state government and local councils, the traditional emirate structure was redefined and given new functions. In each previous NA, an Emirate or Traditional Council was established with the Emir or Chief as chairman. The Council had the following functions:

a) Giving general advice to the local government council concerned;

b) Advising the local government council concerned on proposed development plans;

c) Assisting in the collection of taxes as might be required;

d) Advising on religious matters where appropriate;

e) Promoting and advising on arts and culture;

f) Subject to the law of the state, dealing with and advising on chieftaincy matters and traditional titles and offices;

g) Deliberating and expressing opinions to any organization on any matter which it deemed to be of importance to the area as a whole or which might be referred to it by the government or other organization;

h) Assisting in the mobilization of human and material resources towards self-reliance, community development and welfare within the area; and

i) Such other functions as the Local Government Council may from time to time refer to it.

These functions were incorporated into the 1979 Constitution. The Third Schedule to the Constitution, Part II, Section B also states that "nothing in this Schedule shall be construed as conferring any executive, legislative or judicial powers on a Traditional Council."

Just as the 1976 Reform did away with the emirate as an administrative unit without abolishing the office of emir, so did it abolish the traditional districts as administrative units without abolishing the office of district head. Instead, the office of district head was converted to a public office. That, in effect, meant that the office of district head was, in principle, open to anyone whom the local government service commission deemed fit to occupy it. District heads became employees of the Local Government Service Commission, and they were required to show loyalty to the local governments they were posted to, not their respective emirs. According to the decree on the local government reform, district heads could be transferred to any part of the state (even outside their own emirates of origin).[5] That provision like others in the decree illustrates the emirs' weakened grip on their respective district heads.

The reform also established a State Council of Chiefs at the state level, comprising selected functionaries of each of the emirates or traditional councils in the state. At the national level, it made selected traditional rulers, one from each state, members of the National Council of State. This council comprised of the Head of State, his Deputy, all former Heads of State, all former Chief Justices, the President of the Senate and the House Speaker, all State Governors, and the Attorney General of the Federation. All three councils, to which the traditional rulers belonged, had merely advisory powers. The National Council of State advised the President, the State Council of Chiefs advised the Governor, while the Emirate Council advised the Local Government Chairman. In all cases, the advice could be accepted, ignored, or rejected outright.

The guidelines had also specified that the population of local government areas should be between 150,000 and

800,000. That being so, Kano LGA, with a population of about five million, had to be fragmented. The result, even if unintended, was the break-up of Kasar Kano, or Kano Emirate, initially into sixteen local Government Areas.[6] That, in turn, threatened the organic unity and undermined the institutional and symbolic basis of the emirate as epitomized in the person of the emir.[7]

When Kano city became the capital of the new Kano State in 1968 and also the capital of Kano Metropolitan Local Government Authority later in 1976, its traditional role as the emirate capital was over-shadowed. Others now enjoyed some status symbols that were previously reserved for the Emir alone within Kano, like the use of a flag on his official car, or escorts and sirens to herald his arrival at any function, like the Governor or the State Police Commissioner. Equally, the very presence of the military governor, state commissioners, and permanent secretaries controlling the day-to-day governmental activities in Kano tended to relegate the formerly all-powerful Emir to the background. Added to these was the fact that when Audu Bako assumed duty in Kano as Governor, he came with a clearly defined strategy of how to recruit his cabinet. That strategy was informed by Governor Bako's belief that, although seemingly homogeneous, Kano State was a plural society with various competing interests. Thus, the governor saw the need to form a government that was representative of the various interests within the state.

He identified eight interests that made up the diversity of Kano State and proceeded to create a cabinet that was representative of those interests. The interests were: the four emirates of the state, the disbanded NPC, the disbanded NEPU, traditional institutions, Native Authority workers, the civil service, traders and industrialists. Having designated the interests that he believed had a crucial stake in how the state was governed, Audu Bako approached Mallam Aminu Kano, the four emirs of the state, and his friends and asked them to assist him pick the right individuals to represent those interests.

All appointments reserved for the emirates and traditional institutions were given to the various emirs to dispense. Thus, Umaru Gumel, a Gumel prince, Muhammadu, the Magajin Garin Kazaure, and Muhammadu Gauyama, the Madaki of Hadejia were nominated by their respective emirs. Kano Emirate was not represented as such, but that was offset by the fact that all representatives of the other interests were chosen from among people of Kano Emirate and most of them were related to the ruling families of Kano Emirate. For example, Alhaji Muhtari Adnan, who represented traditional institutions of the state as a whole, was also the Sarkin Bai of Kano and one of the four kingmakers of the emirate. In addition, Yusuf Maitama Sule, who represented the old guard NPC, was the Dan Masanin Kano, and was from the Yolawa ruling family of Kano. Sani Gezawa, who represented the NA interests, was the Mai Unguwar Mundubawa of Kano. Baba Danbappa, who represented the industrialist interest, was related to the Kano royal family through marriage, while Inuwa Dutse, who represented the civil service, was related to the Dutse ruling family. Inuwa Dutse and Tanko Yakasai were said to have been recommended by Mallam Aminu Kano. Aminu Dantata and Baba Danbappa were Bako's own choice. Even though Governor Bako did not give Emir Ado Bayero much latitude to influence key appointments in his government, he did him the courtesy of informing him in advance of making public some key appointments.[8] The Sarkin Bai, Alhaji Muhtari Adnan, who was the pioneer Commissioner for Education of Kano State, for example, recalls that he first heard of his appointment to the Audu Bako cabinet from Emir Ado Bayero. The Emir had summoned him to the palace, where he told him that he had been selected as commissioner in the state government. Twenty-four hours later, the government released the list of the state executive council. And another twenty-four hours later he received a formal letter of appointment.

Increasingly, it became obvious that the centre of power had shifted from the NA office opposite the Emir's Palace to the State Government Secretariat, along Post Office Road, where the new ministries were located. It was there that employments were given. It was there that the millions of Naira of the newfound oil revenue allocated to Kano State as its share were disbursed. It was there that contracts were awarded. At a higher level, it was the Military Governor's Office and not the Emir's Palace that became the locus of recruitment into key positions of state, or representatives of the state at the national level. It also offered the fastest opportunity of making wealth. These realities were not lost on the emerging contractors, professionals, as well as educated and business elite of Kano.

Following on the heels of the 1976 Local Government Reforms, came the Land Reform of 1978. Although the provisions of the reform were not any different from the land tenure law in operation in Kano at that time, they had one important point of difference. Whereas before the reform public land was held in trust by the emir or his representatives, who disposed of it as they saw fit, the reform divested the emir of those powers. The State Governor was now the trustee and allotee of urban lands, while in the rural areas, the chairmen of the local government councils were vested with these powers. In some of the states, the governments established Ministries of Lands to exercise those powers vested in the governor. In others, a Bureau for Lands was established in the Governor's office, while in yet others, special committees—Land Allocation Advisory Committees—were established and given that responsibility.

KANO EMIRATE'S POLITICAL DISPENSATION ON THE EVE OF THE SECOND REPUBLIC

In summary, by the time the soldiers finally left the political scene on October 1, 1979, Emir Ado Bayero was everything but what we described him at the beginning of this chapter. Yet, as we have seen, he played key roles in all the processes that eventually led to his disempowerment. Why would anyone want to lose power? Did he not realize that he owed Gidan Rumfa a duty to preserve its one thousand years of history? Did he not realize that Kano people cherish and are indeed proud of that most important institution that he headed?

When the winds of change began to blow after the first coup, Emir Ado Bayero had given these questions very serious thought. He had reasoned that the character of the Nigerian State was changing very fast, and Kano was not immune to those influences. The age-old value system that had distinguished the Kano man from others was fast giving way to materialism and other un-Islamic mores. The desire to make money, by any means, was beginning to characterize the life of the people and the state was becoming an avenue for making quick money through very dubious means. Then Ado Bayero also recognized that there were many structural limitations to correcting the ills. The judicial system, the English Common Law, which replaced the *shari'ah* was a man-made law and therefore subject to human error.[9] No matter how determined a leader entrusted with political authority may be to do the bidding of the *shari'ah*, he could only achieve his aim within the context of the provisions of the nation's constitution; and that constitution was not Islamic but secular. If the emir were to continue to wield political power, he would be expected to use that power to defend or project issues that Islam might not encourage. Ado Bayero therefore reasoned that in the circumstances it was better for one to be distanced from political power.

Furthermore, the Emir had hearkened to the religious teaching against seeking, or being keen to enjoy, the authority of ruling. The Prophet, Muhammad S.A.W., had said, "Do not seek to be a ruler, for if you are given authority on your demand then you will be held responsible for it, but if you are given it without asking for it, then you will be helped by Allah in it..."[10] In another *hadith* the Prophet had said, "You people will be keen to have the authority of ruling which will be a thing of regret for you on the day of Resurrection..."[11]

With these *ahadith* at the back of his mind, Emir Ado Bayero had asked himself why he should insist on holding on to his powers. He reflected that perhaps those reforms, coming at the time they did, were Allah's way of protecting traditional institutions from the dangers inherent in exercising power in an increasingly corrupt socio-political and economic environment.

Deprived of legislative, judicial, and executive powers, the Emir could not be blamed for the pervasive ills of the society. In contrast to the time before the reforms, when drunks dared not walk the streets of Kano, or women of easy virtue advertise themselves without fear of severe sanctions from the emir, (especially during the time of Emir Ado Bayero's elder brother, Emir Muhammadu Sanusi), the series of reforms absolved the Emir of any responsibility for the reappearance of these evils.

While many traditional rulers were protesting what they perceived as policies designed to marginalize them, and make them irrelevant in the governance of the country, Emir Ado Bayero felt the reforms were truly the saving grace of the institution of traditional rulership. While many were clamoring for some clearly defined constitutional role for them in the 1979 Constitution, Emir Ado Bayero openly opposed any such prescription. His position was that if the occupants of the offices of traditional rulers could not make themselves relevant in their own communities without the government decreeing so, then they had truly lost relevance.

Even though he had always been conscious of the fact that the *raison d'être* of his office is Islam[12], Alhaji Ado Bayero saw the changes of the late 1960s and 1970s as an opportunity to go back to the source of his legitimacy and authority and find relevance there. The Nigerian State, being secular, increasingly capitalistic, and driven by the profit motive, could not be expected to faithfully protect Islam. Emir Ado Bayero therefore began to devote more of his time to Islam—studying it, calling people to it, and promoting it. On his own, and with some of Kano's established Islamic scholars, he spent hours studying various aspects of Islam.

Even though he was the Emir and by now approaching fifty, he was humble enough to take lessons from some of Kano's acclaimed Islamic scholars, namely Sheikh Nasiru Kabara and Mallam Dan Amu, the Chief Imam of Kano City mosque. Both scholars were also considerate enough to go to the palace for the tutorials.[13]

The Emir also began to devote many of his public functions to Islam. He encouraged the wealthy to spend their wealth for the sake of Allah by building mosques, Islamiyya schools, and other projects that would benefit the people. He used every opportunity to make exhortations to the people to live in accordance with the teachings of Islam, and the people responded with enthusiasm. Many wealthy people began to build mosques and Islamiyya schools in Kano and other parts of the emirate, and communities also began to embark on self-help projects, building mosques and Islamiyya schools. Emir Ado Bayero encouraged communities that embarked on self-help projects by striving to be present at the Appeal Fund Launching Ceremonies and in most cases; he was the chairman of the occasion, or the Royal father of the Day. He never failed to make his own modest personal contributions. On some occasions, he made donations on behalf of the Kano Emirate Council. Soon enough, the Emir's daily schedule began to get crowded, since he was being invited almost on a weekly basis to go and formally open mosques and Islamiyya schools in all parts of the emirate. The Emir's evangelical role was also recognized beyond his emirate that Katsina, Katagum, Lapai and Kaduna, among many others invited him to either launch the Appeal Funds for the building of their mosques or to open their new Juma'at mosques.

So important did the Emir take his new mission that everything else was considered secondary. In fact, in 1998 Emir Ado Bayero considered his presence at the formal opening of the College for Islamic Education at Kura, some thirty-five kilometers from Kano, important enough to warrant his excusing himself from a meeting of the National Council of Traditional Rulers and Leaders of Thought in Abuja in order to be there.[14] Much earlier, in 1984, Emir Ado Bayero, in his Sallah address to the people of Kano, renounced the title traditional ruler in preference for religious leader. According to the Emir, he would answer the title of traditional ruler only in so far as Islam is understood to be the tradition of Kano people.

In addition to encouraging the building of Islamiyya schools and mosques, Emir Ado Bayero also promoted *tajweed*, the science of reciting the Holy Qur'an in Islamiyya schools. After the interest of students had been aroused in that aspect of Islam, *musabaqa*t, or competition was introduced among the various Islamiyya schools in Kano State. By the early 1980s, the practice had spread to other states of the federation. That brought out some of the best reciters of the Holy Qur'an in the country. In 1987, Nigeria felt confident enough to enter the world competition on the recitation of the Holy Qur'an for the first time. Subsequently the nation's representatives did Nigeria proud by beating all other competing countries, including Saudi Arabia, to emerge the best *tajweed* students in the world in the competition held in Makkah al Mukarrama, Saudi Arabia in 1998.

Thus by the time the Second Republic was ushered in, Emir Ado Bayero had redefined his role in society. He was no more an agent of the state, did not rule, and did not wield any political power. It was the soldiers, the politicians, and the civil servants who ruled. And he was very satisfied with that arrangement. He saw his role as essentially one of adviser to the powers-that-be, and a guide to the masses of the people. Emir Ado Bayero aptly summarizes the changes his office underwent in those revolutionary years thus, "*Da mu muke yi. Akazo ana yi da mu. To yanzu lokaci yazo, sai dai ayi a fada mana.*" "In the past we were the ones doing it [governance], then came a time when we were just partners [in governance]. Now time has come when it is done and we are simply briefed [about what has been done]."

These fundamental changes notwithstanding, Emir Ado Bayero's stature did not diminish in the eyes of his people. Indeed, that apparent impotence, which distanced him from the state, seemed to have brought him nearer to the people. Many more people could now go to him with their complaints about some agencies of the state like the police, the judiciary, or their employers without any fear that he was part of the system. On his part, he always intervened where he believed agents of the state or other influential persons had wronged his subjects, and in most cases, his intervention yielded positive results. That is not surprising, as the Emir is a skilled administrator who knows the civic rights of citizens as well as the limitations of the state. Moreover, his Council has always comprised some of the most eminent Nigerians in their various fields of vocation. At present, for example, the Council comprises, among other eminent Nigerians, Alhaji Mahe Bashir Wali, the Walin Kano since 1992, who retired from the Nigeria Police Force as Deputy Inspector General. There is the Makaman Kano, Alhaji Abdullahi Sarki Ibrahim, who was Principal Secretary to General Sani Abacha when he was Head of State. There are many others who were close to various Heads of State, such as the Galadiman Kano, Alhaji Tijjani Hashim, who was a godfather to General Ibrahim Babangida, Head of State from 1985 to 1993. There is also the Jarman Kano, Alhaji Muhammadu Adamu Dankabo, who was a confidant and business partner of General Sani Abacha, Head of State between 1993 and 1998. He also has on his Council such statesmen as the Sarkin Bai, Alhaji Muhtari Adnan, a former Party Chief Whip in the Federal Legislature in the First Republic. There is the Magajin Garin Kano, Alhaji Inuwa Wada, who was Works and later Defense Minister of Nigeria in the First Republic. And finally Alhaji Sule Gaya, the Sarkin Fada and Minister of Local Government in the defunct Northern Region, among others whose vast experiences he could tap.

In addition to these, there are also younger professionals in the Emir's Council from whom he could always seek opinions. The *Sarkin Dawakin Tsakar Gida*, Alhaji Sanusi Ado Bayero, is a trained lawyer, the Tafida, Alhaji Nasir Ado Bayero, is a communications expert. In addition, there are others such as Aminu Ahmad, the Zanna; Garba A.D., the Talba; Gambo Danpass, the Dansara; who have made their marks in other fields, like commerce, for which Kano is renowned. Equally strategic for the Emir is the presence of the older generation councilors who, like him, are well versed in Islam, such as the Wazirin Kano Alhaji Shehu Gidado. The senior councilor and Wamban Kano Alhaji Abbas Sanusi's administrative skills are also readily available for the Emir to tap. There is also the young *Sarkin Dawaki Mai Tuta*, Aminu Babba Dan Agundi, who like his late father brooked no nonsense from anyone, including governors of Kano State. On many occasions in the past the elder Babba Dan Agundi had gone to the Government House and seriously tongue-lashed Governor Rimi when the latter was behaving in ways perceived as hostile to the Emir of Kano.[15]

At the state level, but for the brief period between October 1979 and April 1983 when Rimi ruled Kano State, Emir Ado Bayero has always had people who loved and respected him in positions of authority. Nearly half of the members of the Sani Bello Cabinet were in one way or the other related to the Emir. Such commissioners as Mahe Bashir Wali, Abubakar Bashir Wali, Sule Gaya, and Muhammadu Maude, among others were all related to the Kano aristocracy. In other words, though deprived of political power, the Emir was still able to get things done through his goodwill.

That, then, is the picture of the position of Emir Ado Bayero in the political system of Kano State on the eve of the Second Republic.

NOTES

1. For the list, grades and status of the 31 Native Courts operating in Kano at that time see *Northern Nigeria Year Book 1966,* (Zaria, Gaskiya Corporation, 1966), p.88.

2. While the government was known to rely heavily on traditional institutions for support, a few individual traditional rulers were suspected of disloyalty by the Head of State.

3. Interview with General Olusegun Obasanjo, Katsina May 12, 1999.

4. The suffrage was limited to men in Northern Nigeria during those elections. Women were allowed the vote for the first time during the 1979 elections.

5. *Guidelines for Local Government Reforms,* (Kaduna, Government Printer, 1976) Appendix A.

6. Following the 1976 Reform, Kano State was split initially into sixteen and later twenty local government areas. Sixteen of these were in Kano emirate, two in Hadejia, and one each in Kazaure and Gumel. For details of the politics of local government creation in Kano state during that period see Muhammadu Uba Adamu, *The Evolution of Local Government System in West Africa: A Comparative Study of Nigeria and the Republic of Niger,* Unpublished Ph.D. Thesis, Post Graduate School, Bayero University, Kano, 1997.

7. Yaya Aliyu, "As Seen in Kaduna" in Keith Panter-Brick, ed. *Soldiers and Oil: The Political Transformation of Nigeria,* (London, Frank Cass, 1978).

8. Alhaji S.A. Tanko Yakasai traces the problems between Emir Ado Bayero and Governor Audu Bako to this among other reasons. Int. Kano 12:04:97.

9. At the approach of self-government for the North, the Northern Premier, Sir Ahmadu Bello had commissioned a body of jurists comprising Islamic scholars from Sudan. Egypt and Nigeria to review the laws of Northern Nigeria to accomodate certain aspects of the Shari'ah that deal with such matters as marriage and inheritance. To a large extent, the revised laws—called Penal Code—did away with most of the Shari'ah— prescribed punishments for criminal offenses. For example, the penalty for *hadd* offenses—offenses punishable by death

according to the Shari'ah were, with the exception of murder, made prison terms. Similarly, instead of amputation of the wrist for stealing, the penalty was a fine or jail term or both. Although *alkalai* courts were to continue to operate in the Northern Region, litigants were free to appeal against their judgments. Thus, it was clear that the Shari'ah was made subservient to the man-made laws of Nigeria—the Constitution.

10. Sahih al-Bukhari, vol. 9, Book 89, hadith 260.
11. Op. cit., hadith 262.
12. Evidenced for example, in his title, *Amir ul mu'umineen*, leader of the faithful, which was anglicized and shortened to Emir.
13. The practice of the Emir taking lessons in religion has continued even with the approach of his seventieth birthday.
14. It was at that meeting that the elders and traditional rulers endorsed the candidature of General Abacha for the Presidency of Nigeria from October 1, 1998. See Chapter Ten.
15. Governor Rimi had a lot of respect for Babba Dan Agundi for his role in the NEPU.

THE CHALLENGE FROM THE PEOPLE'S REDEMPTION PARTY

GOVERNMENT OF KANO STATE 1979-1983

When General Olusegun Obasanjo lifted the nearly thirteen year-old ban on partisan politics in September 1978, the same old political parties of the First Republic that had been earlier proscribed, re-surfaced and were registered under different names. Chief Obafemi Awolowo's Action Group of the First Republic resurfaced as the Unity Party of Nigeria (UPN), while Dr. Nnamdi Azikiwe's National Council of Nigerian Citizens (NCNC) resurrected as the Nigerian People's Party (NPP). In the same vein Mallam Aminu Kano's Northern Elements Progressive Union (NEPU) was reborn as the People's Redemption Party (PRP) and the late Sardaunan Sokoto, Ahmadu Bello's Northern People's Congress (NPC) resurfaced as the National Party of Nigeria (NPN) with the Turakin Sokoto, Alhaji Shehu Shagari, as its presidential candidate. The Great Nigeria People's Party (GNPP), led by Alhaji Waziri Ibrahim, was an offshoot of the NPP.

The NEPU, as noted in the introduction, espoused an ideology that was against traditional institutions. The PRP during the Second Republic trod the same path and gave vent to the same rhetoric but in a changed socio-political environment. It claimed to be dedicated to the emancipation of the *talakawa* from "domination," "exploitation," and "servitude" by the Northern oligarchy. The analysis of the PRP concerning the nature and characteristics of the *talakawa* as a class remained essentially the same as that made by the NEPU some quarter of a century earlier. But the PRP noted a change in the nature and characteristics of the ruling class; hence their change in terminology of "Northern aristocracy," which the NEPU had used, to "Northern oligarchy." The essential difference between the two, according to the PRP, was that the Northern aristocracy had been wholly dependent on the NA system for its power, and entrance into that class was narrowly restricted, largely through ascription. The Northern oligarchy on the other hand was more broad-based, in the sense that apart from birth other social criteria such as wealth, Western education, position within the State and Federal civil services, the armed forces and parastatals opened the way for easier membership of that class.

In the policies and programs of both the NEPU and the PRP, special reference was made to traditional rulers who were made pointed targets of criticism. In the analysis of the NEPU the traditional rulers or the "Northern aristocracy" had constituted unto themselves a class, the dominant class; and the *talakawa* constituted the other class, the dominated class. NEPU was to dedicate itself to the emancipation of the latter class. The PRP, likewise, identified two classes in Nigeria "locked in a grim struggle for survival." The general program of the PRP stated that:

> Two great forces face each other and are locked in grim strug-
> gle for survival and ascendancy. On the one side, the forces of
> privilege are resolved to protect their interests at all costs under
> the existing social order. These are the conservatives, because
> their political stand is to protect, retain, and sustain the existing
> social order. On the other side, forces of the people are deter-
> mined to replace the existing social order that harbors so much
> hardship and frustration for them with a new social order in
> which there will be equality, liberty, freedom from want, and
> social justice. These are the progressives, because their politi-
> cal stand is to replace a system of oppression and exploitation
> with a new society that guarantees a free and fuller life for all.
> The constant and ever deepening struggle between the forces

of conservatism on the one hand and those of progress on the other is the prime moving force of contemporary Nigerian life.[1]

The PRP is described in the program as the:

> Vanguard of the people in their historic march to establish a new social order which will completely liberate every Nigerian from feudal shackles, from economic exploitation, and privation, from denial of human rights, from ignorance, disease, squalor and want.

According to the PRP the remnants of feudal shackles as they existed in Northern Nigeria in the late 1970s were the members of the traditional ruling class (or the *sarakuna*) of the emirates, namely the emirs, the district, village and ward heads. It was from these functionaries that the PRP promised to liberate the *talakawa*.

Whereas the 1959 Election Manifesto of the NEPU was silent on the issue of traditional rulers, the PRP position was clearly stated in Article 6 Part 5 of the Party's 1979 Election Manifesto thus:

> The problem of chieftaincy in the country has not been seriously studied, let alone scientifically resolved. The chief, according to our tradition is the apex authority in his community. He is the spokesman of his people. He has no will other than the wish of his people. A PRP government will restore chieftaincy to its pristine democratic functions, compatible with respect for fundamental human rights. The authority of the chief will be recognized in the following fields:
>
> i.   Community development
> ii. Maintenance of order and security in their community.
> iii. Settlement of family disputes in the traditional way.
> iv. Preservation and development of the culture of the community.

Elements of continuity from NEPU to PRP included the tradition of protest against the *sarakuna* class, the composition of the leadership of the two parties, and their programs.

Whereas the continuity in the tradition of protest against traditional institutions as well as the parties' programs is fairly clear, the continuity in leadership was not that straightforward. This was because unlike in the First Republic where a political party could limit its electoral focus to only one Region, the electoral laws of the Second Republic compelled political parties to be national in outlook. Section 79 (1) of Electoral Decree No. 73 of 1977 stated that:

> The Constitution and Rules of a Political Party shall ensure that members of the Executive Committee or other Governing Body reflect the federal character.

It further states in subsection 2:

> For the purpose of this section, the members of the Executive Committee or other Governing Body of a Political Party shall be deemed to reflect the federal character of Nigeria if the members belong to different states not being less in number than two-thirds of all the states comprising the federation.

That requirement accounted for an important discontinuity in the composition of the national leadership, but not necessarily the membership and support, of the two parties. New faces from the Southern parts of the country appeared in the national leadership of the PRP.[2] But within the North, the leadership was markedly the same, especially among the founding members of the PRP. Mallam Aminu Kano, the President-General of the NEPU was until his death on Sunday April 17, 1983 the leader of the PRP. Other founding members and activists of the NEPU such as Lawan Dambazau, Mudi Sipikin, Gambo Sawaba, Asabe Reza, Muhammadu Abubakar Rimi, Adamu Gaya, and others were either founding members of the PRP or became active members.

Instances abound where the leadership of the PRP had proudly referred to the party as the reincarnation of the defunct NEPU. For example, Governor Muhammadu Abubakar Rimi in a speech on his first anniversary in office said:

The present struggle between the PRP and the NPN is an extension of the ideological conflict that has existed in this country
since the early fifties between the aristocratic bourgeoisie elements and their benefactors on the one hand, and the forces
demanding for positive changes on the other... Furthermore, it
must be recognized that the PRP, which has its roots in the former NEPU, is a front-line nationalist organization.[3]

In another place Rimi made an even more direct linkage
between the PRP and the NEPU when he pointed out that:

Many of us in the PRP have suffered imprisonment, beating,
torture, and maltreatment in the hands of the British colonialists
and their Nigerian successors. The PRP did not therefore emerge
from a vacuum. It came out of a long tradition of resistance to
feudal and colonial oppression... In our party, we have many
graduates who are highly honored and respected because they
are graduates. But they are not university graduates. They are
graduates of a different kind. They are graduates of colonial
prisons. Graduates of Native Authority prisons....[4]

Other PRP leaders—Mallam Aminu Kano, Lawan
Dambazau, Mudi Sipikin, etc. have all at one time or another
made reference to the linkage between the NEPU and the
PRP.[5]

Although the program of the PRP differs slightly in terms
of social and geographical horizons from that of the NEPU,
its perception of the roots of the people's problems and hence
its analysis of those problems was essentially the same as
NEPU's. This fact may explain the continued theme of feudalism and traditional institutions in the PRP program, while
in fact the said ills of feudalism or traditional chieftaincy
were almost alien to other Nigerian societies like the Igbo, the
Tiv, and to a lesser extent the Yoruba. The point is that the
PRP electoral focus was still the North, where remnants of
feudalism and some aspects of traditional institutions were
live political issues. These were seized upon by the party and
projected as national issues. In the same way the UPN made
free education a national campaign issue even though education was already virtually free in the North in 1979.[6] The

point is that the interest of the electoral focus of each party was projected as the national interest.

In retrospect, it would appear that the most significant contribution of the NEPU to the development of Northern Nigeria, even though it never attained power, was that it seized upon the ills of Northern society perpetuated by the ruling class and made them political issues. It also mobilized the *talakawa* and educated them to oppose those conditions. As Emir Ja'afaru of Zazzau once put it: "The damage done by Aminu Kano was to let the *talakawa* know they could say "no."[7]

With the military take-over in 1966, those social conditions in the North, which the NEPU had succeeded in making political issues, attracted the attention of the politically minded military men. Reforms were introduced removing the powers of the courts, prisons and the police from the native authorities. Further reforms democratized the local governments in 1968, 1972 and 1976. In Kano, the land reform of 1978 divested the Emir and his representatives of the power of land allocation and vested it in the Governor and the chairmen of local governments. Although the *sarakuna* continued to collect the *kharaj*, they had been divested of the power of assessment since 1974. From that year government made *kharaj* a flat rate, and all that the traditional rulers did was to collect it on behalf of the State Government. In short, the thirteen years of military rule witnessed the elimination of virtually all the grievances that the NEPU utilized against the *sarakuna*.

On October 1, 1979, Muhammadu Abubakar Rimi was sworn in as the first civilian Governor of Kano State. He had netted 79% of the popular votes cast in the August gubernatorial elections.[8] The People's Redemption Party, PRP, on whose platform he had contested the elections also, won 123 of the 138 seats in the State House of Assembly. Thus, with both the executive and the legislative arms of the government firmly controlled by the PRP the Rimi government was well placed to carry out its party's programs and designs with respect to traditional institutions. True to its campaign rhetoric, the Rimi administration took on traditional rulers. Within two years of coming to power, the government had introduced the following measures, which many people perceived as aimed at undermining traditional institutions. First, it abolished the *kharaj* and *jangali* taxes and it barred *hakimai* from paying the annual Sallah homage to their emirs. Second, it excised parts of Kano and Hadejia emirates and created four new emirates from them. Third, it abolished distinctions in the grades of the various emirs in Kano State by making all of them first class. Fourth, it ordered the discontinuation of the live transmission of the annual Ramadan *tafsir* from the palace of the Emir of Kano. Fifth, it refused to formally constitute the State Council of Chiefs, and finally it issued an administrative query to the Emir of Kano. Although the first three measures were seemingly directed at the institution in general, it was generally believed in Kano State and beyond that the real target of the government's actions was the Emir of Kano, Alhaji Ado Bayero.

What were the substances of the seven measures? In what way were they directed particularly at the Emir of Kano and not the other emirs? How did Emir Ado Bayero take these measures? What were his responses, and what were the results?

Abolition of the *Jangali* and *Kharaj* Taxes

In his maiden address to the people of Kano State, minutes after he had been sworn in as Governor, Alhaji Muhammadu Abubakar Rimi announced the abolition of the *jangali* and *kharaj* taxes throughout the State.[9] The Governor was later to say that "the abolition of community and cattle taxes ... has rudely shocked and undercut the corrupt feudalistic order."[10]

In neighboring Kaduna State, also controlled by the PRP, the Governor, Abdulqadir Balarabe Musa, described their actions as the greatest blow ever struck against the powers of traditional rulers over the *talakawa*. He further characterized these taxes as "key bastions of feudalism."[11]

The major actors thus portrayed these measures as aimed at redeeming the people from feudal oppression and exploitation purportedly perpetrated in the process of the assessment and collection of the two taxes. We shall examine these measures in some detail.

THE *JANGALI*

The PRP government of Kano State claimed credit for being the first to abolish the *jangali* and *kharaj* taxes in the whole of the Federation of Nigeria. Governor Rimi in a broadcast to the people of Kano State on August 23, 1980 said:

> We have never wavered or deviated from the course of the people's redemption from legacies of imperialism, feudalism, oppression, poverty and the many vices afflicting the generality of our people. In pursuit of the implementation of PRP programs and promises we have among several other things carried out the following:
>
> > a) The total and permanent abolishing of the community and cattle taxes throughout the state. This is something historic, as it has never been done before, from the beginning of colonial rule over one hundred years ago to date.

Perhaps because of the element of surprise[12] in Rimi's announcement, and in part because during their time the military did not politicize their own actions, Governor Rimi's claim to being the first to abolish the *jangali* has gone unchallenged. Yet that claim is not completely justified. Indeed, nobody in Kano State had collected any amount of money in the name of *jangali* for fully five years preceding the advent of the PRP administration. As a matter of fact, the *jangali* was abolished in April 1974 by the then Head of State General

Yakubu Gowon. In his 1974 budget speech, delivered on April 1 that year, General Gowon said:

> Government has agreed, in principle, to abolish throughout the country the age-old cattle tax otherwise known as *jangali*. This will bring some relief to the Fulani cattle owner on his capital and encourage him to keep his cattle within the country.

But the Gowon administration did not give this move legal backing. Neither a corresponding Decree was enacted at the national level nor was any Edict at the state level enacted to formally outlaw the collection of *jangali*. However, the agreement not to collect the *jangali* was adhered to by all the states. Then during the regime of General Olusegun Obasanjo, some of the Northern State governments, particularly those of Gongola, Plateau and Borno appealed to the federal government to allow them to reintroduce the *jangali*. They argued that quite apart from the revenue it yielded for the state, it also served a very important social function. They suggested that the cattle Fulani, who were supposed to be the direct beneficiaries of the abolition, supported the call for the re-introduction of the *jangali*. This was because when the *jangali* was abolished income and property taxes had been introduced among the Fulani to replace it. The net effect, they realized, was that the bond of unity amongst members of their extended families was being shaken. The background to this reaction is interesting.

It had been the practice for members of an extended family or even neighbors or friends to give their cattle or sheep to others to tend. Since the rate of *jangali* was fixed (70 Kobo per head of cattle, and 30 kobo per head of sheep or lamb), they sent the money due on their animals to the person tending them at the appropriate time. But when the *jangali* was abolished and people were taxed according to how much wealth they were seen to have, those who were tending relations', friends', and neighbors' animals began to be over-assessed. Since the taxes were not on the animals per se, but on the individuals, they could not demand reimbursement from the owners of the animals they were tending. The solution, they concluded, was to stop tending for others; and that decision began to have serious negative consequences on the social structure of the nomadic Fulani. The Fulani leaders then met and decided that it was better to reintroduce the *jangali* so that their social organization could be saved.

The Obasanjo regime reviewed the "agreement" and made the abolition optional for those states that felt they needed to reintroduce it. Thus, in his 1978-79 budget speech, the Governor of Gongola State, Colonel Muhammadu Jega, said:

> Furthermore, there is a possibility during this financial year of reintroducing cattle tax – *jangali*—with effect from April 1, this year.

In the same vein, the Plateau State Governor, Group Captain Dan Suleiman said, "the *jangali* or cattle tax which was previously abolished will now be reviewed...."

The Kano State Government on the other hand did not reintroduce the *jangali*. The aspect of the abolition policy for which the PRP government could rightly claim credit was the introduction of a law that made the collection of *jangali* an offense. Legislation No. 18 of 1979 entitled "A Law to Amend the Personal Tax Law" states:

> Any person who demands, receives or instructs any other person to demand or receive community tax or cattle tax shall be guilty of an offense and liable on conviction to a fine of one thousand Naira or to imprisonment for two years or to both such fine and imprisonment.[13]

The soldiers, as noted earlier, did not enact any decree or edict to outlaw the collection of *jangali*. That meant that any government could resume its collection without having to repeal any existing law. In Kano, the PRP government not only did not resume its collection, but also went further and specifically outlawed the tax.

The impact on traditional rulers of the abolition of the *jangali* by the PRP government has been tremendous. However, as we have suggested, it was not so much the substance of the policy that was new, but the psychological impact it made on both the *sarakuna* and the *talakawa*—an impact that came to affect the relations of power between the two classes.

When the military first abolished the *jangali* in 1974, they did not present the policy as an instrument for the liberation of the *talakawa* from the traditional rulers. The PRP on the other hand, presented the measure as the first assault in the class struggle between the oppressed (*talaka*wa) and the oppressors (*sarakuna*). It was, above all, this presentation and the wide publicity given to it—a publicity that helped condition the minds of many people to accept the presentation as true—that tended to undermine the influence of the traditional rulers in the eyes of their subjects.

THE *KHARAJI*

At the same time that the *jangali* was abolished in 1974, the *kharaj* was made a flat rate. In the five financial years from 1974/75 to 1978/79 flat rates varied between four Naira and six Naira for all taxable adult males in Kano State. Prior to this period, *masu unguwa, dagatai, hakimai,* and *wakilan fuskoki,* in the case of Kano City, assessed individuals according to their perceived economic status.[14]

We have noted that the reforms of the late 1960s and 1970s that abolished the Kano NA as an administrative unit, and created in its place a number of local governments, also transferred virtually all the powers of the NA to the State and new local governments. These included the power to assess and collect *kharaj*. Thus, even though the traditional rulers continued to collect those taxes, they did so on behalf of their state and local governments.

Yet when the PRP government abolished those taxes, it deliberately created the impression that the money realized

from those taxes had been going to the Emir and other traditional rulers. Many *talakawa* believed that the *kharaj* they had
been paying every year ended up in the pockets of the *mai
unguwa*, the *dagaci,* the *hakimi* and finally the Emir. Few, if
any, associated the elected local government chairman, or
the State Governor with those taxes. Fewer still associated
those taxes with the social services such as water, medical
care, education, roads, etc.; they were receiving from the
government.

BARRING THE ANNUAL SALLAH
HOMAGE TO EMIRS BY DISTRICT HEADS

In most of the emirates of Northern Nigeria, as in most
Muslim societies, two festivals are annually celebrated with
great pomp and pageantry. These are the two Eids of *Eid al-
Sagir* (Hausa *Karamar Sallah)* and *Eid al-Kabir* (Hausa
Babbar Sallah). The former is celebrated immediately after
the annual month-long Ramadan fast, while the latter is cel-
ebrated a day after the Arafat.[15] In some other emirates the
Maulud, which is the anniversary of the birthday of the
Prophet, Muhammad (SAW), is celebrated with more pomp
and pageantry than the two Eids.

In Kano Emirate the history of the celebration of the
Sallah festivals goes as far back as the reign of Sarki
Muhammadu Rumfa (1463-1499).[16] At each Sallah festival
all the district heads of the emirate would leave their districts
for the emirate capital to attend the celebrations. The district
heads normally went with a large retinue including some of
their important village heads. The occasion was used by the
district heads to pay homage and renew their allegiance to the
emir. The festival lasted about four days, during which period
the emir and the large entourage numbering hundreds on
horseback and thousands on foot went round the city to
receive greetings from his subjects. The first outing, called
Hawan Daushe or *Hawan Mai Babban Daki*, takes them
round some parts of the walled city terminating at the official

residence of the Mai Babban Daki, the Emir's mother. There, the emir alights from his horse, enters his mother's house and pays his respects. *Hawan Nassarawa* takes the emir and his entourage to the settlements outside Kano City; namely Fagge, Sabongari and Nassarawa, with a courtesy call on the State Governor by the Emir.[17] The emir's bodyguards were always gaily dressed and musicians and praise-singers followed the entourage. The emir's subjects came out on to the streets calling *"Ran Sarki ya dade"* meaning "May the Emir live long," *"Allah Ya kiyaye Sarki"* meaning " May Allah protect the Emir," *"Allah Ya ja zamanin Sarki"* or "May Allah prolong the Emir's reign," *"Allah Ya kara ma Sarki imani,"* meaning "May Allah increase the Emir's faith" etc., raising their clenched fists in salutation.

On the last day of the festivities, a durbar was held and all the district heads and titled officials, one after another, came on horseback to pay homage and renew allegiance to the emir. After that they sought permission to return to their respective domains.

The festival afforded the emir an opportunity to go out and see and be seen by his subjects in metropolitan Kano. It also served to reassure him of the continued loyalty of his district heads and other titled officials, particularly those living in far away districts. Most importantly it constituted the most graphic reminder of the existence of Kasar Kano, whose head was none but the emir.[18]

The *Babbar Sallah* of 1979, the first since the PRP government assumed office was celebrated as usual in Kano, likewise the *Karamar Sallah* of 1980. But on October 17, 1980, two days before the *Babbar Sallah*, the speaker of the State House of Assembly, Alhaji Abdullahi Abubakar Karaye, who was holding the fort in the absence of Governor Muhammadu Rimi and his deputy Ibrahim Farouk, made an unprecedented announcement. In a radio broadcast to the people of Kano State, he directed district and village heads not to leave their domains for their respective emirate capitals to celebrate the *Babbar Sallah*.[19] All district and village heads were directed to remain in their domains and celebrate the Sallah with their people.

In justifying that directive, the government explained that it was aimed at redeeming both the subordinate traditional rulers (district and village heads) and the large number of *talakawa* who were obliged to come with them to cater for their horses. The government pointed out that the *talakawa* in the retinue of the district and village heads were subjected to inhuman treatment. For example, while the *talakawa* herded their district and village heads' horses to the emirate capitals, the journeys sometimes lasting two or more days, they could not ride the horses but had to walk beside them for the whole journey. Furthermore, for the four or more days that they stayed in the emirate capitals for the celebrations, neither the emir nor their immediate bosses were responsible for their feeding or accommodation. Thirdly, the government pointed out that the people in the villages also had a right to celebrate those festivities with their traditional rulers. Finally, and I think this point is very significant, the argument was advanced that the district and village heads were employees of their respective local governments, and since their local governments did not extend to the emirate capitals, they had no business leaving their territories for another without the express permission of their employers.

CREATION OF FOUR NEW EMIRATES

On April 1, 1981, Governor Rimi announced the creation of four new emirates in Kano State. Three of the new emirates, namely Dutse, Gaya and Rano were excised from Kano Emirate, while the fourth, Auyo, was excised from Hadejia. That act, according to the Governor, was in pursuance of the redemption programs of the PRP government. The action, Governor Rimi said, was aimed "at returning the quality of traditional and political autonomy to the original source." The government argued that until its subjugation by Kano in about 1450, Dutse had been an independent kingdom.[20] In excising the district of Dutse[21] from the domain of Kano Emirate, the Emir of Kano's area of authority was thus reduced. The creation of Gaya and Rano emirates with the same declared rationale as Dutse has had the same effect on the Emir of Kano, who symbolizes and personifies Kano Emirate as such. The policy is thus one of dismembering the emirate of Kano as a social, political and religious entity.

UPGRADING SECOND-CLASS EMIRS TO FIRST-CLASS STATUS

At independence, Kano Province, which came to constitute Kano State in 1967, comprised four emirates, namely Gumel, Hadejia, Kano and Kazaure. Of these only the Emir of Kano was first-class. The other three were second-class emirs. Successive post-colonial governments until 1981 maintained this status imposed by the colonial regime, until the PRP government of Kano State reviewed the situation. On April 1, 1981 Governor Rimi announced the simultaneous upgrading of four districts to emirate status and the appointment of first-class emirs for each of them, and the upgrading of the existing three second-class emirs to first-class status. By the end of the exercise there were eight emirs in Kano State and each of them was a first-class emir, legally at par with the Emir of Kano.

STOPPAGE OF LIVE TRANSMISSION OF RAMADAN TAFSIR FROM THE PALACE

Traditionally, the Emir's Palace has been a centre for religious activities, especially during the holy month of Ramadan. Every evening during that month tens of thousands of people from the city gathered at the palace to hear the tafsir or exegesis of the Holy Qur'an delivered in the Hausa language by Sheikh Nasir Kabara.[22] The Emir was always in attendance. These *tafsirs* were always transmitted live across the state and beyond on the state-owned Radio

Kano. Thus, many more people who could not come to the palace followed the tafsir from their homes.[23] To many people, the Ramadan tafsir was the only opportunity they have to read through the Holy Qur'an once a year.

In 1979, Radio Kano as usual transmitted the *tafsir*. But in 1980, acting on instructions from above, the technical crew of the radio station failed to turn up at the palace to transmit the *tafsir*.

NON-CONSTITUTION OF STATE COUNCIL OF CHIEFS

The 1979 Constitution stipulated the establishment in each state of the federation of a State Council of Chiefs. Together with the State Governor, its chairman was to represent the state at the National Council of States. But the PRP government failed to constitute the council in Kano, apparently because it was obvious that the Emir of Kano was going to be the chairman. It was speculated in Kano that the upgrading of second-class emirs to first-class status as well as the creation of more first-class emirs may have been undertaken as a way of getting one of them to emerge as the chairman of the State Council of Chiefs when eventually created.

QUERY TO THE EMIR OF KANO

In late June 1981 the Emir of Kano left his domain for a certain ceremonial function outside the State. On his return the Cabinet Office sent him a letter, dated July 9, 1981, in which he was queried about his movements. He was given up to forty-eight hours to show reason why disciplinary action should not be taken against him for leaving his domain without the express approval of the State Government. Alhaji Sule Yahaya Hamma, the Secretary to the State Government, signed the query. It listed the alleged offenses of the Emir, which included travelling out of his domain without seeking approval of the State Government, meeting with President Shehu Shagari without seeking clearance from the State government, failure to turn up at state functions, and general insubordination to constituted authority of the State.

The contents of the query, which either because of oversight or deliberate intent, was not issued under secret cover, leaked to the general public, who interpreted it as an insult to their revered Emir. It was the last straw. Before the deadline for the reply of the query had elapsed Kano was in flames, and property worth ₦ 17,337,868.75 was lost in addition to two lives.[24] That was the last the people heard from the government concerning the query.[25]

In what way were these measures directed at the person of the Emir of Kano and not the other emirs? It has been suggested that Emir Ado Bayero has come to personify traditional institutions not only in Kano State but Hausaland in general. Secondly, it was generally believed that traditional functionaries of Kano emirate were in the past more notorious in the abuse of the assessment and collection processes of the abolished taxes than those of any of the other emirates in the State. Thirdly, the order banning Sallah homage was selectively applied, as the following cases from Gumel and Gaya emirates illustrate.

Of the four emirates in Kano State at the time of the imposition of the ban, two—Kano and Kazaure—were celebrating the Eid festivals, while the other two—Gumel and Hadejia—celebrated the Maulud. The essence of the two celebrations was the same. They afforded the emirs opportunity to meet with their entire district and major village heads so that they could renew their allegiance to them. In Gumel, Hadejia, Daura and other emirates where the Maulud is celebrated, it is called *Sallar Gani*.

With the approach of the 1981 *Sallar Gani*, the Emir of Gumel, Alhaji Ahmad Muhammad Sani, directed that preparations be made for the celebrations. Subsequently, district and village heads converged at Gumel for the five-day affair. At the end of the festival, a durbar was held where the village and district heads went to pay their homage to the emir. Governor Rimi himself was there as the Special Guest of

Honor of the occasion. When asked why Gumel was celebrating the Sallah festival with district and village heads in
attendance, contrary to government directives, the Emir of
Gumel said that he understood the ban order to have specifically mentioned the *Eid* festivals, not the *Sallar Gani*.

Even if the Emir's interpretation of the order was correct, there was still a breach. Gaya, one of the Rimi-created
emirates, set out to celebrate the 1981 Sallah in grand style.
The district and village heads of Gaya emirate converged in
Gaya town on the occasion of the 1981 *Babbar Sallah* festival, and celebrated in exactly the same way that Kano and
other emirates had been barred from doing. When asked why
district and village heads went to Gaya town for the festival
at a time when a ban was supposed to be in force, the Emir,
late Alhaji Adamu Gaya, answered that as far he knew there
was no law prohibiting district and village heads from coming to their emirs on Sallah occasions. What he understood
by that order was that if any emir wanted his village and district heads to come to his capital for the Sallah festival, he
should seek the permission of the employers of the village
and district heads, namely their respective local governments.
According to the Emir, he sought for that permission and he
got it. Not only were his districts and village heads permitted to go to Gaya for the Sallah, but also in fact, the State
Government, through the Cabinet Office, funded the entire
celebrations.[26]

The district heads of Kano did not understand the government's order in the same way. In fact, according to the
Sarkin Bai, the order was categorical; there was no ambigu-
ity. He first heard it over the radio, later a formal directive
came from the Secretary to the Dambatta Local Government
prohibiting any absence from the district during the Sallah
festival without the written permission of the Local
Government Secretary. What is unclear is whether any district head from Kano Emirate did apply and was refused permission to go. When contacted, the Secretary to the State
Government, Alhaji Sule Hamma said that the order was cat-

egorical and that government had banned Sallah homage.[27] Yet government never came out to explain which of the two interpretations of its order was correct. In so doing, it allowed some emirates to flout the order while others complied with it, and that created the impression that the policy was directed not at the institution of traditional rulership per se, but at the person of the Emir of Kano. It was suggested that the behavior of the Emir of Gaya and the government's silence was due to the fact that Alhaji Adamu Gaya was, until his appointment as Emir, a Senator of the Federal Republic of Nigeria on the platform of the PRP. Similarly, Emir Ahmed Muhammed Sani of Gumel was, until his appointment as Emir in 1980, a member of the Rimi cabinet.[28]

All the above acts of provocation from the government notwithstanding, Emir Ado Bayero never for once reacted adversely. While his friends and admirers felt very agitated over what the Rimi government was doing to the Emir, Ado Bayero went about his business as if everything was normal. Even when friends came all the way to Kano to lend him their support and seek his tacit approval to deal with Rimi, he carefully avoided discussing the issue. So concerned were some key traditional rulers in the North about what Rimi was doing to Emir Ado Bayero that one prominent emir sent to Emir Ado Bayero to ask what he was doing about the Rimi provocation. He added that if Emir Ado Bayero was not going to do anything, he should be permitted to do something. Emir Ado Bayero replied that he appreciated the concern of his friend, but added that as far as he was concerned it was a passing phase. More importantly, he noted, two wrongs do not make a right.[29]

The continued silence of the Emir over Governor Rimi's irreverent behavior became a matter of concern among people even outside Kano State. A popular Hausa musician Alhaji Musa Dankwairo, in one of his celebrated songs had to ask why Emir Ado Bayero was treating the Tuareg of Kano (reference to Rimi because of his features) with kid gloves.

Throughout those years, the Emir spoke to only six people on the seeming interminable provocation. The first was his close friend and confidant, the Mai Unguwar Mundubawa, Alhaji Aminu Yusuf. The second, Alhaji Muhammadu Bashar, the Emir of Daura, was also his friend, and had been his best man when he married Saudatu, a daughter of Sir Abubakar III, the Sultan of Sokoto, in 1974. The third person was Mallam Aminu Kano, leader of the PRP and a loyal friend of the Emir. The fourth was Barrister Michael Agbamuche, also an old friend who credits the Emir with having saved his life during the 1966 crisis in the North. The fifth was then Turakin Kano, Alhaji Tijjani Hashim. And the sixth was Aliyu Ibrahim, at that time a State Counsel with the Kano State Ministry of Justice, and son of Matawallen Kano, Ibrahim.[31]

Immediately after reading the query from the State Government, the Emir made a quick decision: he was going to reply as directed. Even though he thought the language of the query could have been more courteous, he reminded himself that it came from constituted authority and that he, as a leader, should not be seen to show disrespect to it. He himself had, after all, always exhorted his people to respect constituted authority. Having resolved to reply, he sent for Aliyu Ibrahim. Aliyu read the query and was baffled. He sought the Emir's permission to go and draft a quick reply and before long he was back with an answer for the government. The Emir studied the reply. The language was intemperate, like that of the query itself. The Emir decided to obtain a second legal opinion. He sent for his lawyer friend, Chief Michael Agbamuche.

Chief Agbamuche took the first available flight to Kano. At the palace, the Emir gave him the nine-paragraph query to study and advise him appropriately. Agbamuche was furious not only at the points raised in the query but also at the language in which it was couched and he did not mince words in saying so. The Emir advised him not to allow his emotions to get the better of him, but to ignore the language of the query, and address the issues raised. Agbamuche not only advised the Emir, but he also drafted a sober reply to the Government.

Turaki Tijjani Hashim was another person the Emir contacted when he received the query. He had telephoned him and requested if he was free to come and see him. It was an unusual request and the Turaki rushed to the palace immediately. There, the Emir gave Turaki the query to read. The Turaki immediately suggested that Mallam Aminu Kano, the leader of the PRP be contacted. Alan Feinstein, Aminu Kano's biographer, who happened to be around when the information about the query got to Mallam Aminu recalls that Mallam Aminu muttered something like, "He's crazy! I'm really worried that there's going to be trouble."[32]

At a point during the never-ending provocations, Emir Ado Bayero gave a serious thought to abdicating the throne. He sent an emissary to his friend, the Emir of Daura, Alhaji Muhammadu Bashar, with a message that he should come to Kano at his earliest convenience. Emir Bashar rushed to Kano, and was pleased to see his friend hale, hearty and lively. The two of them retired into one of the Emir's private rooms. There, Emir Ado opened up to his friend. He started by narrating the obvious, which were the continuous provocations from the state government. He noted that a lot of innocent people were becoming victims of the government's actions, which were directed at him. He felt that he needed to save those people from unnecessary sufferance. According to the Emir, he had given the matter some serious thought, and had come to the conclusion that he should abdicate office. He further told Emir Bashar that he was going to inform his mother, Mai Babban Daki, about his decision. Emir Bashar waited until Emir Ado Bayero had finished saying what he wanted to say. Sounding as serious as Emir Ado, Emir Bashar took a philosophical view of what his friend had just narrated to him. He first reminded Emir Ado Bayero that he was not responsible for the sufferance of the innocent people he mentioned. And he assured the Emir that those people did not see him as the cause of their sufferance. Secondly, he reminded Emir Ado Bayero that he did not seek that office, and that he was thousands of miles away when Allah chose him for the office, even when there were many other eligible princes in Kano at that time. Thirdly, he reminded the Emir that if he abdicated at that time, the institution of traditional rulership, which has served to protect and preserve the religion and culture of Kano people, will be seriously undermined. Emir Bashar implored his friend to look at the cost of his abdicating to Kano people, its society, and its culture. He reassured Ado Bayero not to feel guilty about the travails of some people that the government had targeted for persecution because of their perceived closeness to him, adding that those people believe in a cause for which they were willing to pay the price.

After the meeting with Emir Bashar, Ado Bayero decided to give his friend's advice some more serious thought. Eventually, he agreed that the Rimi years were just a passing phase in his reign.

TOWARDS INTERPRETING THE GOVERNMENT'S ACTIONS

The Rimi government did not have any problem anchoring its actions concerning traditional rulers to the philosophy and campaign promises of the PRP. But the selective application of those decisions left a big question mark over those claims. Of the four emirates in Kano at the time of the proscription of Sallah homage, two—Hadejia and Gumel—did not celebrate the Sallah with the pomp and pageantry that they did Sallar Gani. It was only Kano and Kazaure that celebrated the *Karamar Sallah* and the *Babban Sallah*. Although the directive specifically mentioned *Karamar Sallah* and *Babbar Sallah*, Hadejia, under Emir Haruna Abdulqadir, understood the directive to apply to *Sallar Gani* too. This however was not the understanding of the Emir of Gumel Alhaji Ahmed Muhammed Sani. In other words, the Emirs of Kano, Kazaure and Hadejia understood the directive to apply to them. To further prove this position, when Gaya Emirate was

204

created the ban order, as we have seen, was not applied to the emirate.

It is interesting to note that the Emirs of Kano and Hadejia, the two emirates whose territories were excised to create four new emirates, were perceived by the PRP to be sympathetic to the rival NPN. While there was no concrete basis for that suspicion, the PRP leadership might have constantly borne in mind the fact that Emir Ado Bayero had been appointed by the NPC Government of the First Republic. The relationship between the NEPU and the PRP, as we noted, is similar to that between the NPC and NPN. In fact, speculation was rife in Kano during the 1978-79 election campaign that if the PRP formed the government of Kano State, Emir Ado Bayero was going to be deposed and ex-Emir Sanusi would return from Azare and be re-appointed Emir. Indeed, Muhammadu Sanusi was returned to Kano by the PRP government in December 1979, barely three months after it came to power. But he lived a private life at the Emir's Wudil retreat until he died on April 5, 1991.[33]

The alleged NPN-inclination of the Emir of Kano does not in any case explain the venom with which the Rimi Government acted. The problem appears more deep-seated. It was not simply a class struggle between the *sarakuna* and the *talakawa*, for Rimi himself belonged to the *sarakuna* class, and so did most of the key functionaries of his government. It was more of an intra-class struggle within the *sarakuna* class. To better understand the behavior of the PRP government towards the Emir one needs to understand the dynamics of the politics of the aristocracy in Kano or the politics of *sarauta*.

Almost all studies of Northern Nigerian society have noted that the emirate polities were genuine class societies. There were basically two classes—the *sarakuna* and the *talakawa*. The *sarakuna* comprised (from the top downwards) the emirs, the *hakimai*, *alkalai*, palace scholars, other titled officials (e.g. among royal slaves), village heads and ward heads. A *basarake*, or member of the ruling class, was therefore anyone from any of these groups in the emirates. The other class, the *talakawa*, comprised all others who did not belong to any of the above mentioned families.

But even within the *sarakuna or ruling* class there were gradations. Two sub-classes were distinguishable. The first was what, for lack of a better term, one would call the higher aristocracy. This comprised members of the royal family, those of the *hakimai* and other important titled officials who dealt directly with the Emir. The second was the lower aristocracy, comprising members of the families of village and ward heads. To a large extent, this sub-class executed the policies made by the higher aristocracy, and they related with the Emir almost always through their district heads. The educated children of this sub-class of *sarakuna* were generally more hostile to the higher aristocracy than even the pure *talakawa* were to the *sarakuna* as a class.

Muhammadu Abubakar Rimi typifies the mind-set of this class of people. A son of a village head of Rimi, in Sumaila District of Kano Emirate, Rimi reminisces about his father's experience at the hands of the *hakimi* of Sumaila some forty-five years ago as if it happened only yesterday. He narrates how scared his father was of the *kharaj* season; how he was punished for failing to collect the taxes on time; or how any shortage was visited with severe sanctions. Even as a child, according to Rimi, he grew up to hate the people who made life miserable for his father, namely the *hakimai* and eventually the Emir. That, he said, accounted for his choice of the NEPU when he joined politics during colonial rule.[34]

Luckily for Rimi, whereas people from the *sarakuna* class occupied 67% of all key leadership positions in his government, only 17% of them came from the higher aristocracy. By far the larger percentage was of the lower aristocracy stock. That concentration of the lower level aristocracy in his government emboldened Rimi to take the measures he took against Emir Ado Bayero. At the same time, the government pursued policies that favored the lower aristocracy. For example, when Governor Rimi abolished the *jangali* and *kharaj* with so much publicity, he did not abolish the offices of those directly responsible for its administration, namely the ward and village heads. Instead, in a low-keyed fashion, he directed local government chairmen to include all village and ward heads resident in their local government areas in their payroll. The effect of that directive was to boost the legal sources of the income of that stratum of *sarakuna*. Not a few village heads had their income more than quadrupled as a result of that directive.[35]

Many years after leaving office Rimi still justifies every decision his government took concerning the Emir of Kano. According to him, he acted the way he did because the Emir broke a gentleman's agreement reached between the two of them early in the life of the Rimi administration. Alhaji Muhammadu Rimi says that despite their hostile talk about the *sarakuna* during their campaigns, he was ready to work with the Emir of Kano when he became Governor. Rimi says that a few days after he had become Governor, he sent a confidential message to the Emir requesting a meeting of the two leaders. Rimi added that he would like the meeting to be very private. He therefore ruled out the Government House and the Palace. The Emir suggested his Nassarawa retreat. At the appointed time Rimi drove, supposedly incognito, to this place, which was just a few hundred meters away from the Government House. According to Rimi, he explained to Emir Ado Bayero that the campaigns were over and his duty was to steer the affairs of Kano State for the good of its people. He assured the Emir of his support for his person and the institution. They exchanged telephone numbers, with the understanding that either could call the other whenever he felt it necessary.

According to Rimi, he was dumbfounded when a few days later he heard that he had requested a meeting with the Emir and apologized on behalf of the PRP for all the insults given during the campaign on the Emir and the traditional institutions. As a politician that could be most damaging. Rimi traces his hostility towards the Emir from that day.

Similarly, the Emir recalls the said meeting. He also recalls that there were just the two of them in the room. But he does not recall subsequently discussing the subject of his talk with Rimi with anyone else, and he would not speculate on how the information leaked to the public. There are many possibilities. Could the Governor have been trailed by his security agents to the Emir's Nassarawa retreat? Or could he have been recognized by someone as he drove along the State Road or Sokoto Road to the Nassarawa retreat? Was it just possible that the two most important people of Kano State could meet without anyone knowing? What could they be discussing that they wanted shrouded in secrecy? Was everybody in the Emir's Nassarawa retreat asked to keep away from the house for the period the two were supposed to be there? If so would that not, in itself, make the staff curious to know who was going to be received there? Was it possible that some staff of the palace, excited about a secret meeting between the Emir and Governor could have leaked the information to others? The actual subject of their discussion need not be known for the meeting in itself to be news worthy.

On April 30, 1983, Rimi resigned as Governor to enable him secure a platform to recontest for the office. He had been expelled from the PRP barely a year into his governorship. He secured the ticket of the NPP, but not the mandate of Kano people, and his defeat brought a lot of relief to many of the admirers and loyal subjects of the Emir. But one loyal friend of the Emir was not swayed by the change. Contributing to a discussion on the matter with other councilors of the Emir, the learned *hakimi* had cautioned his colleagues over their pronounced sigh of relief. He had remarked that the ordeal of the Emir of Kano, Alhaji Ado Bayero, was not over with the final exit of Rimi and the arrival of the traditionalist Aliyu Sabo Bakin Zuwo as the chief occupant of the Government House. He added that as a Muslim, who had proclaimed his belief in Allah, and who had also proclaimed his belief in destiny, that is, in nothing happening in the world without Allah willing it to be so, Emir Ado Bayero's belief was constantly going to be tested by Allah. For as long as he lived, Allah would continue to test his faith. The Rimi years were therefore explained as one of those phases of trial by Allah.

To Emir Ado Bayero the Rimi years were no different from any of the years he had spent on the throne. Always guided by the Holy Qur'an, his position was that anyone who believes in Allah and in destiny has conquered fear.[36] His handling of the provocations from the Rimi government endeared him even more to his friends and admirers. Commenting on the issue Chief Ojukwu said, "I was particularly impressed with the way he handled the crisis with Rimi. His reaction was simple—a dignified silence—throughout the period. That was where he demonstrated his nobility."[37] As far as the Emir was concerned there were no nightmares. In fact, at the time of this study, all the years Rimi spent in office are just about one-tenth of the years Ado Bayero has been on the throne. As far as the Emir was concerned, the Rimi years never happened.

NOTES

1. The Platform of the People: *The General Program and Election Manifesto of the People's Redemption Party*, (n.p.n.d.).
2. S.G. Ikoku, an Igbo, from Eastern Nigeria, became the national secretary of the PRP. Other southern faces in the leadership were Comrade Uche Chukwumerije, U.N. Akpan, A.Y. Eke, Chief Michael Imuodu, O. Adeosun, Lekan Balogun, etc.
3. Muhammadu A. Rimi, in Edet Uno ed., *Struggle for Redemption,* (Zaria, N.N.P.C., 1981), p. 278.
4. Op. cit., p.71.
5. See for example, Lawan Danbazau, *Tarihin Gwagwarmayar NEPU da PRP 1950-1981* (Zaria Gaskiya Corporation 1981), Balarabe Abbas Lawan, *Myths and Realities of Our Struggle: Documents from the*

NEPU Days to the PRP Vols. 1 and 2, (n.p.n.d) and Edet Uno ed., *Struggle for Redemption,* op. cit.

6. Candido, a satirical column in the *New Nigerian* attacked the UPN over this when in its column of November 5, 1978 it stated:

> "Parties are now beginning to realize that what they at first considered to be national issues are turning out to be nothing more than sectional interests. Take such red-hot issues like free education, housing, and rural development for example.... Education has always been virtually free in the North anyway (except for the former minority areas) and promising the people of these parts what they already have hardly amounts to a dramatically effective campaign strategy in the circumstances. They (UPN) will have to choose between finding collective issues which are truly national and single issues which have relevance for specific groups in the electorate."

7. Quoted in Allan Feinstein, *African Revolutionary: The Life and Times of Nigeria's Aminu Kano,* Revised edition, (Boulder, Lynne Rienner, 1987) p. 132.

8. The results of the gubernatorial elections for Kano state were as follows: The Great Nigeria People's Party (GNPP) 14,804; the Unity Party of Nigeria (UPN) 8,568; the National Party of Nigeria (NPN) 218,751; and the People's Redemption Party of Nigeria (PRP) 909,118. The Nigeria People's Party did not field a candidate for the gubernatorial elections. Source: Oyeleye Oyediran, ed., *The Nigeria 1979 Elections,* (Lagos, MacMillan Press, 1981), Appendix 4. Also Haroun Adamu and Alaba Ogunsanwo, *The Making of the Presidential System: 1979 General Elections,* (Kano, Triumph Publishing Company, 1981), p. 237.

9. Although the Governor did not have the constitutional power to abolish local taxes, that power having been reserved for the legislature, the platform on which the PRP came to power and the fact that it controlled both the leg-

islature and the executive made the possibility of any challenge to the Governor's unconstitutional proclamation very remote. Indeed, when a member of a rival political party, the NPN, Alhaji Shehu Gaya, threatened to take the governor to court for violating the constitution, he was cautioned by his party against such an action. This was because of the fear by the NPN that the *talakawa* would interpret Shehu Gaya's action to mean actual opposition to the abolishing of the taxes, which they saw as their bane for ages. Interestingly, in Kaduna State where a rival political party controlled the legislature, the PRP Governor, Abdulqadir Balarabe Musa, did not announce the complete abolition of the two taxes at his swearing in. Rather, he presented a bill to the NPN-controlled House of Assembly, which passed it.

10. Muhammadu Abubakar Rimi, "Impeachment of Governor Musa" in Edet Uno, ed., *The Struggle for Redemption,* op. cit. p. 83.

11. Abdulqadir Balarabe Musa, *The Struggle for a new social order: The Policies and Programs of the People's Redemption Party Government 1979-1981,* (Kaduna, Government Printer, 1982), p. 130.

12. There are two opinions about the abolition of the *jangali* and *kharaj* by the PRP government. Whereas Mallam Lawan Dambazau, a leader of the PRP and Alhaji Suleiman M.B., national administrative secretary of the party informed me that at no time before the election did the party leaders agree on abolishing the *kharaj* or *jangali*, Alhaji Muhammadu Abubakar Rimi and Professor Dandatti Abdulqadir, a member of the PRP Think Tank, said a decision to abolish the two taxes was taken long before the elections. Interviews 16-4-83, 15-4-83, 28-2-95 and 21-4-83 respectively.

13. Gazette of Kano State No.18 of 1979, Government Printer, 1979.

14. The method of tax assessment evolved during colonial rule (discussed in the introduction) continued through to

the early seventies with minor modifications. Civil servants paid as they earned, and their taxes were deducted at source. The very wealthy were assessed by the government separately. The introduction of flat rates in *kharaji* in 1974/75 financial year led to a drastic fall in the revenue accruing to the State from that source from N1,869,000 in 1973/74 to N303,000 in 1974/75. Similarly, the actual recurrent revenue of the Kano State Government for the financial years 1971/72 to 1975/76, indicates that N72,000 was realized from *jangali* in 1971/72, N44,000 in 1972/73, N22,000 in 1973/74 and no revenue at all from 1974/75 up to the advent of the PRP government. Source: Kano State Government Estimates Ministry of Finance, cited in *Kano State: A Giant Leap* (The Triumph Publishing Company, 1981), p.111

15. The Arafat day is the 9th day of the month of Zul-hijja. It is the culmination of the many religious rites performed by Muslims on hajj.

16. S.J. Hogben and AHM Kirk-Greene, The Emirates of Northern Nigeria, (London, Oxford University Press, 1966), p. 192.

17. The practice of paying courtesy calls on the colonial Governor or Resident was symbolic of the transfer to the British colonial power of the allegiance that used to be owed to the Sultan of Sokoto. During the First Republic the emirs did not pay courtesy calls on any political leader. But with the creation of states in 1967 Ado Bayero started the practice when he paid a courtesy call on Governor Audu Bako in 1968. That practice continued until the PRP government abolished it in 1980.

18. The splitting of the Kano NA into several local government areas (between 1968 and 1991) did not deny the emir of suzerainty over the areas, as the *Hakimai* of the districts of the various local governments were still appointed by the emir. But with the creation of Jigawa state in 1991, and the excision of Ringim, Garki, Babura, Dutse, Kiyawa, Aujara, Birnin Kudu, Gwaram, and Jahun, districts from

Kano state, the new Jigawa state government took a major step to sever any traditional allegiance those districts owed the Emir of Kano, by creating two new emirates at Dutse and Ringim, and subjugating the other districts to these two. Interestingly, the district heads of Garki and Gwaram appointed by Emir Ado Bayero, voluntarily relinquished their offices in Jigawa State and returned to Kano rather than become district heads outside Kano Emirate.

19. The background to this directive is interesting. According to a key member of the Rimi government, although barring Sallah homage was once discussed with the Governor, no agreement was reached before Rimi travelled out of the country. Taking advantage of the absence of the deputy Governor, who had by then fallen out with the governor, some radical members of the government approached Speaker Karaye and suggested that the directive be issued. Speaker Karaye initially refused to act arguing that he was not aware of any decision by the Governor on that matter. But the radical members had anticipated that. They had come prepared. They told Karaye that escort cars complete with sirens and outriders were outside waiting to take him to the Government House where he would make the broadcast. They added that, in the absence of Governor Rimi and Deputy Ibrahim Farouk, he was the State Governor. The very thought that he was going to be Governor for even one day worked magic on Karaye as he immediately changed his mind and set off for the Government House. (Interview with a cabinet member in Rimi's government. Abuja, 20-3-91).

   On Rimi's return to the country, and upon journalists asking him to comment on the order, he said," the traditional Sallah homage in Kano State has been abolished forever." Reported in *The Punch* 7-11-80.

20. See *Kano State: A Giant Leap*, (Triumph Publishing Company), 1981, p. 33.

21. The excised territory included not just Dutse but also Kiyawa district.

22. Mallam Nasiru Kabara did the *Tafsir* during the reign of Emir Abdullahi Bayero. When Sanusi became emir in 1953, Nasiru became the alternate mallam for *tafsir*. He did the t*afsir* for Emir Ado Bayero. Mallam Nasiru Kabara died in 1997. Seven years before he died he had sought Emir Ado Bayero's permission for his eldest son Karibullah to succeed him in the *tafsir.*

23. An estimated 20,000 people attended the *tafsir* every night. See John N. Paden, Religion and Political Culture in Kano, (Los Angeles, University of California Press, 1973), p. 157n.

24. Kano State of Nigeria Government Views on the Report of the Justice Fernandez Judicial Commission of Enquiry into the July 10th Rampage, White Paper. The White Paper and Report were not officially released. I am grateful to Mallam A.B. Mahmoud, Attorney General and Commissioner of Justice, Kano State, during the aborted Third Republic, for making available to me the original White paper. 19-2-93.

25. Interestingly the reaction of Kano people to the query confirmed the findings of a research conducted by Clive Harber of Birmingham University in late 1978 and early 1979. Harber had administered a questionnaire to 483 primary and secondary school pupils in Kano State. The questionnaire had contained the question "who is the most important man in Kano State?" The response showed that about three-fifths of the respondents thought the Emir of Kano was the most important man. One-fourth named the Governor of Kano State and the remainder named Mallam Aminu Kano. See "Who counts in Kano" in *West Africa Magazine*, 21-28 December 1988, 3033.

26. Ibrahim, Omar F., *The Fabric of Rule: A Study of the Position of Traditional Ruling families in the Politics of Kano State, Nigeria, 1960-1983,* Unpublished Ph.D. Dissertation, Rutgers, The State University of New Jersey, 1988. P.112

27. Interview with Alhaji Sule Yahaya Hamma. May 21, 1983, Kano.

28. Alhaji Ahmed Muhammed Sani, was Hon. Commissioner for Home Affairs and Information in the PRP government. He was a member of the Great Nigeria People's Party.

29. At least three very important personalities in the country had come all the way to Kano to lend their moral support to the Emir. Each had broached the issue while with the Emir, but the Emir would not discuss it.

31. Upon the death of Matawalle Ibrahim, the Emir gave the title to Aliyu. To further cement the bond of fidelity, Aliyu married one of the daughters of the Emir.

32. Alan Feinstein, *African Revolutionary: The Life and Times of Nigeria's Aminu Kano*, (Boulder, Lynne Rienner, 1987), p. 326.

33. Emir Ado Bayero used to visit his elder brother, ex-Emir Muhammadu Sanusi at Wudil. Indeed, he visited him just a few days before Sanusi died. (Interview Ciroman Kano Alhaji Muhammadu Aminu Sanusi, Kaduna June 28, 1998).

34. Int. Kaduna March 18, 1995.

35. Some village heads earning N288 per annum before the abolishing had their salaries increased to N1,248 per annum after the exercise. The huge increase resulted from their being made LG employees and therefore eligible for the minimum wage legislated by the PRP government.

36. The Emir's philosophy is anchored on the ayat "No misfortune can happen on earth or in your souls but is recorded in a decree before we bring it into existence; that is truly easy for Allah" LVII: 23.

37. Interview, March 2, 1997, Abuja.

THE TRIP TO ISRAEL

THE MILITARY AGAIN

The defeat of Alhaji Muhammadu Abubakar Rimi in the August 1983 Kano State gubernatorial elections was hailed by not only the supporters of the victor, Alhaji Aliyu Sabo Bakin Zuwo of the PRP, but also the admirers and sympathizers of the Emir of Kano. The latter group had felt greatly relieved by the final exit of Rimi, whose nearly four years in office had been characterized by his obsessive desire to humiliate the Emir of Kano.

Sabo Bakin Zuwo was sworn in as the sixth Governor of Kano State on October 1, 1983. To symbolize his loyalty to Emir Ado Bayero, he drove straight from the racecourse, the venue of the swearing-in ceremony, to the Emir's palace to pay his homage and to reassure the Emir of his continued loyalty and support.

For the three months that Sabo Bakin Zuwo was in office, he hardly did anything without consulting Emir Ado Bayero, especially on matters of religion and tradition. On the few occasions that he had acted without consulting the Emir, he had assumed that those actions would please the Emir, or that there was just no time for consultation. The first act was the dissolution of the four new emirates created by the Rimi administration and the sacking of their emirs; it was the subject of the very first public policy pronouncement of Sabo Bakin Zuwo as Governor. Thus, immediately he was sworn-in, Sabo Bakin Zuwo dissolved the emirates of Gaya, Rano, Dutse and Auyo and their territories were returned to their original emirates, and directives were given that their staff of office should be collected and deposited in the Gidan Makama Museum. The action was reminiscent of the Rimi abolition of the *jangali* and *kharaj* taxes.

Furthermore, Governor Sabo Bakin Zuwo dismissed from office the two Rimi appointees to the traditional office of Wambai and Durbi, Alhaji Abubakar Bayero and Alhaji Maikano Gwarzo respectively.[1] The two had been in the good books of Governor Rimi, who had promoted them to those offices without recourse to the Kano Emirate Council. Governor Bakin Zuwo also set out to depose the Emir of Gumel, Alhaji Ahmed Mohammed Sani, whom he saw as a Rimi appointee.[2] In addition, Governor Sabo Bakin Zuwo annulled the order barring district and village heads from going to their respective emirate capitals for the Sallah celebrations.

From all indications things appeared to be moving very well for Emir Ado Bayero and his sympathizers and admirers. Then the military struck again on the eve of 1984. The Federal and all the State Governments were toppled in a military coup, the fourth successful coup in the history of the then twenty-three-year old independent nation.[3] General Muhammadu Buhari, from Daura, the legendary source of the kings of the seven Hausa states, emerged as the new military Head of State. He appointed Air Commodore Hamza Abdullahi, from Hadejia in Kano State, as the State Military Governor.

As with the previous military regimes, the Buhari government looked up to the traditional rulers for support and advice. It saw them as the fathers of the people and treated them as such. In his first address to his governors, General Buhari emphasized the need for them to cultivate the goodwill of their respective traditional rulers. As soon as he had settled down to business, he undertook a tour of the country, where he made it a point to visit the key traditional rulers in each state. When General Buhari came to Kano he briefed the Emir about the programs of his government, especially the War against Indiscipline, WAI, and sought his support.

RED CARPET AT BEN GURION
INTERNATIONAL AIRPORT

About eight months into the Buhari regime, on August 5, to be precise, Emir Ado Bayero flew to London. While there, his friend the Ooni of Ife, Oba Okunade Sijuwade Olubuse II, informed him that he was going to Israel, and wondered if Ado Bayero would like to visit there. Ado Bayero reflected on the invitation. He still had a few more days to spend in London before returning home. Furthermore he did not have any engagements to attend to. But most importantly, Ado Bayero had, for many years, been looking for an opportunity to go and pray in Islam's third most sacred mosque, the Masjid al-Aqsa.[4] He had prayed inside Masjid al-Aqsa before, some twenty years earlier, when he had spent barely one year on the throne. But since then he had come to learn that the tomb of Prophet Musa (May Allah's peace be upon him), was in the vicinity of the mosque which he wanted to visit. Ado Bayero accepted his friend's invitation. The two friends flew to Cyprus at the invitation of Mr. P.C. Leventis, a mutual friend of both the Emir and the Ooni, to see a modern farm he had established. Meanwhile, a small group of the Emir's friends and *hakimai* sat in the ante room of the house that the Emir usually stayed in when in London, discussing the implications of the proposed visit by the Emir to Israel. The group was made up of the Emir of Daura, Alhaji Muhammad Bashar, Alhaji Tijjani Hashim then Turakin Kano, and Alhaji Hamidu Bayero then Barden Kano. The owner of the house, Alhaji Tijjani Hashim had, as a mark of respect for the Emir, reserved a section of his spacious house exclusively for his use. Nobody uses that section but the Emir. Alhaji Aminu Dantata, a wealthy Kano businessman and member of the Kano Emirate Council, who also has a very spacious house in the heart of London, accords the Emir the same honor.

They concluded that it was not politically advisable for Emir Ado Bayero to go to Israel. In the first place Nigeria had severed diplomatic relations with Israel following an Organization of African Unity (OAU) Resolution to that effect in October 1973.[5] The Resolution followed Israel's refusal to return parcels of land annexed from Egypt, a member state of the OAU, during the Arab-Israeli war of 1973. Secondly, Israel was accused of supporting the apartheid regime in South Africa. In fact between 1979 and 1980 the international media reported that Israel and apartheid South Africa were collaborating in developing nuclear missiles as well as other nuclear delivery systems. Given Nigeria's strong anti-apartheid posture, it was feared that in the event of apartheid South Africa acquiring superior military capability, Nigeria would be its first victim. Therefore any state that assisted apartheid South Africa in enhancing its military capability was seen as an enemy of Nigeria. Furthermore, Israel practiced Zionism, a version of apartheid, which Nigeria was dedicated to fighting. Indeed, so strong was Nigeria's position on apartheid that its permanent representatives to the United Nations occupied the Chair of the United Nations Special Committee against Apartheid continuously for over ten years.

The group then delegated Emir Ado Bayero's best friend, Emir Muhammad Bashar, to call and advise Emir Ado Bayero accordingly. Emir Bashar reached Ado Bayero on phone and advised him against making the trip. Bashar argued that given the relationship between Nigeria and Israel, Emir Ado Bayero's presence in Israel could be given some political meanings. Bashar said that he was not sure the government at home would take kindly to Ado Bayero going to Israel.

Ado Bayero gave his friend's advice some serious thought. But he concluded that since he was going on a religious pilgrimage, and as a private citizen, there was no cause for alarm. After all, the Ooni and himself were going to be there for only two days. Ado planned to spend most of his time inside the Holy Mosque of Al-Aqsa. He had planned to offer all the obligatory prayers in congregation in that mosque.

Emir Muhammad Bashar reported to Turaki Tijjani Hashim that he had spoken to Emir Ado Bayero, as they agreed, but his impression was that Ado Bayero was not convinced with the arguments against his going to Masjid Al-Aqsa. Turaki Hashim then began frantic efforts to reach the Emir on phone at Cyprus, but in vain.

Emir Ado Bayero and his friend Oba Sijuwade flew from Nicosia to Tel-Aviv, aboard an El-Al airliner. The Ooni's trip was private, not official. He was making a pilgrimage to Mount Zion, a religious ritual he had performed regularly for over twenty years. Emir Bayero's visit was making a pilgrimage to the nearly 1,500 years old Holy Mosque in Jerusalem.

As soon as the plane landed at Ben Gurion international airport, Tel-Aviv, the airline crew announced the presence of some very important dignitaries on the plane, and all passengers were requested to remain seated until the dignitaries had disembarked and the airport reception formalities had been completed. Everybody on board was wondering who those VIPs were. Emir Ado Bayero looked around the first class cabin, where they were seated, for any sign of some VIPs.

Looking through the window, Ado Bayero saw a red carpet laid from the stairs of the plane to the terminal building. There was also a guard of honor. Turning to the Ooni he asked who the important dignitaries on the plane were. Just before the Ooni could answer, some protocol officers approached them and very respectfully told them that they could disembark and that all arrangements for their reception had been concluded. Ado Bayero was baffled. How did the Israeli government know he was coming there? He was coming as a private citizen of Nigeria, on a pilgrimage to

Masjid al-Aqsa. He had no business with the government of Israel, either privately or on behalf of the Nigerian government.

For some time Ado Bayero just could not move from his seat. He understood the political implication of being received as a guest of the Israeli government. But he could not continue to sit in the plane when all the passengers were waiting for them to disembark. The two eventually climbed down the stairs on to the red carpet. Feeling very uncomfortable, Ado Bayero went through the brief airport reception of inspecting a guard of honor, wishing that all would end as quickly as possible so that he could be left alone. But hardly had the airport reception finished when another difficult demand was made on him. He was told that the Head of State, the Prime Minister, and some other key Israeli government officials would like to meet with them. Again, it was one of those requests that left one with no real option. As Ado Bayero reasoned, "You can't go to a country for the Head of State to say he wants to see you and for you to say no. It is not done." Reluctantly, Ado Bayero agreed to meet with President Chaim Herzog and the Prime Minister, but no others.

Luckily for Ado Bayero, the day was a Friday and he quickly excused himself to attend the Juma'at prayers, which are offered in the early afternoon. After the Juma'at prayers, he decided to stay inside Masjid Al-Aqsa for the Asr (late afternoon), Maghrib (dusk) and Isha'i (night) prayers. That, in effect, kept him in the mosque from the afternoon until night. Early the following morning too, Ado Bayero went to the mosque for the *Subh* (dawn) prayers. He stayed inside until sunrise before he came out. He spent some time going round the vicinity of the Holy Mosque. He entered the Mosque again about *Zuhr* time and stayed inside till after Isha'i. On the day they were leaving Israel, some pressmen requested the Emir for an interview, which he granted. In the interview, Ado Bayero lamented the sorry state into which the Holy Mosque of Al-Aqsa had been allowed to fall, presumably by the Israeli government. He then called on Muslims the world over to go and save the Mosque from total collapse. He called on well to do Muslims to contribute towards rehabilitating the Holy Mosque of Al-Aqsa, implying that the Israeli government that had forcefully occupied it, was not taking good care of it.

SANCTIONS: SUSPENSION AND RESTRICTION

The visit of the two dignitaries from Nigeria was given wide publicity in the Israeli news media. The news was also carried by a number of important Western media houses. The British Broadcasting Corporation (BBC) reported on August 20, "the Emir of Kano, Alhaji Ado Bayero and the Ooni of Ife, Oba Okunade Sijuade are now in Israel on a private visit." The report added that the two traditional rulers had held talks with Israeli leaders. "The talks" it added, "centered on bilateral issues and other areas of co-operation."[6] The reaction of the Nigerian government to that news report was swift. The Buhari regime which was fast establishing a reputation as a "no nonsense" government, reminiscent of the Murtala Muhammed administration of a decade earlier, had just taken some very important foreign policy decisions. One of them was the recognition of the Palestinian Liberation Organization, with which successive governments of Nigeria had sympathized without having the courage to accord official recognition to for fear of adverse reactions from the major nations of the Western world. Another was the recognition of the Saharawi People's Democratic Republic (SADR). Thirdly, General Buhari and President Dauda Jawara of the Gambia had barely two weeks earlier concluded a summit where they issued a communiqué which, among others, called on Israel to withdraw from all occupied Arab territories.[7]

These foreign policy initiatives by General Buhari portrayed his regime, in the eyes of the international community, as a reincarnation of Murtala Muhammed's. Given those foreign policy postures of the regime, the report of the visit to

Israel by two of the most important traditional rulers in Nigeria was viewed with all seriousness by the Federal Government. The foreign Minister, Professor Ibrahim Gambari, told the press that the visit of the two royal fathers had embarrassed the Federal Government, adding that they had not consulted the government on the visit nor obtained approval.[8]

On their return home from the trip, the two royal fathers were queried by their respective state governments. That action was followed by the announcement, simultaneously, by Governors Oladayo Popoola of Oyo State and Hamza Abdullahi of Kano State of the imposition of sanctions on the Ooni and the Emir respectively. They were suspended from the chairmanship of their respective State Councils of Chiefs for a period of six months. Secondly, they were both confined to their domains – Emir Ado Bayero to Kano City and Ooni Sijuwade to Ile-Ife—for the same period. Thirdly, their passports were withdrawn. Emir Ado Bayero was moreover removed as the Chancellor of the University of Ibadan.[9]

The government's action sent shock waves not only through the domains of the two traditional rulers but throughout the country, for the duo was inarguably two of the most influential and prestigious traditional rulers in Nigeria. The message sent by the government's action was clear: nobody was too big to be disciplined by the government.

Many questions arise out of this trip to Israel. How did the Israeli government get to know in advance that the two royal fathers were visiting Israel? Why did the Israeli government accord the visit by the two royal fathers diplomatic status when

1. They knew that the two were coming to Israel on private visits, and
2. The Ooni had been there many times in the past without the Israeli Government according him such a privilege?
3. How and why was the decision to discipline the two traditional rulers taken?

4. How did Emir Ado Bayero take the government's action? Did he see in Governor Hamza Abdullahi the spectre of another Rimi?

5. How did he relate to General Muhammadu Buhari; his Deputy, Brigadier Tunde Idiagbon; and Air Commodore Hamza Abdullahi, the Governor who announced the sanctions both during the period of the sanctions and after its expiration?

6. And how did he relate to them after all three had left office?[10]

It is not easy to unravel the reasons for the Israeli government's action. But one can hazard some guesses.

When the Ooni and Emir applied for a visa to enter Israel, the Israeli embassy in London had immediately informed Tel-Aviv and requested clearance especially as the pair were very important personalities coming from a country perceived in Israel as unfriendly. The embassy was cleared to issue them with the visas.

From that request the Israeli government came to know of the planned arrival of the Emir of Kano and the Ooni. Israeli intelligence knew who Emir Ado Bayero was. He was one of the three most important traditional rulers of Nigeria; he was from the predominantly Muslim North, which has traditionally been sympathetic to the Arabs in the conflict between Israel and the Arabs; and he was someone respected by Nigeria's political leaders. The Israeli authorities decided that the visit could not be allowed to remain private: Emir Ado Bayero was too important to be allowed to "sneak" in and out of Israel without the government taking advantage of his presence on Israeli soil.

He could either be used to influence the Nigerian government to change its hostile policy towards Israel, or he could be used to embarrass the Nigerian government by showing to the world that despite Nigeria's unfriendly foreign policy stance, its leaders relate well with the Israeli government. By receiving the two royal fathers as government guests, the Israeli government could ridicule the hard-line stance of the Buhari government.

Equally by publicizing the visit of especially Emir Ado Bayero, the Israelis could hope to boost the morale of their own citizens by showing that even their publicly sworn-enemies paid them nocturnal visits. Furthermore, the publicity could be a source of embarrassment to the Arab nations who took Nigeria's support for granted. In that way, a wedge could be planted between Nigeria and the Arab nations. This objective could have been a real possibility as the Buhari regime, under pressure from the International Monetary Fund (IMF) had turned to Saudi Arabia for financial support to enable it to reject the IMF conditionalities.

The Buhari regime had made the War against Indiscipline, WAI, a cardinal program[11]. Both General Buhari and his deputy, Brigadier Tunde Idiagbon, were firmly convinced that the bane of Nigeria's underdevelopment was indiscipline, which manifested itself in many ways—official corruption, nepotism, lack of patriotism, disorderliness, moral laxity, and lack of a sense of direction among the generality of Nigerians. They believed that once they had succeeded in instilling discipline among Nigerians, a major part of the hurdles to socio-economic development would have been scaled. And for the twenty months they were in office, they registered some success in instilling discipline among a majority of Nigerians of all social strata. Top government officials went to work on time and stayed until closing hours, sometimes longer, in order to clear their desks. Inflation of contract amounts by government officials, a practice that had become a norm in the civil service and parastatals, suddenly disappeared. The practice whereby contractors collected mobilization funds from the public treasury and abandoned their projects only to come back later asking for a variation of cost also became a thing of the past. Down the line, WAI ensured that the once rowdy motor parks in the cities, where passengers or commuters physically struggled to get a seat on any commercial vehicle, were made orderly places, where people joined queues and waited for their turn to catch the bus, train or taxi. Similar orderliness replaced the rowdiness at the nation's airports. For the first time in many years, Buhari's WAI guaranteed every potential passenger who had a boarding pass a seat on the plane. People were afraid to be caught doing the wrong thing. It was in that political atmosphere that the news of the traditional rulers' trip was reported in the international media.

Although the governors of their respective states announced the sanctions, the directive came from Dodan Barracks, the seat of the Federal Military Government. Brigadier Tunde Idiagbon, Buhari's immediate lieutenant and the officer in charge of state administration, was thoroughly embarrassed on hearing the news of the trip. He instantly summoned the two relevant military governors to Dodan Barracks. They were directed to investigate the matter—who authorized the trip, what the pair went to do, what they did, and what they said while there. They were to come down to Lagos with their reports. Governor Abdullahi did as directed. He met with the Emir and the two discussed the trip at length. The Emir narrated everything to Governor Hamza, right from the invitation up to his return. He expressed his regret over the misunderstanding, emphasizing that he went to Jerusalem as a private citizen and on pilgrimage and nothing more. He narrated the embarrassment he felt when he realized that he was being received as a guest of the Israeli Government. He also explained that his acceptance of the invitation to inspect a guard of honor at the airport and later to meet with the Israeli President and Prime Minister, even though he did not have prior knowledge of those arrangements, was to accord respect to constituted authorities. He apologized for any embarrassment his trip unwittingly had caused the federal government.

Governor Abdullahi took his report to Lagos. Upon seeing him in Dodan Barracks Brigadier Idiagbon presumptuously demanded to know what the traditional rulers were still doing in office. He added that the governors should have sacked the traditional rulers before leaving their states to come for the meeting. Meanwhile, as Governor Abdullahi was waiting for Governor Oladayo Popoola to come so that they could go and formally submit their reports to Brigadier Idiagbon, he managed first to see General Buhari. He informed the Head of State about his encounter with Idiagbon. He also briefed Buhari about his discussion with Emir Bayero. He added that from what he knew of the Emir and the discussion he had had with him, he was convinced that the Emir had not meant to embarrass the government. General Buhari appeared sympathetic to the royal fathers, but there was little he could do to save their necks. Formally, the Office of the Chief of Staff, Supreme Headquarters, was responsible for state administration. All the governors reported to the Chief of Staff, Supreme Headquarters, and Buhari, a stickler for formality and proper procedure, was not going to interfere in a matter that was not strictly in his schedule. In any case, he believed the matter was already in the hands of his very able lieutenant. Furthermore, their government had started the WAI and it was yielding positive results. Any action taken to protect the traditional rulers was bound to create the impression that some Nigerians were above the law, and that WAI was for some categories of Nigerians only. Although Idiagbon's argument was hinged on WAI, other factors came into play in aggravating the situation.

Early in their administration, General Buhari and his deputy, both of whom were Muslims, had agreed that Idiagbon would perform the pilgrimage in 1984, and Buhari in 1985. As the Chief of Staff, Supreme Headquarters, which was the equivalent of vice-president of Nigeria, Idiagbon expected the Saudis to accord him some important privileges including entrance into the Holy Ka'aba. All arrangements had been completed for Brigadier Idiagbon's trip when the news of the traditional rulers' visit to Israel, a state that was literally at war with Saudi Arabia, was relayed by the international media. The Saudis reacted immediately. They informed the Nigerian government that they could not guarantee the safety of Idiagbon while he and his team were in the Holy Land. Idiagbon was furious. He decided that the two traditional rulers who had ruined his chance of seeing the inside of the Holy Ka'aba must pay for their action.[12]

Governor Abdullahi's meeting with Buhari helped the cause of the traditional rulers, as the earlier hard-line stand of the government was mellowed. Buhari, for once, intervened on behalf of the traditional rulers. Other key officers of the government who sympathized with the position of the traditional rulers, although it is not clear whether they succeeded in influencing the outcome of the final decision, included the then Chief of Army Staff, Major-General Ibrahim Babangida, and Air Vice Marshal Mukhtar Muhammed, a member of the Supreme Military Council, the highest ruling body of the government. The two were contacted by Turakin Kano, Tijjani Hashim, who flew into Lagos as soon as he learned that the Federal Government was displeased with the visit of the two royal fathers.

When he received the letter of discipline, Ado Bayero harbored no hard feelings towards anyone—Buhari, Idiagbon, Abdullahi, or anyone of those who had participated in the decision to impose sanctions on them. In fact, he saw these people as instruments in the hands of Providence to further test his faith. Emir Ado Bayero had seen the crisis coming the night before his departure from Israel. In his sleep that night, Emir Ado Bayero had dreamt that there was a lot of commotion in Kano City. He saw himself standing on one side of the big ponds at Kofar Wambai wanting to cross it. There was *kainuwa,* specie of water lettuce, on the pond, which he wanted to step on to cross. But he was afraid that the *kainuwa* could not carry his weight. He stood there contemplating what to do. Suddenly, he heard some voices saying, *"Taka daidai, Me kayi? Taka da 'karfin ka. Babu abin da zai same ka. Hayaniya kawai za'a yi."* Meaning (Step right on it. What have you done [wrong]? Step on it with confidence. Nothing will happen to you. It is just a commotion, which will come to pass.") That exhortation emboldened him to step on the *kainuwa* and walked on the water to safety on the other side of the pond. The Emir's interpretation of that dream was that there would be a problem awaiting him at home, but nothing serious would come of it. Everything would come to pass.

Emir Ado Bayero did not think that he deserved the sanctions imposed on him, especially when he was aware that the Security Report prepared for the Federal Government had indicated that even the Israeli Government was not happy with him over his reluctance to meet with their leaders. Neither were they happy about the statements he made about the sorry state of the Holy Mosque of Al-Aqsa. Nevertheless, he understood the need for the government not to send the wrong signal to the public about its resolve to instill discipline in the society. Emir Ado Bayero took it that the sanctions they had received were their own contribution towards instilling discipline in the Nigerian society. It was not going to help the cause of WAI, he reasoned, for the government to absolve them at that time, particularly given the wide negative publicity the trip had received at home. Emir Ado Bayero understood that in administration, some decisions are taken for their symbolic value, for the message they will send to the generality of the public. The sanctions meted out to them were one such decision, he concluded.

Except for the media publicity that followed the announcement of the sanctions, nobody would have known, during the six months the sanctions were in force that the Emir was under such restriction. This is because his daily routine for over two decades did not change during that time. He was normally up early enough for the Subh prayers, the time of which varies with the seasons, from 4.30 a.m. to 5.30 a.m. He would read the Holy Qur'an until about 7 a.m. when he would move to his private office to receive early morning visitors. He would be there until 9.30 or 10 a.m. when he would return to the house and prepare to come out to receive formal guests or attend Council meetings or hold court. That would last until about 1 p.m. or 1.30 p.m. when he retired into the house for meals, prayers and some rest. He would come out again about 4.30 p.m. to attend to visitors sometimes until

Maghrib, the time of which varies from about 6.15 to 6.45 p.m. depending on the season. If he had an appointment he would come out again in the night. Every Friday that he is in town, he would spend between an hour and an hour and a half in the morning, usually between 9 a.m. and 10.30 a.m. seeing members of the royal household and other residents of the Palace. He would also give alms to children, the sick, and the needy. Thereafter, he would sit on the throne in one of the spacious halls in the palace to receive homage from his subjects. On that occasion, protocol was observed very strictly. The most senior *hakimi,* currently the Waziri, was the first to go and pay homage. He was followed by the Galadima, the Madaki, the Wambai, Wali, and Makama in that order until all the *hakimai* had paid their homage. Next come the *dagatai* and the *masu unguwa,* then the *talakawa.* Sometimes, prominent sons of Kano of aristocratic or commoner background precede the *dagatai* in paying homage.

During the period of the sanctions also, the Emir continued to preside over the meetings of the Kano Emirate Council, which met more regularly than the Kano State Council of Chiefs, (the latter sometimes does not meet for a whole six months). Just a few weeks into the sanctions, Governor Hamza Abdullahi received Emir Ado Bayero at the Government House when he paid a courtesy call during the Babbar Sallah. In his speech on that occasion Emir Ado Bayero commended the federal and state governments for the steps they had taken to ameliorate the suffering of the masses of the people. The Governor had announced that essential commodities worth seven million Naira (eleven million USD) had been purchased by the state government for sale to the public at affordable prices. Thus, in effect, for the whole period the Emir was under sanctions he was not kept idle.

Two events have left indelible impressions about Emir Ado Bayero on General Buhari. The first occurred when Buhari was still in office, as Head of State. Barely two months after the expiration of the sanctions, which his government had imposed on Emir Ado Bayero and the Ooni, General Buhari decided to visit Kano. The reception he received from the Emir at his palace, including a mini durbar surpassed anything Buhari imagined he would get from a traditional ruler his government had just disciplined. After all, even though he sympathized with the traditional rulers over their fates, he never publicly or even in private dissociated himself from those penalties.

The second incident occurred in 1992 when the Emir was bereaved. General Buhari, whose government was toppled seven years earlier, went to Kano on a condolence visit. Traditionally, when the Emir of Kano leaves his court at about 1 p.m. and retires into the house, he does not come out again until after the Asr prayers. But on this particular occasion, even though it was not normally done, information was passed to the Emir that General Muhammadu Buhari had come on a condolence visit, and the Emir came out and received him. Those two acts of the Emir have left indelible impressions about Emir Ado Bayero on General Buhari.

Although General Idiagbon refused to talk about the past until he died on March 24, 1999, it is on record that when Emir Ado Bayero visited Ilorin in 1992 for the installation of late Alhaji Aliyu Abdulqadir as the Emir of Ilorin, Idiagbon went and paid him homage. [13]

NOTES

1. See chapter ten for details.
2. We noted in the previous chapter that Alhaji Ahmed Muhammed Sani, was in Governor Rimi's cabinet, when his father died. When the Kano State Government delegation was going to Gumel on a condolence visit, Governor Rimi had directed the leader of the delegation and Commissioner for Local Government Affairs, Shehu Muhammed Shanono to inform the Wazirin Gumel that Ahmed Muhammed Sani's name must be included in the list of nominees for the office of Emir that would be forwarded to the Governor for selection and approval. It is widely believed that but for that inter-

vention the Gumel Emirate Kingmakers would not have included Ahmed Muhammed Sani on the list.

3. Between independence in 1960 and 1998, Nigeria experienced six successful coups de tat. These were on January 15, 1966; July 29, 1966; July 29, 1975; December 31, 1984; August 27, 1985; and November 17, 1993. There were many abortive ones.

4. The first and second are the haramaini, namely the Holy Ka'aba in Makka al-Mukarrama and the Holy Prophet's mosque in Madinatu al-Munawwara. The significance of Masjid al-Aqsa in Islam lies in the fact that it is the only mosque after the Ka'aba mentioned in the Holy Qur'an. It is as Allah (SWT) says, "a Mosque whose precincts We did Bless..." (HQ XVII:1) Equally significant about Masjid al-Aqsa is the fact that Prophet Muhammad (May Peace and Blessings of Allah be upon him) made the miraj, or ascension through the seven heavens to the Sublime Throne from that mosque. For details on the miraj see HQ XVII, and especially Abdullah Yusuf Ali's introduction to that chapter. See *The Holy Qur'an: Text, Translation and Commentary*, (Beirut, Dar Al Arabia, 1934).

5. Before that time Israel had a diplomatic mission in Lagos, the federal capital. But Nigeria did not open a mission in Tel-Aviv.

6. See *New Nigerian* of 21st August 1984, p.1 story titled "Bayero, Sijuade in Israel." It is interesting to note that the BBC reported that the visit was private. And at the same time claimed that talks were held that centered on bilateral issues and other areas of co-operation.

7. "OAU I'll Survive" *Daily Sketch*, July 24, 1984, p.1.

8. "FMG Unhappy with Bayero, Sijuade, over Israeli Visit." *New Nigerian*, August 22, 1984, p. 1.

9. *The Daily Times* of September 1, 1984 had the following for its headline: Oni, Bayero Disciplined. Ado Bayero is currently the Chancellor, University of Maiduguri.

10. Hamza Abdullahi eventually retired from the Nigerian Air Force wearing the rank of Air Vice-Marshal.

11. General Muhammadu Buhari's government did not last long enough to actualize Rousseau's advice to political leaders to the effect that "the strongest is never strong enough to be always the master, unless he transforms strength into right and obedience into duty." The regime had launched the 3rd phase of WAI, which focused on fostering stronger sense of nationalism and patriotism among Nigerians. Its objective was to inculcate in people the inherent virtue of discipline, so that it would become part of the people's way of life, instead of the situation then in existence where people obeyed the laws more out of fear of reprisals from the government than any belief in the inherent goodness of obeying the laws. But a palace coup on August 27, 1985, led by Buhari's Army Chief of Staff, Major General Ibrahim Badamasi Babangida terminated the life of the regime.

12. The following year General Idiagbon was invited by the Saudi government to perform the pilgrimage. Ironically, it was while he was there that General Babangida conducted the coup against their government.

13. Sadly, I could not get General Idiagbon to speak to me on this project as all efforts, which included five visits to his Ilorin home over a period of three years (1994-1997) and the personal intervention of his good friend and colleague, General Muhammadu Buhari, could not get him to open up on their years in government. Idiagbon died on March 24, 1999.

THE NEW TITLE HOLDERS

THE QUEST FOR TRADITIONAL TITLES

There has in recent years been a resurgence of interest in the acquisition of traditional titles by people who are not ordinarily from royal, aristocratic or other traditional ruling families. Retired military officers, civil servants and businessmen of commoner ancestry who have achieved some level of recognition in their chosen professions, or have come into wealth, want to cap it with a traditional title.

The rate at which chieftaincy titles are given to this class of people, especially in the Southern parts of the country, has become a matter of serious concern among both admirers and critics of traditional institutions. A number of state governments in the aborted Third Republic proposed steps they considered necessary to save the institution from itself. Governor Bamidele Olumilua, for example, proposed the imposition of a N5,000 levy on every chieftaincy title awarded in Ondo state. Edo State made it mandatory for all traditional title holders to register such titles with the state government before they could use the prefix "Chief" before their names. Put in other words, the conferment of a chieftaincy title by a properly constituted awarding authority did not make such an award valid until a certificate of chieftaincy had been secured from the government. Governor Michael Otedola of Lagos State also stated his intention to come up with a proposal to curtail the cheapening of the title of "chief."

While the quest for traditional titles cut across the nation, the indiscriminate awards have been more pronounced in the Southern states of the country. In the emirate states of the North, where emiral authority has continued to carry some weight, some efforts have been made to save the institution from becoming an all-comers affair. Particularly in Ado Bayero's Kano, concerted efforts have been made to maintain the respectability of the institution and the titles it awards by restricting such awards to hereditary families.

Up to the end of the 1980s Emir Ado Bayero carefully avoided succumbing to the enormous pressure from Kano's *nouveaux riches* to admit them into the aristocracy. He ensured that, up to that time, everyone to whom he gave a traditional title could lay historical claims to it.[1] However, after 1990, in very quick succession, the Emir gave the titles of Talba, Ajiya, Zanna, Kacalla, and Kaigama to people who were perceived as *shigeges*. A *shigege* is a new entrant into the aristocracy, whose claim to the office is not hereditary but achieved. In other words a *shigege* is someone who, on his own merit and not because of his pedigree, is given a traditional title. The opposite of a *shigege* is a *karda*, or one who gets a title purely on ascription.[2]

Not a few people have expressed their concern at the conferment of titles on some of these new title holders. A few more have questioned the rationale of Emir Ado Bayero appointing, for example, Alhaji Garba A.D. as the Talban Kano, or Alhaji Aminu Ahmed Maiturare as the Zannan Kano, or Alhaji Muhammadu Dansarari as the Ajiyan Kano, or Alhaji Mustapha Galadima as the Kacalla. Some have even questioned the appointment of Alhaji Abba Ahmed as the Ma'ajin Watari and Alhaji Muhammadu Adamu Dankabo as Jarma even though neither appointee is a *shigege* as such. To these critics, the common denominator to all these new title holders is their wealth. Each and every one of them belongs to the *nouveaux riches* of Kano.[3]

THE RATIONALE FOR THE
CONFERMENT OF TITLES

To Emir Ado Bayero's critics, the conferment of titles on these prominent Kano citizens of humble origin is one sure way of cheapening the titles. But is the practice of conferring traditional titles on people of non-aristocratic background a new phenomenon in the history of Kano? Is Emir Ado Bayero doing anything different from what some of Kano's greatest rulers of the past did? What are its perceived dangers, and what are its advantages?

Although Hausa society has for long been recognized by some as a class society, it was by no means a caste society. Indeed, Kano's greatness from the fourteenth century down to the twentieth can rightly be attributed to, among other factors, its ability to co-opt peoples of various ethnic nationalities, assimilate them and indigenize them. Many of the prominent wards in Kano City such as Alfindiki and Alkantara, Unguwar Ayagi and Tudun Nufawa, Yakasai and Zangon Barebari, Agadasawa and Arzai were founded by settlers. After a generation or less, these settlers came to acquire the same rights as their hosts. In fact, they came to be considered indigenes. Where foreigners came in large numbers to settle in Kasar Kano, they were usually given land on which to build their own villages. The villages of Hungu, Faragai and Sayasaya are examples of such settlements that came to be integral parts of Kano with their residents having the full citizenship of Kasar Kano. The important factor determining assimilation appeared to be Islam. Once an individual or a group of people is Muslim, other differences, like ethnicity or race became unimportant.

In the same way that individual foreigners or large numbers of settlers were accepted and assimilated into Kano culture, so did the rulers co-opt commoners and even settlers into the ruling class. For example, Sarki Abdullahi Burja, who ruled Kano between 1438 and 1452, appointed Gwauran Duma, a Borno settler in Kano, to his Council of State. Similarly, Amir Muhammad Bello (1882-1892) appointed

Garba Mai Jonijoni, also from Borno, the Sarkin Balare and later Sarkin Gaya. Even as late as the reign of Sarki Alu (1892-1903), Dandalma Makwalo, another settler from Borno, was appointed Sarkin Gaya, Kura and Garko at different times.[4] In 1933, Mallam Sulaimanu, a scholar of commoner descent, was co-opted into the aristocracy when he was made Ma'ajin Kano by Emir Abdullahi Bayero. Five years later, in 1938, the office of Wali was created and Ma'aji Sulaimanu became the first Wali of Kano. In all cases where commoners or even settlers were co-opted into the aristocracy the most important consideration was their contribution, real or potential, to the development of the emirate, and sometimes their loyalty to the head of the emirate. Sulaimanu commended himself to Emir Abbas and later Emir Abdullahi Bayero because of his learning. He was reputed to have been very learned even as a young man.[5]

How does Emir Ado Bayero justify his choice of new titleholders? In what ways can Emir Ado Bayero's appointees be said to have contributed to the development of Kano Emirate? Emir Ado Bayero and members of his emirate council have justified the choice of the recipients of each and every title that they have given especially to the non-hereditary titleholders.

They have noted, for example, that the decision to honor Alhaji Garba A.D. with the title of *Talba* was to show appreciation to Alhaji Garba for his untiring efforts in making Kano excel in at least four areas. First, he was one of the pioneer industrialists of Kano. By spear-heading the establishment of industries in Kano, Alhaji Garba A.D. sought to diversify the economic base of the State and at the same time provide job opportunities to Kano people, especially graduates of tertiary and secondary institutions of learning. Secondly, Alhaji Garba A.D. sought to train Nigerians particularly Kano people to handle most of the operations of his factories. He recruited many secondary school graduates and sent them to Europe and Japan to train in handling the various machines in the various factories he had established in

Kano. Thirdly, Garba A.D. has been one of the three key philanthropists of Kano.

The other two being Aminu Dantata and Isyaku Rabi'u. He has built many schools and clinics and mosques across the emirate. He has also to his credit provided deep-water wells in many villages and even within metropolitan Kano to areas with water problems. He imported merchandise in large quantities which he gave out to scores of Kano's rising business class who became distributors. Many of these distributors did not have to make any deposit before they were allowed to collect the goods. These distributors, in turn, have many people working under them as retailers. Garba A.D. was also known to have fulfilled every pledge he had made for assistance towards community development. And finally and perhaps most importantly, despite his commoner ancestry, Alhaji Garba had shown reverence and great personal commitment to the institution of *sarauta*. He was one of the few rich people in Kano who took great pride in the institution of Kano *sarauta* and spent from his wealth to ensure that the institution was sustained at its most critical time. Palace sources recall that at one time all the vehicles used in conveying the *dogarai* and other palace officials when the Emir went to some function outside the palace were grounded. The State Government was not ready to repair them, nor was any group or institution. The palace did not have the resources as there was at that time no constitutional provision similar to the five percent that the Abacha administration introduced for traditional institutions. Traditional institutions were, to a large extent, left at the mercy of the state governments. When Garba A.D. heard about the situation, he provided the palace with two new air-conditioned luxury Asia buses each capable of conveying 35 people. Furthermore, he undertook to maintain the vehicles. He went further and renovated parts of the Kano palace and built a new gallery over-looking the durbar ground so that the Emir could be more dignified when he hosts dignitaries to a durbar. But most important of all, his massive wealth notwithstanding, Alhaji Garba was humble enough to visit the palace on Fridays, and just like any subject of the emir await his turn to pay his homage to Emir Ado Bayero. The difference between Alhaji Garba A.D. and other wealthy Kano people who also contributed to the development of Kano but were not given traditional titles was in the public interest and commitment shown to the institution of *sarauta* by Alhaji Garba.

Whereas, Alhaji Garba A.D. would go to the palace and take his turn behind the *hakimai*, some of whom might have been beneficiaries of his generosity, and remove his shoes and sit on the carpet to pay homage to Emir Ado Bayero who would be sitting on the throne, the other wealthy people would rather pay private visits to the Emir.

Alhaji Aminu Ahmed Maiturare's choice for the title of Zanna was informed by similar considerations as Alhaji Garba A..D.'s. Aminu Ahmed is a businessman and a youth leader. He is reputed to have helped many Kano young men set up their own businesses through the Kano Traders' Association in the 1970s and 1980s. He had extended credit facilities to many of Kano's young traders. Aminu had saved many traders whose businesses were collapsing. Aminu Ahmed's actions were all geared towards ensuring that Kano retained its pre-eminent position as the commercial nerve centre not only of the Northern states of Nigeria but the neighboring states of Niger, Chad and Cameroon. So popular did he become among the young and rising commercial class in Kano that a delegation of this class went to the Emir and thanked him for the assistance Aminu Ahmed was giving to them. It was this same group that later made a case for the conferment of a title to Alhaji Aminu Ahmed. According to palace sources however, it was not enough for people to make a case for another person. That person must show serious commitment to the institution. And Aminu had for years shown in words and deeds that he was a traditionalist and was ready to defend the institution at all times. Apart from his public show of commitment to traditional institution, he also spent from his wealth to build Islamiyya schools and mosques. Since the office of emir was essentially a religious office, anyone who supported the cause of Islam was helping the emir in his work of propagating the religion and was so recognized.

The Ma'ajin Watari, Alhaji Abba Ahmed, is not really a *shigege*. He is a descendant of Amir Sulaiman, the first post-jihad Amir of Kano. The title of Ma'ajin Watari had been held by the descendants of Sulaiman for some time after Dabo became emir. But after a while the title became moribund, perhaps because the lineage of Sulaiman would rather focus on scholarship than earthly authority. When in the last quarter of the twentieth century, a descendant of Amir Sulaiman showed keen interest in the title therefore, it was only natural that he was considered for it.

The award of the titles of Ajiya, Kacalla and Jarma on Muhammadu Dansarari, Mustapha Galadima and Muhammadu Adamu Dankabo respectively among others has also been rationalized on similar grounds. Muhammadu Adamu Dankabo's contribution to the improvement of the life of the people, not only of Kabo, his village, nor even Kano his state, but Nigerians in general is public knowledge. He has been described as a good ambassador of Kano. He has built mosques not only in Kano emirate but also in other states of Nigeria. He has also built hospitals and Islamiyya schools. Adamu Dankabo is a *karda* in the sense that he came from an aristocratic family. What Emir Ado Bayero did was to upgrade him from the status of *dagaci* to *hakimi*, as a result of the creation of Kabo local government, from the then Gwarzo local government, with Kabo village as headquarters.

All of Emir Ado Bayero's appointees have been people who have shown great reverence to traditional institutions. All of them have contributed immensely of their time, resources and energy towards protecting, promoting and dignifying the institution. Many have spent a lot of their personal wealth to dignify the institution. Others have done a lot of community service, providing for the people of their locality and the emirate in general services that touch on the lives of many ordinary citizens. It is these services, coupled with a demonstration of a sufficient interest in the institution that have recommended them to Emir Ado Bayero for the award of titles. While inheritance still plays a key role, Emir Ado Bayero believes that Kano society is not a caste society, where people were condemned to their stations at birth. Kano's progress, argues the Emir, could not have been achieved without the rulers giving due recognition to those people of commoner descent including settlers who demonstrated commitment to the development of the emirate.

Interestingly, the Emirate has used the institution of marriage to both further cement the bond of fidelity between the aristocracy and the palace and to assimilate titleholders of commoner descent into the aristocracy. It is important to note the common denominator in the characteristics of all the commoner titleholders. The differences in position, temperament, wealth, level of education and other factors among the awardees notwithstanding, the common factor among them, and which more than anything else recommended them for the titles, is their recognition and show of respect to the person and office of the Emir of Kano. The greatest show of respect to the Emir of Kano is not in what you do or say to him in private, but that public acknowledgement of his suzerainty, as in paying homage to the emir while he is on the throne, or coming out to the street to salute the Emir when he is passing by.

NOTES

1. It is pertinent to note that not all the claims could be substantiated. But the important thing was that the awardees always laid such claims and it was usually on the basis of such claims, that the Emir conferred the awards.
2. It should be pointed out that since the title given to the *shigege* is personal to him, it couldn't be transferred to

his offspring. But a *shigege* who lives up to the expectations of the emir and has offspring who exhibit qualities of their father could succeed in making the title hereditary to his family. Similarly, although karda is ascriptive, the element of competition for all offices introduces the achievement factor.

3. A probable exception is the Kacalla, Alhaji Mustapha Galadima, whose appointment was influenced by the then head of state, General Sani Abacha, who came from the same local government—Fagge—with the Kacalla. Indeed, the conferment of that title was one of the few instances when the Emir had reluctantly succumbed to external pressure. According to palace sources, when Fagge Local Government was created the people of the area made a request to the Emir that they would like a district head from among residents of the area. The Emir had already decided that he was not going to post a district head to Fagge, but appoint one from there. He had not however, decided on the person when the request from the then Head of State came. Perhaps even without Abacha's intervention the Emir would still have appointed Mustapha Galadima.

4. Alhaji Sule Gaya, Sarkin Fadan Kano, "The Contribution of Kano Traditional Institutions to Social Integration and National Unity" Paper presented at the Workshop Organized by the Kano State Constitutional Conference Committee, April 5-14, 1994.

5. For a fuller account of the life of Wali Sulaiman, see Alkali Hussaini Sufi, *Musan Kammu: Wali Sulaimanu a Tarihin Kano*, (Kano, Mai-Nassara Press, 1983).

THE QUIIAL ADO

THE MAN BEHIND THAT MASK

Just who is the man behind that mask? Who is Alhaji Ado Bayero? What qualities of his are most admired by those who know him, and what qualities are only tolerated? I have put these questions to everybody that I have talked to while writing this project. The refrain has been the following: Emir Ado Bayero is a principled, peace-loving, humble, trustworthy, law-abiding, patient, God-fearing, honest, non-covetous, helpful, dignified, proud, broad-minded, progressive, far-sighted and honorable person. But I have not been satisfied with the simple enumeration of these qualities by scores of respondents even though most of them are very responsible people in our nation. I have asked them to give me concrete reasons to justify each of the qualities they attribute to the emir. The following are some of the anecdotes given to justify the above characterizations of the emir.

A MAN OF HONOR

The Adamu Gaya Story

Adamu Gaya was three years ahead of Ado Bayero at the Kano Middle School. For the two years they spent together at the school, 1944-1945, Adamu Gaya, despite his being Ado's senior, both in age and in school, treated Ado with some deference. He never sent Ado on an errand as other senior students were wont to or treated him the way senior boys normally treated their juniors. A day before Adamu passed out of school, in 1945, he called Ado to bid him good-bye. After wishing Ado well in his school life, Adamu made one request. He said, "My wish is that you will appoint me Sarkin Gaya, when you become the Emir of Kano."

Ado was only 15 at that time. He had nearly a dozen elder brothers, and another dozen younger brothers, scores of nephews and cousins and a number of uncles each of whom could legitimately stake a claim to that office. Yet there he was, being told to look forward to becoming the Emir of Kano some day. Young Ado, as is natural with all princes, wished he would one day become Emir. But the sheer number of eligible contenders, coupled with his age, did not give him cause to be encouraged. All the same, he felt that Adamu Gaya, who had been so nice to him for the two years they spent at the school together deserved an answer from him, and a favorable one for that matter. So he told Adamu Gaya that if he became Emir and a vacancy existed, he would grant his wish.

Seventeen years later, in 1963, Ado Bayero became Emir of Kano. Not too long after that, in 1968, the Sarkin Gaya died. While many contenders appeared for the now vacant office, Emir Ado remembered his promise. He looked at the names of the short-listed candidates, but did not find Adamu Gaya's name. By now, Adamu Gaya had taken up a job as an assistant medical dispenser.

To the surprise of everyone, Emir Ado Bayero asked for Adamu Gaya who, like all the others, was also a legitimate heir to the vacant office of Sarkin Gaya. When Adamu came, Emir Ado told him that he had gone through the list of candidates for the office, but did not see Adamu's name; that was why he had called him to find out if he really was not interested in the office. He reminded Adamu that he had given him his word, and that for as long as Adamu was interested in the office, he would not give it to anyone else. Adamu then told the Emir that he had not indicated interest in the office, first because he was not sure the Emir would remember the promise, especially as it was made a very long time ago. Secondly, because he reasoned that even if he got the office, he did not have the money for the elaborate celebrations that go with the formal installation.

Emir Ado Bayero then approved the appointment of Adamu Gaya as Sarkin Gaya. To take care of Adamu's second fear, the Emir offered to write off the expenses of the celebrations. In return, Emir Ado Bayero requested Sarki Gaya Adamu to be God-fearing and just in the administration of his people. Adamu Gaya remained a loyal hakimi of the Emir of Kano until 1981 when the Rimi administration excised Gaya from Kano emirate and made it an independent emirate. The PRP Senator Adamu Gaya, who was appointed the Emir of Gaya by Governor Rimi, decided to appoint Adamu Gaya (the Emir of Kano's hakimi) his hakimi with the title Wambai and made District head of Gaya city. Many admirers of the Emir of Kano felt that by accepting to remain a hakimi in the new Gaya emirate, Sarkin Gaya, Adamu Gaya had betrayed Emir Ado Bayero. This feeling was accentuated by the fact that the excision exercise was generally perceived to have been done to spite the Emir of Kano, as discussed in chapter eight. There is also the fact that two *hakimai* appointed by the Emir of Kano to territories that came to be part of the new Jigawa State opted to return to Kano for re-posting by Emir Ado Bayero instead of remaining at their posts.

When Sabo Bakin Zuwo became Governor and immediately abolished the Rimi-created emirates in 1983, many people expected Emir Ado Bayero to sack Sarkin Gaya, Adamu Gaya by withdrawing his traditional title. But Emir Ado Bayero did not do that. Realizing that Adamu Gaya had lost face among his own people in Gaya for what he did to his benefactor, the Emir of Kano, Ado Bayero decided to post him to Kunci with the new title of Katukan Kano. Adamu Gaya died at Kunci.

The Babba Dan Agundi Story

Alhaji Babba Dan Agundi was in the 1950s and early 1960s a leader of the Northern Elements Progressive Union, NEPU, the main opposition party in the North. Among his schedules was applying for permission for the NEPU to hold political rallies or meetings in Kano emirate. Babba would normally write the application and take it to the office of the Chief of the NA Police for approval. Since Ado became Police Chief, Babba did not have to see the Police Chief before his applications were approved. One day when Babba took his application to the office, he requested to see the Police Chief. The secretary collected the application, entered it in the records, filed it, and took it to the Chief. Within minutes, it was out with the Chief's approval. But Babba wanted to see the Chief.

When he was ushered before the Police Chief, Babba told Ado that he had come to see him for two reasons; first, to express his appreciation for the prompt way his applications had been receiving attention from the Police Chief; and secondly, to request that Ado Bayero should make him Sarkin Dawaki Mai Tuta on his becoming Emir of Kano. That was at a time when the powerful Emir Muhammadu Sanusi was on the throne. Emir Sanusi was, unarguably, the most powerful traditional ruler in Nigeria at that time, and nobody was thinking of when the office of the Emir of Kano was going to be vacant. Moreover, like Emir Abdullahi Bayero before him, Emir Sanusi was grooming one of his sons to succeed him.

Ado felt the request was awkward. But it had been made, and the man making it appeared serious. He would not leave that office until he had an answer. Ado tried to brush the matter aside, but Babba insisted on getting an answer. Ado then said to him, "Okay." Babba then left. About four years later, Ado became Emir. Another fifteen years later, in 1978, Sarkin Dawaki Mai Tuta, Bello Dandago died. While many eligible contenders for the title were busy out-doing each other in competition for the office, Babba sought audience with the emir.

Emir Ado Bayero did not need to be reminded about his word to Babba Dan Agundi. Ado recognized that Babba was a non-conformist, and at one time had been a radical critic of traditional institutions. But then he had made a promise, even though at the time he had thought that the probability of being asked to redeem it was very remote.

And that was how Babba Dan Agundi became the Sarkin Dawaki Mai Tuta of Kano and one of the staunchest defenders of traditional institutions until he died nearly twenty years later.

A Man of Principles

Opposition to Traditional Rulers
Endorsement of Abacha for President

Critics of traditional institutions accuse traditional rulers of general lack of principles, saying that they always dance to the tune of the government of the day. The critics argue that it is not what the traditional rulers believe is right, or what their subjects think is right that they ask for, but what the government of the day tells them it wants to do. This perception of traditional rulers gained wide currency especially when the General Abacha government-created Committee of Traditional Rulers and Leaders of Thought came out and publicly endorsed the General's bid to transform himself from a military Head of State into the civilian President of Nigeria's Fourth Republic. Many people, all over the country, criticized the traditional rulers for that stand, which was widely believed to be at variance with what they knew to be in the national interest as well as what their subjects wanted.

The impression Nigerians got was that there was unanimity in the decision of the traditional rulers to endorse Abacha. But that was not the case as the following two incidents indicate. Early in 1998, the Head of state had sent his

249

aide to the Emir with a request that the Emir should endorse Abacha's plan to transform from a military to a civilian ruler. He was also requested to appeal to his colleagues, other emirs, and chiefs to do the same. The aide told the Emir that a presidential jet had been parked for him at the Kano airport. He was also told that there was enough money in the plane to take care of the assignment he was being asked to do. After the aide had finished speaking the Emir replied that he was not a politician and would not dabble in partisan politics. Abacha's aide, who incidentally was from Kano Emirate, appealed to the Emir to reconsider his position as the Head of State would not be happy to hear that the Emir did not support his moves. When the pressure was becoming too much the Emir told the aide that he did not think that it was proper for Abacha to want to transform to a civilian president, adding that those people who were advising him to do so were not sincere to themselves. He asked the aide to go away with his plane and money.

When Abacha was told about the Emir's reaction to his request, he was livid. Sensing the mood of the General, his advisors suggested that he should remove the Emir from office. General Abacha expressed fears about the social consequences of taking such an action. He was reminded that he had ordered the removal of Sultan Dasuki two years earlier and nothing happened. It was also pointed out that the removal of the powerful Emir of Kano, Muhammadu Sanusi by Premier Ahmadu Bello did not lead to any crisis engulfing Kano. Abacha told his advisors that he was not satisfied with those two examples. As a compromise, it was agreed that the Emir's territory was going to be balkanized and two new emirates created and given to loyalists of Abacha. That decision was leaked to the Emir. In the calculation of Abacha's strategists, the realization that government was contemplating breaking up his emirate might make the Emir co-operate. However, at a meeting of the Northern members of the Committee of Traditional Rulers and leaders of Thought held at Kaduna in preparation for the general meeting, Emir Ado

Bayero cautioned his brother emirs and chiefs against dab-
bling in politics to the extent of endorsing a presidential candidate. When a few days later, a meeting of the full committee was convened at Abuja Emir Ado Bayero did not want to
go because he sensed that the Committee's endorsement of
Abacha was a foregone conclusion. Yet, he did not want to
appear as an open critic of the Government. To the government any expression of dissenting opinion, no matter how
rational, was regarded as disloyalty or even sedition. He went
to Abuja where he monitored the trend of the discussion at the
meeting on the first day. He was right. The discussion was
building up for a resolution to endorse Abacha. That evening
Emir Ado Bayero met the chairman of the committee and
requested permission to be absent at the following days' sessions, due to previous commitments.

When Abacha was briefed about the details of what had
transpired at the Kaduna and Abuja meetings he was out-
raged to hear that the Emir of his birth-city had opposed his
bid. He swore to get even with the Emir.[1] All arrangements
were concluded for the deposition of the emir, so as to clear
the way of all potential opposition, when Abacha mysteri-
ously died on Monday June 8, 1998.

Reports coming out of the Presidential Villa, and carried
in some of the nation's newspapers, confirmed that Emir Ado
Bayero had opposed the succession plan of General Abacha.
For daring to do that, he was slated for deposition the very
week that Abacha died.[2]

The Deposition of Sultan Ibrahim Dasuki

On April 20, 1996, the Sokoto State Government announced
the deposition of the 18th Sultan of Sokoto, Alhaji Ibrahim
Dasuki, and his banishment to Zing in Taraba State. It was
widely believed that Governor Yakubu Muazu's action complied with a directive from Abuja. Immediately the government announced the appointment of Alhaji Muhammadu
Maccido as the new Sultan, traditional rulers from different

parts of the country began to troop to Sokoto to congratulate the new Sultan. But Emir Ado Bayero did not go. The Federal, Kano, and Sokoto State Governments felt very uncomfortable with the absence of the Emir of Kano from Sokoto. An emissary was sent to the Emir.[3] The emissary appealed to the Emir to consider going to Sokoto as the authorities wished him to go. Politely but firmly, Emir Ado Bayero refused. He still would not budge even when he was reminded that the Shehu of Borno, the Emirs of Zaria, Gwandu and other important emirs as well as obis and obas from the South had all gone. He was also told that the federal government had directed the state governments to ensure that their key traditional rulers went to Sokoto, but still he refused.

After the emissary had made his points, Emir Ado Bayero made three observations. First, he noted that it was not the tradition of Kano emirs to go and congratulate a traditional ruler on the announcement of his appointment.[4] Kano Emirs only attend the official ceremony for the presentation of staff of office. Secondly, the emir noted that the procedure adopted in deposing Sultan Dasuki was wrong. He was not informed of why he was being deposed; neither was he given the opportunity to defend himself. Finally, he told the emissary that his refusal to go to Sokoto should not be construed to mean a personal animosity towards the new Sultan. He reminded the emissary that he, Emir Ado Bayero, was closer to Sultan Muhammadu Maccido than any of those showing concern about his refusal to show up at Sokoto. He reminded them that he had married Sultan Maccido's younger sister.

A MAN OF PEACE

The Assassination of General Murtala Muhammed

When General Murtala Muhammed, the Kano-born Head of State of Nigeria between August 1975 and February 1976, was assassinated in an abortive coup, a palpable fear enveloped the country. Many people in the North saw the

Dimka-led abortive coup as another January 1966, where northern leaders were targeted for elimination. Within a few hours after the confirmation of the death of Muhammed, many Southerners resident in the North, but especially in Kano, began to flee back to the South. Many Northerners had prepared to avenge the death of Muhammed; but Emir Ado Bayero came out and addressed the people. The abortive coup, he said, was neither ethnic nor religious. Those responsible were being rounded up and the government would deal with them according to the laws of the land. He appealed to the people against taking the law into their own hands. He also appealed to those fleeing to stay, assuring them of their safety, and the safety of their property.

The Emir's appeal was broadcast over the radio and television at regular intervals until the tension eased off completely.

Not too long after that, however, a very senior military officer of northern origin came to see the Emir. He took the opportunity to express his displeasure, and that of his colleagues, presumably from the North, at the Emir's role in containing the situation in the North when Murtala was assassinated. According to the officer, the Emir's act indicated to them that should any of them be assassinated, the Emir would not see to it that their death was avenged.

And Bringing Peace to Yoruba and Ibolands

In 1976, after many fruitless attempts by various concerned individuals and groups in Yorubaland to bring two important Yoruba Obas, the Alaafin of Oyo, Oba Lamidi Olayiwola Adeyemi and the Shoun of Ogbomosho, Oba Oladunni Oyewunmi Ajagungbade III to reconcile over some misunderstanding, Yoruba leaders decided to invite Alhaji Ado Bayero to come and settle the two obas. Prior to that formal invitation from Yoruba leaders the Emir had tried to bring reconciliation between the two obas when a clash had erupted between their supporters at the University of Ibadan where the Emir who was chancellor had gone to open the new mosque of the university. The two obas were among the dignitaries present. On that occasion, the Emir had taken the Alaafin in his car to his residence, and got the Shoun to also come there. It appeared that peace had been restored in Yorubaland. But not too long after that a clash erupted again. That was when the Yoruba leaders decided to call Emir Ado Bayero to make peace between the two royal fathers.

On another occasion in the early 1970s, the Administrator of the East-Central State Chief Ukpabi Asika called Emir Ado Bayero and requested his royal intervention to settle a rift between the Obi of Onitsha and his chiefs. Emir Ado Bayero went to Onitsha where the Onitsha chiefs, including the Owelle, Nnamdi Azikiwe, met him at the Onitsha end of the Asaba Bridge. The Obi was conspicuously absent. The chiefs wanted to host the Emir at some place different from the Obi's palace. The Emir asked the Owelle in Hausa why he joined the chiefs to rebel against the Obi. Turning to the chiefs, Emir Ado Bayero directed that their first place of call should be the Obi's palace. At a closed-door session, the Emir was able to reconcile the two parties.

And June 12, Too...

After ten years of another bout of military rule, Nigerians were again given the opportunity to choose their president. They went to the polls on Saturday, June 12, 1993, to choose between the Abeokuta-born Chief Moshood Kashimawo Olawale Abiola of the Social Democratic Party, SDP, and the Kano-born Alhaji Bashir Othman Tofa of the National Republican Convention, NRC. Four days after the elections, and as the election results from the states began to trickle in, the Babangida administration first directed the National Electoral Commission of Nigeria (NEC) to suspend further announcement of the results. Then on June 23, it announced the annulment of the elections.

The aftermath of that annulment was a serious political crisis in the country. Disintegration appeared imminent. The Western part of Nigeria threatened to secede from the federation because, as they argued, Abiola was being denied the opportunity to rule Nigeria because he was not from the North. For many days, the economy was at a standstill. Many lives were lost, especially in the Western part of the country.

To many Southerners, Northern leaders supported Babangida's annulment of the elections and that was why they did not do anything to resolve the crisis.[5] Not many people know that Alhaji Ado Bayero took a very major step towards resolving the crisis. Few people know, for example, that it was the Emir who brought the two leaders face to face for the first time since the crisis began in order to find a solution. Emir Ado Bayero, like most Nigerians was very disturbed about the situation in the country and felt obliged to intervene. He made contact with Chief Abiola and requested a meeting at Abuja. He made a similar contact with President Babangida and asked for the same. From both leaders the Emir asked for confidentiality in the matter. To make sure that the meeting was truly confidential, the venue chosen was the Presidential wing of the Abuja International Airport, and the time fixed was late enough in the night not to attract public attention. Abiola flew in from Lagos to Abuja, and Babangida left Aso Rock, the official residence of the President, and arrived at the Abuja international airport incognito. The three sat down to business. The Emir exhorted the two leaders to iron out whatever differences there were between them that were threatening the survival of the nation. He told them that he believed that between the two of them they could come up with a solution that would be acceptable to the nation. He then retired into one of the presidential guestrooms leaving the two gentlemen to deliberate.

About two in the morning, there was a tap on his door. He opened and saw the two gentlemen. He asked if a solution had been found. They answered in the affirmative. They wanted to explain, but he did not think it was necessary. What he needed was a solution. Since it had been found, he did not think it was necessary to go into the past again.

Abiola flew back to Lagos that night and Babangida drove back to Aso Rock while the Emir went back to sleep in the guestroom. He left for Kano early the following morning. Emir Ado Bayero felt very relieved and accomplished as he flew back to Kano. He was expecting a public announcement of the outcome of that meeting, but it never came. Then he realized that the problem was more fundamental than he had assumed.

On another occasion, the Nigerian Supreme Council for Islamic Affairs, NSCIA, the umbrella organization for Muslim groups in Nigeria was meeting in Kaduna when a member brought up the issue of Chief Abiola's incarceration by the Abacha administration. The member suggested that the Council should intervene to get Abiola released. That suggestion appeared to have had the support of most of the members from the Western part of the country, the home of Chief Abiola. But an equally large number of members opposed the suggestion. According to the latter group, the Council was a religious body and it should steer clear of politics. From the exchanges on the floor, it was apparent that if the matter was put to vote the nays were going to have it. Indeed, Sultan Ibrahim Dasuki who was chairing the occasion was about ruling so when Ado Bayero, who was sitting next to him, leaned towards him and whispered to him to adjourn the meeting for five minutes. While they were on break, Emir Bayero met with Sultan Dasuki and advised him not to rule against the minority. Emir Ado Bayero reminded Sultan Dasuki that Chief Abiola was not only a member but also a Vice President of the Council and whose financial contribution to Islam was more than what any of them had made. Emir Ado Bayero further reminded the Sultan of the N 5 million donation Chief Abiola gave the previous year towards the cause of Islam. Finally, Ado Bayero noted that Islam stood for justice and does not distinguish between religion and politics. The issue of Abiola, reasoned Ado Bayero, should be discussed at the meeting.

Thus, when the meeting resumed Sultan Dasuki ruled that the matter be formally tabled for discussion and it was. Although the communiqué did not go as far as calling on the government to release Chief Abiola, probably due to the opposition of a large number of the members which could also be traced to their fear of the government, the fact that it was tabled and discussed at all, was because there were the likes of Ado Bayero.[6]

A LAW-ABIDING EMIR

Presentation of Staff of Office to Emir of Hadejia, Alhaji Abubakar Maje Haruna

Emir of Hadejia, in old Kano state, Alhaji Abdulqadir Maje Haruna died on August 22, 1984. About a week later, on August 31, the Kano State government imposed sanctions on the Emir of Kano over his trip to Israel.[7] Among the penalties was the restriction of the movement of the Emir to Kano City for a period of six months.

While that restriction was in force, arrangements were made for the presentation of the staff of office to the new Emir of Hadejia, Alhaji Abubakar Maje Haruna. The organizers of the event concluded that the presence at the ceremony of the Emir of Kano, who was also the substantive Chairman of the Kano State Council of Chiefs, would add colour to the occasion. They therefore requested the Military Governor, Air Commodore Hamza Abdullahi, for special permission for the Emir of Kano to travel to Hadejia to grace the occasion. Governor Hamza, who hailed from Hadejia, granted the permission. Indeed, it was Hamza himself, who went to the palace and invited Emir Ado Bayero to Hadejia.

Emir Ado Bayero reminded the Governor that his movements had been restricted. Governor Hamza told the Emir that for that special occasion, the restriction had been lifted.

But Emir Ado Bayero politely told the Governor that it would amount to indiscipline and disrespect for law and order for the government to waive the restriction at that time. He noted that the sanctions and their duration had been made public. How could he, or the government, justify to the people his presence in far-away Hadejia before the time publicly announced for his restriction had expired? As a result of the Emir's stand on the matter, the ceremony was shifted to March 4, 1985, four days after the expiration of the sanctions. Thus, Emir Ado Bayero gladly graced the ceremony, his first outing since the expiration of the restriction.

A MAN OF PATIENCE

The Rimi Years; Silence As The Greatest Weapon

Throughout the Rimi years, and despite all the provocations from government, which have been discussed in some detail elsewhere in this book, Emir Ado Bayero did not respond either in words or actions even for one day. The Emir could have responded in kind, knowing very well that the Governor did not have the capacity, even if he had the authority, to depose him or indeed harm him in any way. The Emir knew, for example, that the Governor did not control the police or the army, the ultimate instruments of coercion at the disposal of the State that could compel obedience to whatever the Governor decreed.[8] Yet not only did he not respond, he actually discouraged others from taking on the Governor on his behalf. With time, everything came to pass.

A GOD-FEARING LEADER

An Encounter with Mai Babban Daki

Sometime in 1964, when emirs were still the *de facto* and *de jure* rulers of their people and presided over cases in their courts, an important person from Kano was brought before

Emir Ado Bayero's court over some offense. The accused, knowing the reputation of Emir Ado Bayero as a just ruler, rushed to the Emir's mother requesting her to intervene to ameliorate the punishment, if he was found guilty. Mai babban Daki sent a message to the Emir to temper justice with mercy.

The Emir, whose love and respect for his mother knew no bounds, decided there and then that he must stop people from trying to pervert the course of justice by indirectly talking to his mother, who, by nature, was very helpful to anyone who went to her with problems. The Emir went to his mother, sat down and quoted the section of the Qur'an, which enjoined children to obey their parents, love them and respect them. He added that there was nothing she would want him to do that he would not do. But he had come to ask for one favor. She should allow him to rule according to the laws of Allah. She should kindly limit her intervention in his life to what was purely private. He requested her not to entertain anyone who went to her intent on influencing him through her. He reminded her that on the day of judgement Allah would call him to account for his stewardship. The mother promised to do just that; and to her credit, Mai Babban Daki, never again tried to intervene in what were purely administrative or political matters. The Emir remained ever grateful to her for the rest of her life as a result.

Returning to the court, the trial was concluded and the Emir jailed the man. Many people were surprised because news had spread that the man had seen Mai Babban Daki, whose wish was known to be law to her son, the Emir.

A CONTENTED, NON-COVETOUS LEADER

"Emir Ado Bayero never asks for personal favors. For the whole period I was Governor of Kano state, and as Minister of the Federal Capital Territory, the Emir never, even for once, requested me for a personal favor." That was Air-Vice Marshal Hamza Abdullahi. The same observation was made by all his predecessors and successors that I spoke with while working on this project. Colonel Sani Bello, who governed Kano State during the Murtala-Obasanjo years, also sees that quality of the Emir as one of his greatest strengths. He recalls that before the 1978 Land Reform, traditional rulers allocated land within the walled city of Kano. After the reform, however, the State Government took over that function. In many states, where that had occurred, the government had given the traditional rulers a number of plots to assuage their sense of loss. When the Sani Bello government took over the functions of land allocation in the then new layout at Sani Mai Nagge, which was within the walled city, the Emir of Kano never indicated any interest in acquiring any plot from the new layout.

Alhaji Kabiru Gaya, Governor during the Babangida years, also hails the Emir for his non-covetousness. "Emir Ado Bayero," he said, "is a contented person. For the nearly two years I was Governor of Kano State, the Emir never asked me for a personal favor. Neither did he send anybody close to him, with a request for a favor. He never takes advantage of people. He never takes advantage of his position. He is always ready to sacrifice even what he has for his community."

The Emir of Daura, Alhaji Muhammad Bashar, commented that, "I once asked Emir Ado Bayero why he was not interested in making money or doing business. He said to me "my father always told us not to expect to inherit wealth from him. It was a good lesson."

The Yeriman Zazzau, Alhaji Mannir Ja'afaru, a Zaria prince, who headed the National Maritime Authority during the Babangida, Shonekan, and Abacha years, recalls that because of the respect and admiration he has for Emir Ado Bayero, many people seeking some favors from him went through the Emir. He used to send them down to him at Lagos, with introductory letters, signed by his Secretary. But the Emir never himself asked directly, nor sent any close relation or friend for any form of assistance.

Indeed, even at the highest level, President Ibrahim Babangida, who ruled Nigeria for eight years, credits Emir Ado Bayero for his non-covetousness. In a British Broadcasting Corporation (BBC) interview after he had left office, Babangida said that Ado Bayero was unique among Nigeria's traditional rulers. He never asks for any favor from anyone. At least he never asked Babangida for any favor throughout the eight years that he was president.

Just as he is not covetous, Emir Ado Bayero is also not known to be as generous as his father, Emir Abdullahi Bayero. Emir Ado Bayero is perceived as parsimonious with his personal wealth. Not a few people have noted that the Emir would usually go out of his way to assist people to get assistance from third parties, but not directly from him.

Some explanations have been offered for that seeming parsimony. It has been suggested that the environment in which Emir Abdullahi Bayero operated was radically different from that in which Emir Ado Bayero operates today. For example, during the time of Emir Abdullahi Bayero many people still brought *zakkah* to the palace to be distributed according to Islamic injunctions. But no one brings *Zakkah* to the palace any longer.[9] It is therefore unfair to use Emir Abdullahi Bayero as a yardstick for assessing his son's generosity.

Another explanation is that during the time of Abdullahi Bayero, whoever went to the Emir seeking personal assistance had to be truly be in need of such assistance. Today, however, people have lost their sense of pride and are ready to go a-begging anywhere. Emir Ado Bayero's undeclared policy is to assist people find a means of making a legitimate living. As a rule, he does not encourage giving the needy fish. What he does is to make it possible for them to fish.

But Ado Bayero has been exceptionally generous to individuals and groups whose circumstances dictated such generosity. He has, for example, given out at least a score of houses to various people whose circumstances necessitated that. He has paid for many men to get married. He has made many anonymous donations to individuals and groups in Kano and outside. And, as we noted in Chapter Eight, he gives *sadaqat* every Friday.

Many people have also observed that during his reign Kano witnessed the greatest strides in socio-economic development. The standard of living of the average Kano man has improved greatly. Social amenities, roads, hospitals, educational institutions, and means of communications have seen great advances. A lot more Kano people can be classified as rich than before his time. All these are attributed to the vision of the Emir in ensuring the creation of an enabling environment for commerce and industry to thrive in Kano.

A HELPFUL LEADER

A Day in the Court of the Emir

The number of daily visitors to his palace attests to his empathy for mankind. On an average morning, including Saturdays and Sundays, the emir sees about thirty people in camera. A majority of these people are meeting him for the first time. They come from every nook and corner of Nigeria. They come for his royal intervention. They have either been terminated at work, or they are looking for work. Some come seeking the emir's intervention in some contract they are pursuing with the governments or some companies. Others come because they have some problems with the government or their bosses.

At other times, these visitors seek audience at court, where they lay their complaints to the Emir in public. Depending on the nature of their request, the Emir would act immediately or cause one of his advisors to investigate the complaint before he would take any action. There was a case of a police sergeant whose appointment was terminated on the advice of his immediate boss. The sergeant was convinced he had not done anything to deserve a termination of appointment. But the police authorities had acted on false information. He lodged a complaint with the Emir. The Emir did not intervene until he had got the Walin Kano, Alhaji Mahe Bashir Wali, to investigate the matter and advise him accordingly. Wali, an ex-policeman, who had retired from the force as the Deputy Inspector General of the Nigeria Police Force, investigated and advised the Emir on the merit of the sergeant's case. The Emir then caused a letter to be written to the State Police authorities, requesting them to kindly investigate the allegations made against the sergeant, which had led to his dismissal. The police did so and found those allegations baseless. The sergeant was given back his badge.

And Sarkin Kudu Lamido

In the early 1970s, the office of Sarkin Kudu, District Head of Birnin Kudu, became vacant. The most qualified person for the office happened to be too poor to join the race for the office. When news got to Emir Ado Bayero about why Alhaji Lamido, had not shown a keen interest in the office, he offered to foot the whole bill of the ceremony. He provided the new Sarkin Kudu with horses, clothes, turbans, and all that a District Head needed to appear respectable and dignified.

THE PEOPLE'S EMIR

A few days after the *Karamar Sallah* of the year 2000, Emir Ado Bayero fell ill and was hurriedly flown abroad for treatment. Many Kano people had been taken by surprise at the news of the Emir's sudden illness especially that he had only a few days earlier toured the emirate capital on horseback as part of the *Sallah* celebrations. He had looked hale and healthy, not betraying any sign of sickness; not even fatigue.

The emir was away from Kano for nearly two months. For the whole of the period the emir was away, virtually all mosques in Kano regularly prayed for the emir's safe return to Kano. Many people were calling a London hospital where he was receiving treatment to monitor how he was responding. In most of Kurmi, Kwari, Sabon Gari, and Kofar Wambai markets, the mosques, and the schools as well as other places where a group of five or more people congregated, the chances were that 80% of these groups were discussing the emir. There was so much concern in Kano many elders of the city noted that the only time people had shown as much concern about the health of their emir was during the reign of late Abdullahi Bayero.

When news got around that the emir was returning to Kano, the whole city was agog. Hundreds of thousands of people from Kano and outside trooped to the Mallam Aminu Kano International Airport to receive him. Tens of thousands more lined up the streets of Kano from the airport to the palace to welcome their emir. So big was the crowd at the airport and enroute the palace that it took the emir's convoy three hours to get to the palace, a distance of about three miles. All the markets in Kano were virtually closed as the traders trooped to the airport or the streets. Indeed, for about six hours on that day, all activities in Kano were at a standstill.

The spontaneous reception accorded to the emir really sent the message across that Emir Ado Bayero is loved, adored, appreciated, and respected by his people.

A PROUD EMIR?

A Matter of Orientation

An emir of one of Kano's neighboring states and a one-time Governor of Kano state have described Emir Ado Bayero as a proud person. According to the emir, Emir Ado Bayero is not easily accessible to his subjects. The Kano palace, he noted, is too full of protocol. One cannot just walk in and see the Emir. One has got to seek an appointment, which, he said, could take days or weeks to get. He contrasts the Kano palace with his own, where even unscheduled visitors are received by the emir.

The ex-Governor also noted that the protocol at the Kano palace scares people away. The Emir's subjects find it difficult to reach him. They only see him from a-far. He wished the Emir would be less distanced from the people.

But how correct are these perceptions of the emir? To some extent, they are correct. But it is not a characteristic of Emir Ado Bayero as a person. Rather, it is the characteristic of the institution of *sarauta* in Kano. We noted, in the introduction, the reasons for the re-introduction of some of Al-Maghili's precepts by Amir Dabo after 1819. A little over a century later, Emir Abdullahi Bayero in a conversation with his counterpart from Katsina, Emir Muhammadu Dikko, noted that Katsina emirs were too playful with their subjects and that could cause some loss of respect between the rulers and the ruled. Emir Dikko acknowledged the observations of Emir Bayero, adding that it was normal for Katsina emirs to go to the market to buy what they needed. On some very rare occasions, he said, some subjects behaved in ways that were less than respectful to the emirs. On those occasions, he added, the rulers meted out most severe punishments to the subjects concerned. In other words, a *talaka* who has been interacting with an emir jovially could find himself, within the twinkling of an eye, being severely sanctioned for improper behavior. Emir Abdullahi Bayero then explained that in Kano, the emirs keep their distance from the *talakawa* so as not to tempt them to do anything that could be construed as disrespectful of *sarakuna*, and which could earn them severe sanctions. Furthermore, by keeping their distance from the *talakawa*, they are able to dispense justice without any fear or favor, as no *talaka* could claim to be close to the rulers and therefore influence their decisions in any way.

The different orientations of the *sarauta* houses notwithstanding, the specific charges made against Emir Ado Bayero can be easily faulted. We have noted that there are two avenues of meeting the Emir by his subjects. One is private, which because of the very tight schedule of the Emir, an appointment normally takes some time to get. But he endeavors to see anyone who requests to have a private audience with him. The second is to meet him at court. For that, no prior appointment is needed. One simply goes to the palace on any of the days the emir sits at court. The person would normally tell the palace officials his mission. There is a waiting room where people with more or less similar problems wait for the court session to begin. One after the other these people are called before the Emir to lodge their complaints or say what they want to say. Indeed the number one rule of Gidan Rumfa is that no subject who wishes to see the Emir should be turned away. According to the Emir, all members of the palace staff know the rule and the consequences of breaking it.

Most of the people who come to the Emir with financial problems—requiring money to buy drugs, pay hospital and medical bills, or provide food for a family whose male bread-winner has left the family to another town in search of work – are advised by the Emir to go the private office. There, one of the Emir's staff is directed to assess their real need and from the personal wealth of the Emir, they are provided for. Indeed, on at least three occasions, when I was at the court, some women had come asking for separation from their husbands because they had left their towns for years without making provisions for the upkeep of the family. The court had asked the women how long they had been married to their respective husbands and whether they had children with them. One was married to her husband for ten years, another for fifteen years and a third for four years. All of them had children ranging from two to six with their husbands. They were asked if they wanted divorce because they did not love their husbands any more. All of them said they loved their husbands, but could not continue to live without food. When asked if their husbands had always been uncaring all of them said that their husbands were very caring until the economic situation in the country made their businesses collapse and they decided to go elsewhere to work and make money. The embargo placed on employment by the government had sent them to the labor market in other towns.

On hearing these, the Emir directed that pending the return of their husbands their feeding had become his responsibility. He directed one of his officials to ensure that those families were not left without food and other necessities. About six months later, the Emir ensured that two of the husbands who came to Kano to see their families were rehabilitated by giving them working capital.

THE FORGIVING SPIRIT

The Case Of Sarkin Dawaki Mai Tuta, Alhaji Bello Dandago

Another attribute of Emir Ado Bayero acknowledged by many people is forgiveness. Most people who have done him some mischief have been amazed at his large-heartedness. Where they expected the emir to exact retribution, he extended the hand of forgiveness. A number of them have openly expressed their amazement at his forgiving spirit, as the following state-ment from the then Sarkin Dawaki Mai Tuta of Kano, Alhaji Bello Dandago, reveals:

> *"Da ba dan na samu sarki mai adalci ba da kashi na ya bushe"*
> (tr. But for the fact that I have a judicious emir, I would have been in serious trouble).

The background to that statement was as follows: Alhaji Bello Dandago was the Sarkin Dawaki Mai Tuta of Kano from the1950s to 1978. As Sarkin Dawaki Mai Tuta, he was at once a member of the Kano Emirate Council and one of the four kingmakers of Kano Emirate. In addition, he was the District Head of Kano City.

We have noted that not too long after Audu Bako had assumed duty as the Governor of the newly created Kano State, people came between him and Emir Ado Bayero. Before long, the relationship between him and the Emir began to get sour. Soon enough there emerged two camps in the political leadership of Kano. There were those who were considered to be the mod-ernists and who sided with the State Governor, and there were the traditionalists who sided with the Emir. Among the people seen as loyalists of the Governor was the Sarkin Dawaki Mai

Tuta. Many traditionalists felt disappointed and embarrassed by the Sarkin Dawaki's behavior, and some were even suggesting that he should be sanctioned. The Emir ignored the pressure.

If people thought that the Emir had ignored the pressure to sanction the Sarkin Dawaki because he was afraid of some repercussions from Governor Bako, they were proved wrong when the Sarkin Dawaki fell out of favor with the Governor. The Sarkin Dawaki apparently did something that so displeased Governor Bako that he advised the Emir to un-turban him. But the Emir did not act. A few weeks later, the Governor called the Emir and enquired why the Sarkin Dawaki was still in office. The Emir simply told him that they were looking into the matter. Realizing that the Emir was not in a hurry to act, Governor Bako got the government to make a formal case for the un-turbanning of the Sarkin Dawaki.

At the Emirate Council meeting, where the matter was tabled and discussed, the evidence against the Sarkin Dawaki was overwhelming. The traditionalists thought that they had their chance to pay the Sarkin Dawaki back in his own coin. But when it came to taking the final decision, the Emir said, "the Sarkin Dawaki is human, and like all humans is prone to making mistakes. Nobody is perfect. What we should all strive to do is to learn from our mistakes and those of others. We think that un-turbanning the Sarkin Dawaki is too severe a sanction. We hope that the Sarkin Dawaki Mai Tuta will learn some lessons from these events."

When Governor Bako heard that the Sarkin Dawaki was saved by none other than the Emir, he called Emir Ado Bayero and asked, "How can you save somebody like that? Do you know what he was saying to me about you?" The Emir replied, "I don't. But even if I did it has not changed anything, has it?"

And The PRP Prince

Another episode that readily illustrates the Emir's spirit of forgiveness happened during the years when the PRP was in power in Kano State. We have earlier discussed the frosty relationship between Governor Rimi and the Emir. It was generally believed that Governor Rimi was intent on removing Emir Ado Bayero. A brother of the Emir, then Danburam of Kano, took advantage of the soured relationship between the Governor and the Emir and tried to endear himself to Governor Rimi, expecting that when the Emir was deposed, he would be made the new Emir. It was generally believed that the Danburam even went to the extent of asking the Governor to depose his brother and appoint him. Rimi was also believed to have advised him to go and secure the support of his brother princes first.

The younger prince went to the eldest surviving son of Emir Abdullahi Bayero, Alhaji Sani Bayero, Galadiman Kano, and told him his mission. The Galadima asked for time to think about it. A few days later, the Galadima requested a private audience with the Emir, to which meeting he invited the younger prince. The elder prince then asked the younger one to repeat what he had come to tell him a few days earlier. The younger prince felt highly embarrassed and started begging for forgiveness. The elder brother insisted that the younger one should repeat what he had said.

Emir Ado Bayero intervened and asked the elder prince to forgive and forget whatever mistake the younger one had committed. The elder brother then narrated the story to the Emir. When he had finished, he turned to the younger prince and asked him whether what he had narrated was true or not. Before he could answer, the Emir looked at his elder brother and told him that he had over-reacted. He then asked the Galadima if there was any true prince who did not harbor the ambition of becoming Emir some day. As far as he was concerned, the younger prince's ambition was a legitimate one. Moreover, Emir Ado Bayero asked if it was not going to be better for the son of their father to inherit him than for the office to go somewhere else.

In grooming the Danburam for the office of Emir, the Rimi government unilaterally elevated him to the title of Wambai without recourse to the Kano Emirate Traditional Council. Not too long after that the tables turned. Rimi, who contested the 1983 elections on the ticket of the NPP, lost to Sabo Bakin Zuwo, of the PRP, who immediately on assuming office sacked the Wambai among other traditional titleholders appointed by Rimi.[10] Emir Ado Bayero was not consulted before Governor Sabo Bakin Zuwo took that action. He wished he had been consulted; he would have advised against sacking him. The opportunity came with the December 1983 coup. When Zuwo left the political scene, the Emir decided to rehabilitate his younger brother. He returned him to the office of Danburam, which he was holding before Rimi decided to elevate him against tradition. He was also transferred from Bichi, where Rimi had posted him, to Gwarzo.

Saving the Throne of the Emir of Gumel, Ahmad Muhammad Sani...

Alhaji Ahmad Muhammed Sani was a member of Muhammadu Abubakar Rimi's cabinet. Although he was not a member of the avowed anti-tradition party, the PRP, but the GNPP, which was fairly conservative, he was known to be quite close to the Governor, and although he was a prince of Gumel, he was known to be critical of many aspects of traditional institutions. Indeed, Ahmad Muhammad Sani was in the cabinet that took most of the decisions on traditional rulers discussed in Chapter Seven. When Emir Muhammad Sani died, Governor Rimi directed the Kano State government delegation to the funeral of the late emir to inform the Gumel kingmakers that they should ensure that the name of Ahmad Muhammad Sani is included in the list they were going to submit to him for selection and approval as new emir of Gumel. That was how Ahmad Muhammad Sani, who was not in the race at all, found himself becoming the next Emir of Gumel.

For the nearly three years Ahmad Muhammad Sani was Emir of Gumel and Rimi was Governor of Kano State, he had unlimited access to the Governor and his opinion, especially on traditional institutions, carried strong weight in the government.

It was even speculated that if Rimi had constituted the State Council of Chiefs, Emir Ahmad Muhammad Sani would have been made chairman. After all, he had been promoted a first-class emir.

Then Rimi failed to secure the people's mandate in 1983. Sabo Bakin Zuwo, a loyalist of Emir Ado Bayero became the new chief tenant at the State House. As soon as the *hakimai* of Gumel saw that Rimi had been defeated in the elections, they began to troop to the Emir of Kano's palace with serious complaints against their Emir. They complained that he was removing district heads appointed by his father without any just cause. They also complained that he had no respect for them. There were many other things they complained about. They wanted Emir Ado Bayero to get their emir sanctioned, preferably deposed.

But to their surprise Emir Ado Bayero told them that as elders, they were supposed to exercise patience and put the young Emir on the right path. He also told them that they were not being realistic by expecting the young, Western-educated emir to behave in the same way that they, the elders, without Western education or even exposure to the outside world, had been behaving for many decades. He seriously advised them to try and adjust and move with the times.

Not too long after that incident, Governor Sabo Bakin Zuwo came to Emir Ado Bayero with a proposal. He wanted to remove the Rimi- appointed Emir of Gumel, as he had removed the Emirs of Gaya, Dutse, Rano and Auyo. But Emir Ado Bayero advised against that. He told Governor Sabo Bakin Zuwo that even if Emir Ahmad Muhammad Sani's appointment was irregular, he was the son of the late emir, and therefore a legitimate heir to that throne. He added that since he had been in office for a couple of years, it was not proper to remove him. Sabo was not happy with the Emir's advice, but he accepted it and therefore abandoned the idea of removing Alhaji Ahmad Muhammad Sani from the throne of Gumel.

AN EMIR WITH A NATIONAL OUTLOOK

Choice of Friends

Ask Emir Ado Bayero or anyone who knows him well to tell you whom his best friends are, and you are sure to get a long list. For sure, the following names would be included; Alhaji Muhammadu Bashar, the Emir of Daura, Oba Okunade Sijuade Olubuse II, the Ooni of Ife, and Chief Chukwuemeka Odumegwu Ojukwu, the Ikemba of Nnewi. There would also be Obi Ofala Okagbue II, the Obi of Onitsha to mention a few. Emir Ado Bayero's friendship with each of these gentlemen dates back to over thirty years. To the Emir, there is a lot of symbolism in whatever leaders do. The choice of his friends is deliberately made to send a message to the people. He owes Nigeria a duty to integrate its people, to build one nation out of the various nations that occupy the land of Nigeria. The emir reasons that example is the best teacher. If he has the Ikemba, or the Ooni or the Obi among his best friends, what stops the average Hausa man from making friends with the average Igbo, or Yoruba person?

AN EXEMPLARY LEADER

Public Education for the Princes and Princesses

For the thirty-six years he has been on the Kano Throne, all the Emir's children have attended public schools—from primary to the university or other tertiary institutions. Not that Emir Ado Bayero cannot afford to send his children overseas, nor to some of the expensive private institutions in the country as is the norm with the upper class of the Nigerian society. From his eldest son, Sarkin Dawakin Tsakar Gida, Alhaji Sanusi Ado Bayero, a barrister-at-law, to the youngest school-aged child, all attended the native authority (which later became local authority) primary schools, the various government secondary schools, and the public universities or polytechnics.

When asked why he sends his children to public schools especially at a time when the standard in those schools is generally believed to have fallen, the emir replied that if every important man is to remove his children from public schools, the standard would be worse than what it is today. He reasoned that it is because most of those who are in a position to make the quality of education in public schools better have no personal stakes in those schools that their standards are falling. According to the emir, he cannot morally justify going round the emirate appealing to parents to send their children to (public) schools if by his behavior he indicates that those schools are not good enough for his own children.[11]

A HUMBLE LEADER

Honoring the Summons of Governor Audu Bako

Late one morning during the early years of the Audu Bako administration, Emir Ado Bayero received a summons to the Government House. The letter did not give reasons for the invitation, and the Emir was directed to be there that afternoon. It was a very unusual letter, but the Emir decided to go to the Government House immediately. On his arrival, Governor Bako and some of his commissioners went out and received the Emir. There was bewilderment on the face of the Governor. Equally perplexed were some of the commissioners. It was apparent that they were not expecting the Emir, or at least not so soon, for no arrangements had been made to receive him, and there was no agenda for them to discuss. After a brief stay, the Emir took his leave of the Governor.

As soon as the Emir left, attention focused on some members of the cabinet who, earlier that morning, had forcefully argued that the Emir had no respect for the Governor and therefore would not honor an invitation from the Governor at short notice even if he was not busy. That invitation was meant to prove their point. But as it turned out, the Emir went.

And Apologizing to Kano Butchers

The Kano State Government decided in the late 1970s to build a new, more modern abattoir as the one in use was getting too small for the increasing population of Kano. When the abattoir was built the butchers refused to move there for a number of reasons. First, they claimed the new abattoir was too far away from the center of the city. Secondly, they claimed that the animals were going to be slaughtered by machines, which was against religion.

All pleas to the butchers from the authorities fell on deaf ears. Then government threatened to shut down the old abattoir. The butchers decided to go to the palace and make their case. On getting there, in their hundreds, they created a rowdy scene. The palace *dogarai* felt the butchers were a nuisance and chased them out of the palace. They did not get the opportunity to make their case to the Emir, who was inside the palace. When the Emir heard about what had happened, he invited the butchers to the palace and apologized to them for the behavior of his *dogarai*.

Given the low position butchers occupy in Hausa traditional society, the public apology by the Emir was considered a very significant development.

AN EVER GRATEFUL PERSON:
CONDOLENCE TO BAKIN ZUWO'S RESIDENCE

Traditionally every Kano citizen is either a son or a daughter of the Emir. For this reason, whatever befalls any citizen of the emirate by extension affects the Emir. Hence, whenever a son or a daughter of Kano excelled elsewhere, it was to the Emir that commendations were sent. Similarly, wherever, a son or a daughter of Kano went and disgraced himself or herself, it was to the Emir that complaints were lodged.

In more recent times, this tradition is expressed particularly when important Kano citizens die. On those occasions, apart from the immediate families of the dead, condolence is also paid to the Emir. In fact, depending on the status of the deceased, and especially if he or she has died outside Kano, the corpse is delivered to the Emir. When General Murtala Muhammad was assassinated in Lagos in February 1976, his body was flown to Kano where the final rites, including funeral prayers, were offered at the Emir's palace. Likewise, when General Muhammad Haladu, former Industries Minister died in 1998, his body was flown to Kano and presented to the Emir, who organized the final rites and burial. On both occasions, as with all previous cases from the time of Bagauda, the Emir stayed in his palace for people, including the immediate family members of the deceased, to come and offer their condolences to him.

But, the death of Alhaji Aliyu Sabo Bakin Zuwo, Ado Bayero broke that age-old tradition. The Emir who received the news of the death at the airport while on his way to overseas delegated his Senior Councillor to represent him at the burial. On his return to Kano, instead of staying in his palace to receive condolence visits, he went straight to Bakin Zuwo's house and condoled the family. After that, he moved to his palace and started receiving people coming on condolence visits.

Many perceptive observers of Kano tradition have attributed the Emir's action to the high respect accorded him by Sabo, particularly when he was Governor. It has been argued that Emir Ado Bayero is a very appreciative ruler who strives to please those who try to please him. People noted, for example, that Murtala Muhammad was closer to the royal palace of Kano than Sabo, yet it was not to Murtala's house that the Emir went but to Sabo's.

A PROGRESSIVE EMIR:
THE UBA LIDA PARTY

Bayero University, Kano, held a special convocation ceremony in 1994 and awarded an honorary doctorate degree to Emir Ado Bayero. The extraordinary event attracted very important personalities from all walks of life, in and outside Nigeria. For many reasons, many people had for a long time expected Bayero University, named in memory of Emir Abdullahi Bayero, father of Emir Ado Bayero, to recognize and confer an honorary degree on Emir Ado Bayero. This was especially so since some universities that are geographically far away from Kano, had many years earlier recognized the Emir's contributions not only to his immediate community but also to the nation and humanity at large, and awarded him various honorary degrees.

The occasion was celebrated with enthusiasm by the people of Kano. Many individuals and organizations sent congratulatory messages to the Emir in the newspapers and electronic media. Many more went to the palace and congratulated the Emir. One Kano businessman, Alhaji Uba Lida, felt the award called for more than just a congratulatory message. He decided to celebrate it in style. He organized a dinner party for the emir at the exclusive Chinese Restaurant, Bompai, in the Government Reservation Area of Kano. Invitations were sent to a select few of the Emir's friends, admirers, top government officials, industrialists, and businessmen. Thereafter, Alhaji Lida and a few friends requested a private audience with the Emir. At the meeting, they intimated the Emir of the arrangements they had made. They ended by requesting His Highness to kindly grace the occasion.

After they had left, the Emir informed his key councillors of their mission, and the request they had made. All over the palace, people felt it was an insult for a *talaka* or an ordinary subject of the Emir to invite the Emir of Kano to a function. Moreover, Uba Lida was not even a government official party, but simply a wealthy businessman. The opposition, especially among the councillors and palace officials, to the Emir going to a restaurant in Kano, was overwhelming. It had never happened before in the one thousand years of the establishment of kingly authority in Kano, and they were not going to let it happen in their time. Immediate family members of the Emir, upon hearing about it, also opposed the idea.

For some time the Emir was uncertain what to do. If he decided not to go, he would not have broken any word, as he had never told them he had accepted their invitation. Neither had he told them he was not going to attend. It was up to him to decide.

To the delight of the organizers of the dinner and all who honored the invitation, Emir Ado Bayero showed up at the Chinese restaurant. He did not stay long, but his presence made all the difference. The cream of Kano society was all gathered there. Everybody who was anybody in the business class, which prided itself as the movers and shakers of Kano, Nigeria's center of commerce, was there.

To Emir Ado Bayero, a leader must know when to adapt to the demands of the times. The survival of the institution depended on how it adjusts and makes itself relevant in changing socio-political environments.

NOTES

1. The refusal to be associated with the endorsement move was the last straw. Earlier in 1996, the emir had refused to go to Sokoto to congratulate the newly appointed Sultan Maccido, a position General Abacha took offense to. Equally, he had expressed his concern over Abacha's attempt to interfere in what he believed was purely the prerogative of the Kano Emirate Council, in the choice of a District Head for Fagge Local Government. See supra.

2. See lead story titled "Abacha Planned to Depose Emir of Kano" in *The Guardian* on Sunday, August 2, 1998, p.1. See also the cover story of *Tell* Magazine, No. 33, August 17, 1998. Many other papers later reported the stories.

3. The emissary was Alhaji Guda Abdullahi, then Secretary to the Kano State Government.

4. This tradition may have had its roots in the Prophet's advice that Believers should hasten visits of condolence or commiseration but delay those of congratulations.

5. That perception was wrong as some of the earliest critics of the annulment were from the North. Mallam Adamu Ciroma, Abdulqadir Balarabe Musa, Muhammadu Abubakar Rimi, and the Sultan of Sokoto, Ibrahim Dasuki.

6. Interview with Alhaji Ibrahim Dasuki, 18th Sultan of Sokoto, Kaduna, November 18, 1998.

7. Discussed in detail in the Chapter Eight.

8. This fact became even more evident when during the July 10 rampage, the security agents just looked the other way when Kano state government property were set ablaze, and two lives were terminated. Even after a judicial panel of enquiry had identified the perpetrators of the rampage, the state government was helpless. It could not order their arrest, as it was clear to the government that the police were not going to heed its directives at that time. Thus, despite the damage done by those people they were never punished.

9. The only exception, in recent times, was an octogenarian who used to drop bags of grain at the palace every year. The man died about two years ago.

10. Within a year of his assumption of office, a serious rift developed in the PRP, which led to the splitting of the party into two: the original PRP, or the Tabo faction, led by Mallam Aminu Kano and the splinter group, or Santsi faction, led by Chief Michael Imoudu. Rimi was with the Santsi faction. In 1983, the Federal Electoral Commission refused the Santsi faction of the PRP recognition. And the Tabo faction refused to endorse Rimi for a second term. He thus, joined the NPP for the purpose of contesting the elections. He lost to Aliyu Sabo Bakin Zuwo of the PRP Tabo.

11. The only exception to the rule was Alhaji Ahmad Ado Bayero, the Dan Ruwatan Kano, who had his secondary education in Egypt. But even with Ahmad, it was not the emir who sent him there but Alhaji Uba Ringim.

POSTSCRIPT

Just when this book was going to press, the Kano State Governor, Dr. Rabi'u Musa Kwankwaso announced the resolve of his administration to reintroduce shari'ah in the governance of the state. This decision had followed an earlier one by the Zamfara State Government under Ahmad Sani Yariman Bakura. Governor Ahmad Sani had on January 27, 2000 declared the shari'ah legal system operational in Zamfara State.

Since the relaunch of the shari'ah in Zamfara state, there has been increasing agitation among the Muslim population of the northern states for their governments to do the same. Initially considered, even by President Obasanjo, as something that will, with time, fizzle out, the agitation has grown and now appears beyond the control of any of the governments—state or federal. Virtually all the predominantly Muslim populated states of the North have signified their intention to re-introduce the shari'ah.

All across the North, Islamic scholars have been lending their support to the call for the relaunch of the shari'ah. Many emirs too have openly supported the call even when they know that the federal and some of the state government are not comfortable with the agitation. For the ulama, the reintroduction of the shari'ah is a dream come true. They have lived under the Penal Code more out of duress than choice. And for the emirs, many see the reintroduction of the shari'ah as a vindication of the system their forefathers practiced and on which their legitimacy was initially hinged, but which colonialism came and uprooted.

Indeed, as noted in the introduction, the title emir, which the traditional rulers of the North bear is originally Amir al Mu'umineen, leader of the faithful. This is because the states were Islamic states and in Islam, there is no dichotomy between state and religion. The Amir is both religious and political leader. But when Britain, a Christian state, conquered the emirate states of the caliphate, it introduced the dichotomy between the state and religion as practiced in Britain. And with that dichotomy, the powers of the emirs overs many matters of governance were limited.

How will the emirs fare in the new dispensation? It is too early to predict. But the following factors may, to a large extent, determine the course of events for the emirs. If shari'ah is applied and the emirs are seen as religious leaders, the extent to which they will remain in their offices and be respected will be determined by how much knowledge of Islam they are perceived to have, how much of their public and private lives are lived according to the shari'ah, and most importantly how the age-old debate between Shehu Usman Danfodio and his brother Shehu Abdullahi Danfodio on the place of monarchy in Islam is resolved.

Did Emir Ado Bayero foresee the reintroduction of shari'ah in his lifetime? Why did he insist decades ago that he was not a traditional ruler but a religious leader? Why has he for decades concentrated his attention and resources to Islam and the society?

The challenge, one can safely say, is not for Emir Ado Bayero, for he saw it coming. The survival of the institution will to a large extent depend on how much of Emir Ado Bayero's admirable qualities his successors exhibit.

APPENDIX I

WATHIQAT AHL AL-SUDAN

(THE MANIFESTO OF THE JIHAD)

Know then my brethren:

1. That the commanding of righteousness is obligatory by assent;
2. And that the prohibition of evil is obligatory by assent;
3. And that flight (al-hijra) from the land of the heathen is obligatory by assent
4. And that the befriending of the Faithful is obligatory by assent;
5. And that the appointment of the Commander of the Faithful is obligatory by assent;
6. And that obedience to him and to all his deputies is obligatory by assent;
7. And that the waging of the Holy War (al-Jihad) is obligatory by assent;
8. And that the appointment of the emirs in the states is obligatory by assent;
9. And that the appointment of judges is obligatory by assent;
10. And that their enforcement of the divine laws (*ahkam al-sharia*) is obligatory by assent;
11. And that by assent the status of a town is the status of its ruler: if he be a Muslim, the town belongs to Islam; but if he be heathen the town is a town of heathendom from which flight is obligatory;
12. And that to make war upon a heathen king who will not say "There is no God but Allah" is obligatory by assent, and that to take the government from his obligatory by assent;
13. And that to make war upon the heathen king who does not say "There is no God but Allah" on account of the custom of his

(*bisababi urfi' i-baladi*), and who makes no profession of Islam, is also obligatory by assent; and that to take the government from him is obligatory by assent;

14. And that to make war upon the king who is an apostate (*al-malik al murtaddu*) and who has abandoned the religion of Islam, for the religion of heathendom is obligatory by assent, and that to take the government from him is obligatory by assent;

15. And that to make war against the king who is an apostate—who has not abandoned the religion of Islam as far as the profession of it is concerned, but who mingles the observance of heathendom, like the kings of the Hausaland for the most part—is also obligatory by assent;

16. And that to make war upon backsliding of Muslims (*al-Muhammalin min al-Muslimin*) who do not owe allegiance to any of the emirs of the faithful is obligatory by assent, if they be summoned to give allegiance and they refuse, until they enter into allegiance;

17. And that the anathematising of Muslims on a pretext of heretical observances is unlawful by assent:

18. And that the anathematising of Muslims for disobedience (*takfir al-muslimin bi 'l-ma'asi*) its unlawful by assent;

19. And that residence in enemy territory (*fi bi lad al-harb*) is unlawful by assent;

20. And that refusal to give allegiance to the Commander of the Faithful and to his deputies is unlawful by assent;

21. And that to make war upon the Muslims who are residing in Muslim territory is unlawful by assent; and that to wrongfully devour their property is unlawful by assent;

22. And that to enslave the free born amongst the Muslims is unlawful by assent, whether they reside in the territory of Islam or in enemy territory;

23. And that to make war upon the heathen to whom peace has been granted (*al-kuffar ahl al-amen*) is unlawful by assent; wrongfully to devour their property is unlawful by assent, and to enslave them is unlawful by assent;

24. And that to make war upon the congregation of the apostates (*jama't al-murtaddin*) is obligatory by assent; and that their property is booty (*faitun*) and that in the matter of enslavement there are two opinions, the widespread one being its prohibition, and the other one that the perpetrator of this act does

not disobey (the law) if he is following authority which asserts its lawfulness;

25. And that to make war on the congregation of the warmongers (*juma at al-muharibin*) is obligatory by assent, and that their property is booty, and that their enslavement is unlawful by assent;

26. And that to make war upon the oppressors (*al-bughat*) is obligatory by assent, and that wrongfully to devour their property is unlawful by assent, for, use is made of their armour against them, and afterwards it is returned to them; and their enslavement is unlawful by assent;

27. And that in the matter of the property of Muslims who reside in enemy territory there are two opinions, the second one being that (its seizure) is permitted.

REFERENCES

Al-Maghili, Sheikh Muhammad, *The Obligations of Princes: An Essay on Moslem Kingship tr. by T.H. Baldwin, (Beyrouth, Imperial Catholique, 1932).*

Abdullahi, S.U., *On the Search for a Viable Political Culture: Reflections on the Political Thought of Sheikh Abdullahi {anfodio* (Kaduna, New Nigerian newspapers, Commercial Press, 1984).

Abdullahi, Abba; Tanko Yakasai: *Politics in Politics,* (Kano, Associate Media 1996)

Adeleye, R.A., *Power and Diplomacy in Northern Nigeria 1800-1906* (London, Longmans Group Limited, 1971).

Aborisade, O., *Local Government and Traditional Rulers in Nigeria* (Ile-Ife, University of Ife Press, 1985).

Ali, S.H., *Alhaji Ado Bayero: Symbol of Royal Justice, Wisdom and Patience,* (n.p., 1988).

Abdul, M.O.A., *Selected Traditions of Al-Nawawi* (Lagos, Islamic Publications Bureau, 1982).

Aliyu, Y., "As Seen in Kaduna" in Keith Panter-Brick, ed., *Soldiers and Oil: The Political Transition of Nigeria* (London, Frank Cass, 1978).

Adamu, H. and Ogunsanwo, A., *The Making of the Presidential System: 1979 Elections* (Kano Triumph Publishing Company, 1981).

August, T.G., The Selling of the Empire: British and French Imperialist Propaganda, 1890-1940 (Westport, Connecticut, Greenwood Press, 1967).

Azarya, V., *Aristocrats Facing Change: The Fulbe in Guinea, Nigeria and Cameroon* (Chicago, Univ. of Chicago press, 1978).

Barkindo, B., ed., *Studies in the History of Kano* (Ibadan, Heinemann Educational Books, 1983).

Bayero, Ado., *Mai Martaba Sarkin Kano Alhaji Ado Bayero* (Northern Nigeria Historical Documentation Bureau, 1992).

Bello, Ahmadu. *My Life*, (Cambridge University Press, 1962).

Burns, A., *History of Nigeria* (London, George Allen and Unwin, 1964, first published 1929).

Buckle, H.T., *A History of Civilization* 2nd ed., (New York, Appleton and Company, 1910, first published 1857).

Bagehot, W., *Physics and Politics: Thoughts on the Applications of the Principles of Natural Selection and Inheritance to Political Society* (New York, Appleton and Company 1876).

Blackwell, H.F., ed., *The Occupation of Hausaland 1900-1904 Being Translation of Arabic Letters Found in the House of the Waziri of Sokoto Buhari* (London, Framnk Cass, 1927).

Busia, K.A., *The Position of the Chief in the Modern Political System of Ashanti* (London, Oxford University press, 1951).

Bello, Ahmadu, *My Life* (Cambridge, Cambridge University Press, 1962).

Callaway, B.J., *Muslim Hausa Women in Nigeria: Tradition and Change*, (Syracuse, Syracuse University Press, 1987).

Cartey, W., Kilson, M., *The Africa Reader: Colonial Africa*, (New York, Vintage Books, 1970).

Campbell, M.J., *Law and Practice of Local Government in Northern Nigeria,* (London, African Universities Press, 1963).

Curtin, P.D., ed., *Imperialism* (New York, Walker and Company, 1971).

Crowder, M., and Ikimi, O., Eds. *West African Chiefs: Their Changing Status under Colonial Rule and Independence* (Ile-Ife, University of Ife Press, 1970).

Cartey, W., and Kilson, M., *The Africa Reader: African Reaction and Adaptation: Emergence of Masses, Formation of National Institutions* (New York, Vintage Books, 1970).

Coleman, J.S., Nigeria: Background to Nationalism (Berkeley, University of California Press, 1958).

Diamond, Larry, Kirk-Greene, A., and Oyediran O., *Transition Without End: Nigerian Politics and Civil Society Under Babangida*, (Boulder, Lynne Rienner, 1997).

Dokaji, Abubakar, *Kano Ta Dabi Cigari*, (Zaria, Northern Nigeria Publishing Company, 1958).

References

Elaigwu, J.I., *Gowon*, (Ibadan, West Books Limited, 1985).

Fika, A.M., *The Kano Civil War and British Over-rule 1882-1840* (Ibadan Oxford University Press, 1978).

Feinstein, Alan, *African Revolutionary: The Life and Times of Nigeria's Aminu Kano*, revised ed., (Boulder, Lynne Rienner, 1987).

Gummi, A.M. and Tsiga, I.A., *Where I Stand* (Ibadan, Spectrum Books, 1992).

Henderson, Michael. *The Forgiveness Factor: Stories of Hope in a World of Conflict*, (London, Grosvenor Books, 1996).

Heussler, R., *The British in Northern Nigeria* (London Oxford University Press, 1968)

Imam, Ibrahim, *The Biography of Shehu Othman Dan Fodio*, (Zaria, Gaskiya Corporation, 1966).

Last, Murray, *The Sokoto Caliphate*, (London, Longmans, 1967).

Low, V., *Three Nigerian Emirates: A Study in Oral History* (Evanston, Northwest University Press, 1972).

Lugard, Lady, *A Tropical dependency: An Outline of the Ancient History of the Western Sudan with and Account of the modern Settlement of Northern Nigeria* (London, Frank Cass, 1974).

Muffette, D.J.M., *Let Truth be Told: The Coup d'etat of 1966* (Zaria, Hudahuda Publishing Co., 1982).

Obi-Mbata, R.A., *Alhaji Ado Bayero and the Royal Court of Kano*, (Kano, Capricorn press, 1994).

Obasanjo, O., *Nzeogwu*, (Ibadan, Spectrum Books, 1987).

Paden, J.N., *Religion and political Culture in Kano* (Berkeley, University of California Press, 1973).

——, *Ahmadu Bello Sardauna of Sokoto: Value and Leadership in Nigeria* (Zaria, Hudahuda Pub. Co., 1986).

Pearson, J., *The Selling of the Royal family: The Mystique of the British Monarchy* (New York, Simon and Schuster, 1986).

Rabi'u Fatima, *Sarkin Kano Alhaji Ado Bayero: Tarihin Rayuwarsa Tun Daga Haihuwa Zuwa Yau*, (n.p. 1994).

Rivkin, Arnold, ed., *Nations by Design: Institution Building in Africa* (New York, Anchor Books, 1968).

Rufa'i, R.A., *Gidan Rumfa: The Kano Palace*, (Kano, Triumph Publishing Co., 1995).

Rustow, D.A., Philosophers and Kings: Studies in Leadership (New York, George Braziller, 1970).

Sklar, R.L., *Nigerian Political Parties: Power in an Emergent African Nation* (NOK Publishers, Lagos, 1983).

Sufi, A.H., *Mu San Kammu* (Kano Mai Nasara Press, n.d.).

Sulaiman, Ibraheem, *The Islamic State and the Challenge of History: Ideals, Policies and Operation of the Sokoto Caliphate,* (London, Mansell Publishing, 1987).

Smith, Abdullahi, *A Little New Light: Selected Historical Writings of Abdullahi Smith* (Zaria, Abdullahi Smith Center for Historical Research, 1987).

Yahaya, A.D., *The Native Authority System in Northern Nigeria,* (Zaria, Ahmadu Bello University Press, 1980).

Zawiya, S., and Sadauki T., *Jigatau Dan Bayero: Sir Muhammadu Sanusi, K.B.E., C.M.G. (Kano, Zawiya Enterprise 1991).*

REPORTS AND OTHER DOCUMENTS:

Report of Tribunal of Inquiry on Kano Disturbances (Maitatsine) Printed by the New Nigerian Newspapers Press, Kaduna 1981.

Myths and Realities of our Struggle: Documents from the NEPU Days to the PRP, Gaskiya Corporation, Zaria, n.d.

Northern Nigeria Local Government Yearbook 1966.

Index

Index

Index

Index